W

Big Ben.
imageBROKER/hemis.fr

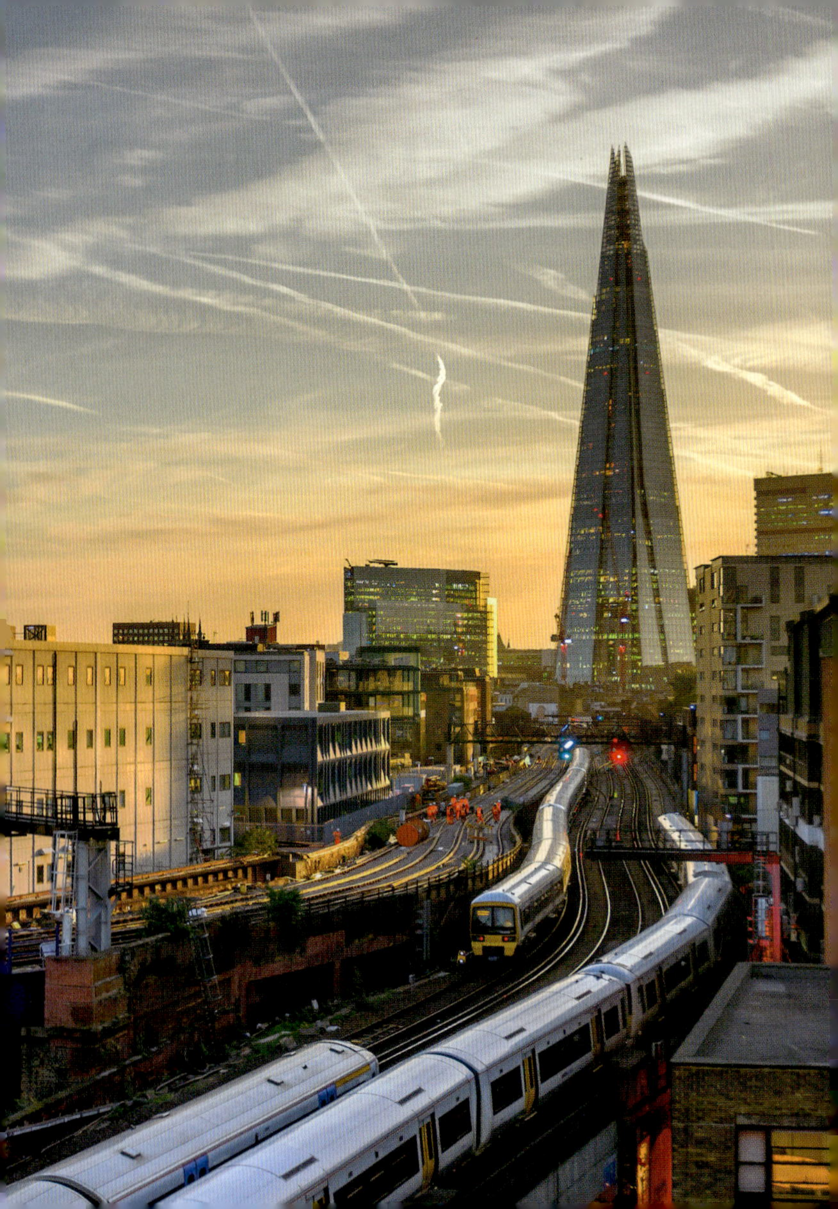

Arriving in London

By Train
Eurostar trains arrive at St Pancras International station.

By Coach
Coaches arrive at Victoria Coach Station.

By Plane

From Gatwick
Airport – www.gatwickairport.com.
Gatwick Express (train) – www.gatwickexpress.com. 30min to Victoria Station *(5:40AM–11:10PM, every 30min)* – from £20.40.
Thameslink (train) – www.thameslinkrailway.com. 30 to 50min to Blackfriars or London Bridge *(24/7 every 15min to 1hr)* – from £14.40.
Taxi – £95–130 to the center (1hr).

From Heathrow
Airport – www.heathrow.com.
Piccadilly Line (subway) – 50min to Piccadilly Circus *(5AM–11:45PM, every 5min, all night Fri. and Sat.)* – £6.70 (£5.60 with contactless card or Oyster Card). **Elizabeth Line (subway)** – 30min to Paddington *(5:15AM–12AM, every 15min)* – £12.80 – www.tfl.gov.uk.
Heathrow Express (train) – 15min to Paddington Station – *(5:10AM–11:50PM, every 15min)* – £25 – www.heathrowexpress.com.
Taxi – £56–105 to the center (50min).

The tracks at London Bridge Station and The Shard, designed by Renzo Piano Building Workshop.
Jon Arnold Images/ hemis.fr

From London City
Airport – www.londoncityairport.com.
Docklands Light Railway (DLR) – 21min to Bank *(5:35AM–12:15AM, every 8–15min)* – £6.70 (£3.70/£5.20 with Oyster Card).
Taxi – £40–50 to the center.

From Luton
Airport – www.london-luton.co.uk.
Train – www.thetrainline.com. Luton Dart shuttle to Luton Airport Parkway station (10min); from there, train to St Pancras Int. – approx. 35min, from £10 (when booked in advance).
National Express (bus) – www.nationalexpress.com. To Paddington (1hr20) and Victoria (1hr45) *(24/7, every 15 to 30min)* – £12–16.
Taxi – min £88 to the center (1hr40).

From Stansted
Airport – www.stanstedairport.com.
Stansted Express (train) – www.stanstedexpress.com. 45min to Liverpool Street Station or Victoria Station *(5:30AM–12:30AM, every 15min)* – £23.
Taxi – approx. £90 to the center (1hr15).

From Southend
Airport – www.londonsouthendairport.com.
Train – www.greateranglia.co.uk. 53min to Liverpool Street Station *(5:30AM–12:30AM, every 15 to 30min)* – £20.90.
Taxi – £80–100 to the center (1hr15).

↻ Public transport, p. 158.

Our must-sees

our selection of the most beautiful sites

★★★ **The City**
Map GH3–4 – p. 48

★★★ **The National Gallery**
Map E4 – p. 21

★★★ **Westminster and Big Be**
Map E5–6 – p. 14

★★★ **The British Museum**
Map E3 – p. 46

★★★ **Changing of the Guard
at Buckingham Palace** – Map
D5 – p. 25

★★★ **The Tower of London**
Map H4 – p. 58

★★★ **The Great Museums of South Kensington**
Map AB6 – pp. 76–78

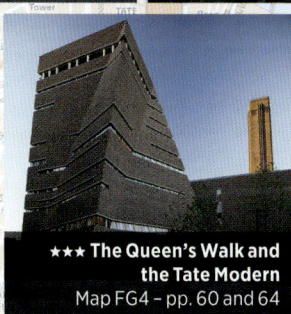

★★ **Notting Hill**
See map p. 83 – p. 82

★★★ **The Queen's Walk and the Tate Modern**
Map FG4 – pp. 60 and 64

★★★ **Regent's Park**
Map BC1-2 – p. 88

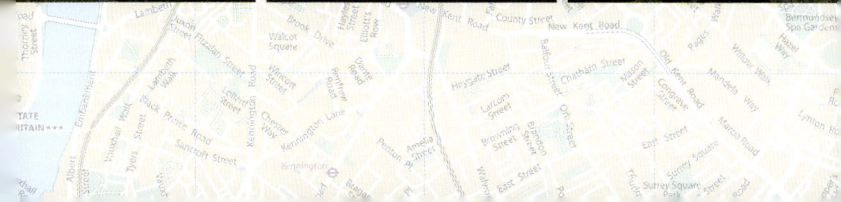

Our favorites

💛 **Treat yourself to a relaxing walk** along the canals of Little Venice (*p. 82*) to Camden (*p. 90*), enjoying the view of colorful boats and Regent's Park along the way. The route can also be done by boat (*see Jason's Trip p. 161*).

💛 **Stroll through the flea markets** in one of London's two iconic locations: Fridays and Saturdays at Portobello (*Notting Hill*) and weekends at Camden Town (more lively than on weekdays). Browse the stalls and stores for great deals, vintage clothing, antiques, or collectibles. *See pp. 82 and 90.*

💛 **Have a pint** at one of the city's historic pubs at the end of the day, for instance in Hampstead. Cozy and lively havens, some boast leather benches, large mirrors, and antique woodwork, while others feature mismatched decor, an old jukebox, candlelight, or a fireplace. *See p. 131.*

💛 **Keep your eyes open for London's street art**. Artists offer guided tours through the streets of Spitalfields and Shoreditch to help discover urban art treasures: traditional graffiti, collages, stencils, sculptures. Art thrives outdoors! *See p. 100.*

💛 **Indulge in the ritual of afternoon tea** in the elegant setting of a prestigious hotel. It is tradition to have tea around 4–5PM, served with finger sandwiches and delicious scones with strawberry jam and clotted cream. *See pp. 130 and 185.*

💛 **Lunch at Borough Market** to soak up the unique atmosphere of London's oldest food market, dating back to the Middle Ages. This typical British gourmet stop is where top chefs come to shop. *See p. 62.*

💛 **Feel the pulse** of a transformed neighborhood around the British Library and the stations of St Pancras and King's Cross. Repurposed industrial buildings, now home to housing, offices, schools, stores, trendy cafés, and restaurants, create a new living space along Regent's Canal. *See p. 92.*

💛 **Embark on a music tour** through the city, tracing the footsteps of The Beatles at Abbey Road, Pink Floyd at Battersea Power Station (*p. 103*), David Bowie in Brixton (*p. 102*), or Amy Winehouse in Camden (*p. 92*). If you're in town in late August, be sure to check out the Caribbean music at Notting Hill Carnival (*p. 164*). *See also p. 181.*

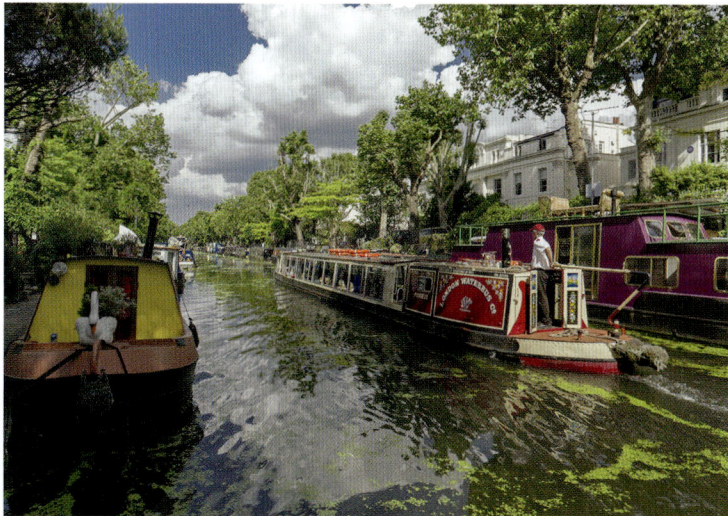

Ph. Renault/hemis.fr

Boats at the junction of the Grand Union Canal and Regent's Canal.

💜 **Visit Sir John Soane's Museum** to experience a spectacular cabinet of curiosities. For an even more mysterious atmosphere, take advantage of the candlelit evening tours. *See p. 43.*

💜 **Take in the view from the top** of the Shard, the Walkie Talkie (Sky Garden), the London Eye, St Paul's Cathedral, or the Tower Bridge walkway to admire the London skyline. Looking for a new perspective on the capital? Head to the former Battersea Power Station's chimney for a 360° panorama. *See pp. 103 and 177.*

💜 **Get a breath of fresh air** in the neighborhoods of Hampstead and Highgate. The former boasts a charming village feel with cobblestone streets, beautiful gardens, and homes where poets and artists once lived, as well as the heath. Highgate is mainly known for its cemetery, the resting place of many famous figures. *See pp. 94 and 95.*

💜 **Visit the West End,** renowned for its excellent musicals. For a discounted ticket, visit the TKTS booth in Leicester Square or go to the theater's box office in the morning. Consider seeing an Elizabethan play at Shakespeare's Globe. *See pp. 63 and 144.*

Three days in London

Day 1

▶ Morning

Start the day at **Westminster Abbey★★★** (*p. 16*), not far from **Big Ben★★**, the **Parliament★★★** (*p. 14*), and **Whitehall★** (*p. 19*). After a walk in **St James's Park★★** (*p. 25*), don't miss the **changing of the guard★★★** (*p. 25*) in front of Buckingham Palace starting at 11AM.

▶ Noon

Have lunch around St James's Park, Trafalgar Square, or Piccadilly (*p. 117*).

St Paul's Cathedral from the Millennium Bridge (Foster+Partners).

Tolga_TEZCAN/Getty Images Plus

▶ Afternoon

Stroll around **Piccadilly Circus★** (*p. 30*), **Regent Street★★** (*p. 31*), and **Oxford Street★** (*p. 84*) to discover London's department stores: Fortnum & Mason, Liberty, Hamleys, Selfridges, etc. Indulge in the tradition of afternoon tea at one of the neighborhood's elegant hotels (make sure to book well in advance) (*p. 130*).

▶ Evening

End this first day by watching a musical in the **West End** (*p. 144*). Want to continue the night? Head to **Soho★** (*p. 31*), known for its clubs and wild nights (*p. 143*).

Day 2

▶ Morning

A visit to **Tate Britain★★★** (*p. 18*) is a must to discover a fascinating panorama of English and British art up to the mid-20th century. Prefer contemporary art? Head to **Tate Modern★★★** (*p. 63*). You can also combine the two visits by taking the river shuttle (*p. 161*).
From Tate Modern, follow the **Queen's Walk★★★** (*p. 60*), the riverside promenade, toward **Shakespeare's Globe★★** (*p. 63*) and **Southwark Cathedral★★** (*p. 62*). For an impressive view of the river and city skyline, climb to the top of The **Shard★★** (*p. 61*).

▶ Noon

Have lunch at **Borough Market** or one of **Southwark**'s charming pubs (*p. 120*).

▶**Afternoon**

Walk past **City Hall** (*p. 61*), cross **Tower Bridge**★★ (*p. 59*), and visit the **Tower of London**★★★ (*p. 58*). Stroll through the **City**★★★ (*p. 48*) among the skyscrapers and ancient churches. Go during the week: the area is deserted on weekends. Wrap up with a visit to **St Paul's Cathedral**★★★ (*p. 48*).

▶**Evening**

End the day with a cocktail at the top of the **Heron Tower** (*see SushiSamba p. 135*) or the **Oxo Tower** (*p. 121*), from where you can enjoy the evening view.

Day 3

▶**Morning**

After visiting the **National Gallery**★★★ (*p. 21*) or the **British Museum**★★★ (*p. 46*), take a stroll to **Covent Garden**★ (*p. 33*) close by, then head on a Friday or Saturday to the **Portobello Road**★ flea market (*pp. 82 and 140*) in Notting Hill. On Sunday, opt for **Camden Lock Market** (*p. 90*) or the flower market on **Columbia Road**★★ (*p. 142*) in the East End, lined with lovely stores, from where you can reach **Brick Lane**★ (*p. 97*) and **Spitalfields** (*p. 96*).

▶**Noon**

Have lunch in Notting Hill, Camden, or Brick Lane (*pp. 122, 125, and 126*).

▶**Afternoon**

Stroll along the canals from Camden to **Little Venice**★ (*p. 82*) or vice versa, and the paths of **Regent's Park**★★★ (*p. 88*), or head toward **Highgate**★ (*p. 94*) and **Hampstead**★★ (*p. 94*), charming neighborhoods with a village feel.

London in All Weather

If it rains... Explore other museums based on your interests: **Victoria and Albert Museum**★★★, **Science Museum**★★★, **Wallace Collection**★★★, **Imperial War Museum**★★★, **The Courtauld Gallery**★★, **Museum of London Docklands**★★, **Sir John Soane's Museum**★★, etc. Head to a pub, browse the covered markets, or go shopping at **Harrods**★★, in **Covent Garden**★, or under the impressive spaces of **Battersea Power Station**★.

If it's nice out... London's parks are full of activities, and it's such a joy to relax there! Hop on a bike, have brunch on a terrace, take a canal boat ride, stroll along the **Queen's Walk**★★★ by the Thames, explore the **Docklands**★, and wander the lawns of **Greenwich**★★★, the paths of **Highgate Cemetery**★★, or the heath at **Hampstead**★★.

▶**Evening**

Stay a while longer in a traditional pub (*p. 131*) or try the bars and clubs of **King's Cross** (*p. 92*), Islington, or Clerkenwell.

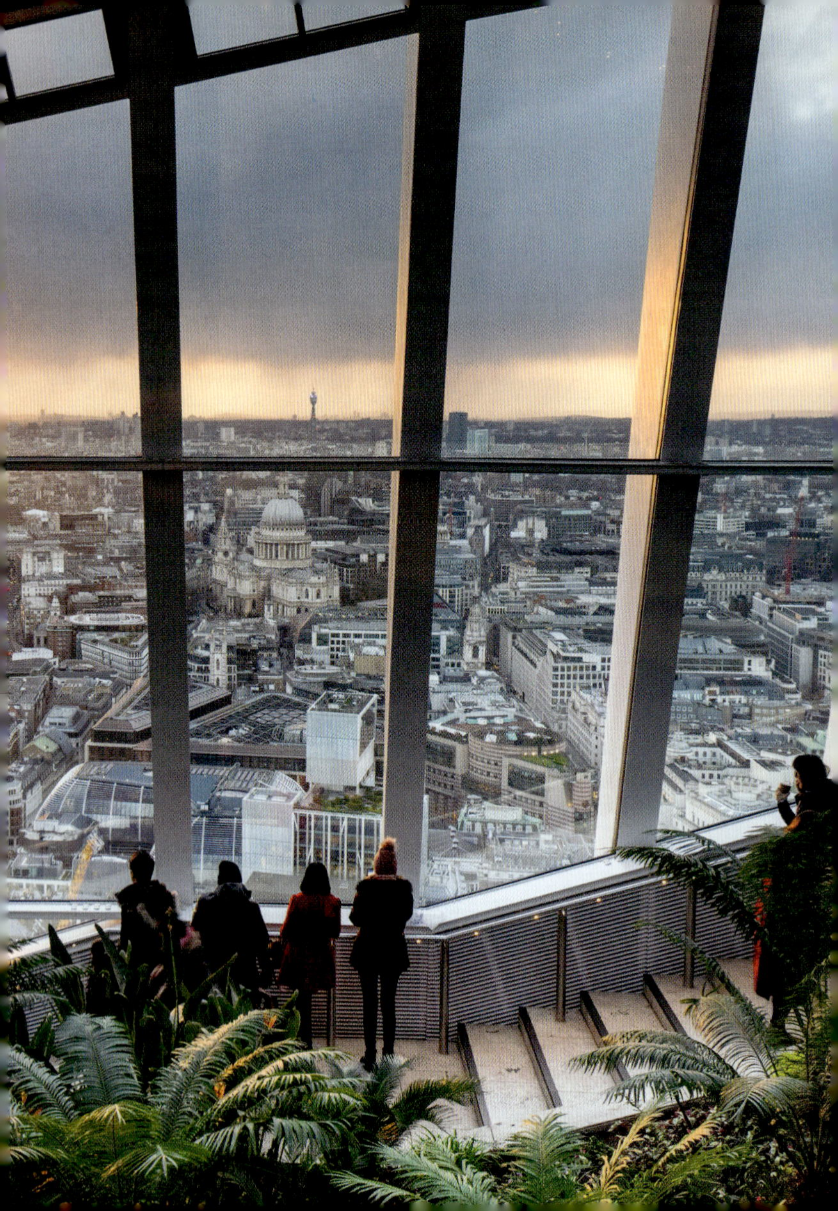

VISIT LONDON

The Sky Garden at the top of the Walkie-Talkie, by architect Rafael Viñoly.
Jon Arnold images/hemis.fr

London today

Eccentric and classic, traditional and quirky, calm and lively, eternal and ever-changing, London is a cosmopolitan city with indelible charm. There's the royal London, in red and gold, of Westminster and Whitehall; the colorful and bustling London of Brixton and Brick Lane, with markets and street vendors; the festive London of Soho, Covent Garden, and Camden, full of musicals and clubs; the chic London of Chelsea and Mayfair, with colonnaded patrician houses; the historic London of the Tower; the trendy London of Notting Hill; the administrative and financial London of the City, dominated by a legion in charcoal suits...

Reaching for the sky

Full of contrast, immense, and ever-changing, London is also undergoing a transformation. You can take in the view (from the London Eye, the Shard, the Sky Garden at the Walkie-Talkie) to better grasp the changes underway: this city with its Victorian houses of two or three floors is now shooting upwards, with futuristic skyscrapers rising in the heart of the City, at Canary Wharf, on the south bank of the Thames... The construction frenzy gripping the city, partly due to demographic growth (with the population expected to increase from 9.65 million to 10 million by 2030), is radically transforming its appearance. The cranes piercing the sky are a testament to the city's astounding ability to breathe new life into abandoned places. Whatever you may think, there is an incredible vitality emerging, proving that London is not just a museum city!

Center and outskirts

We distinguish between **Inner London**, which encompasses 13 boroughs plus the City, and **Greater London**, which includes 19 suburban areas. Each borough consists of distinct neighborhoods with strong identities. It is at the scale of these "villages" that the city should be explored.

The West End and the North

The neighborhoods of **Soho** and **Covent Garden** will plunge you into a whirlwind of nightlife and music halls. To the west and north of **Piccadilly Circus** stretch two of London's most famous streets, Piccadilly and Regent Street, marking the boundary of the very chic quarter of **Mayfair**. To the north, **Oxford Street**, with its plethora of stores, will make your head spin. From **Trafalgar Square**, a famous gathering place, you can reach the institutional districts stretching further south: **Westminster**, its palace (the Parliament) and its abbey, **Buckingham Palace**, and the upscale **St James's** district. Further west, dominated by the department store Harrods, the chic neighborhood of **Knightsbridge** is renowned for its luxury boutiques. To the south, another refined area, **Chelsea**, has long been loved by artists. Less elitist but equally elegant, **South Kensington** is home to three of London's largest museums, including the Victoria and Albert Museum.

Northwest of **Hyde Park**, the residential neighborhood of **Notting Hill** attracts a bohemian crowd with its village-like charm, trendy bars, stores, and restaurants.

To the north, the affluent area of **Marylebone** and the beautiful **Regent's Park** offer delightful surprises like the Wallace Collection. Not far away, **Camden Town** enjoys its reputation as an alternative area and is popular for its flea markets. Further east, the congested areas of **King's Cross** and **St Pancras**, built up around their monumental train stations, are gradually shedding their tarnished reputations. Further north, **Hampstead** and **Highgate**, separated by Hampstead Heath, a preserved heathland with ponds, provide some greenery.

At the eastern limit of the West End, the peaceful neighborhoods of **Bloomsbury** and **Holborn** maintain their intellectual aura around the British Museum, the British Library, and the University of London.

The City, yesterday and today

The historic center of the capital, the City is today its economic heart. Amid the skyscrapers stand the Tower of London, one of the city's oldest buildings, and St Paul's Cathedral. North of the City, Clerkenwell and Islington are among the trendiest neighborhoods.

Reclaiming the East and South

The **East End**, once a poor working-class area, today boasts several trendy neighborhoods like **Spitalfields** (vintage and designer stores), Whitechapel, and **Shoreditch** (hipster through and through). However, driven out by rising real estate prices, the hipsters are setting their sights on other popular areas, and gentrification (☛ *p. 178*) now spreads to the south of the capital, particularly **Brixton**. Before long, these areas may also become unaffordable....

Renaissance along the river

Long ignored, the former industrial neighborhoods of **South Bank** and **Southwark** now embody modernity. Redeveloped, these cultural and tourist hotspots are complemented by a picturesque riverside promenade along the Thames. To the west, around the old Battersea Power Station, the brand-new neighborhood of **Nine Elms** is emerging. To the east, repurposed old docks neighbor the futuristic towers of **Canary Wharf**, such as One Canada Square, which rises to 772 feet tall. On the opposite bank, **Greenwich** is a UNESCO World Heritage site because of its remarkable architecture. In short, you'll need more than a weekend to fully grasp all that this ever-moving global city has to offer.

Westminster★★★

The name Westminster evokes monarchic and political history: coronations and other prestigious royal celebrations are held at Westminster Abbey, and parliamentary sessions open with great pomp in the palace. During state visits, royal figures and dignitaries are accompanied by an impressive escort and welcomed by the cavalry. The Palace of Westminster, with Big Ben as its beacon, captivated Monet, who found inspiration in the combination of monumental stonework, the river, and the ever-changing sky for one of his most famous series of paintings.

▶**Access:** ⊖ Westminster, Pimlico, Victoria.

Neighborhood map p. 17. Detachable map E5–6–7.

▶**Tips:** Parliament is only open to the public during the parliamentary holidays, and on Saturdays during the rest of the year: reserve your ticket. After visiting Tate Britain, head to Tate Modern (◉ p. 63) by taking a Thames Clippers river shuttle (◉ p. 161). ◉ Where to Go pp. 116 and 131.

Palace of Westminster ★★★
(Parliament)

E5–6 *Parliament Square – ⊖ Westminster – ✆ 087 0906 3773 – www.parliament.uk/visiting – ♿ – Aug.–Oct.: Mon.–Fri. 10AM–5PM; rest of the year: schedule online (parliamentary sessions and sittings) – £26 audioguide included. Tickets available at Victoria Embankment.*

In medieval times, the kings of England expanded and beautified the palace of **Edward the Confessor**, though most of the old buildings, later occupied by Parliament, were destroyed by fire in 1834. After the fire, Charles Barry and Augustus Pugin were tasked with redesigning the palace, which then became known as the **Houses of Parliament.** They built a magnificent neo-Gothic palace, a masterpiece of Victorian architecture, completed in 1860. The building contains over 1,000 rooms, 100 staircases, and 2 miles of corridors, covering a total area of 7.4 acres.

Big Ben★★ (Elizabeth Tower)

Reservations required, several months in advance, at www.parliament.uk/visiting/visiting-and-tours/big-ben-tour – £30.

☺ *There are 334 steps to climb, and access is prohibited to those under 11 years old.*

This iconic symbol of the city was completed in 1859. The name originally referred to the enormous bell (weighing 13.5 tons) housed in the 315-foot tower. The light above the clock remains lit during sessions of the House of Commons.

The Palace of Westminster and the iconic Big Ben

Westminster Hall★

Spared by the fire of 1834, this great hall, added to the palace by William II between 1097 and 1099, is the oldest part of the structure. Westminster Hall, where royal banquets and jousts took place in the Middle Ages, was transformed between 1394 and 1399, at which time a splendid wooden ceiling reminiscent of an inverted ship's hull ★★★ was designed by the king's master carpenter, Hugh Herland, and adorned with flying angels. This is where the coffin of **Elizabeth II** lay for four days in 2022 to allow Britons to pay their final respects to their queen. The turnout was so large that some had to wait over 24 hours at the end of a line stretching as long as 10 miles along the Thames!

House of Commons★

Destroyed in a bombing raid in 1941 and rebuilt in 1950, the **House of Commons**, simply decorated, features the chair for the speaker at one end beneath a canopy. The government and majority sit to the right of this canopy, with the opposition and "shadow cabinet" to its left. The red lines bordering both sides of the green carpet mark the uncrossable boundary for members addressing the House.

House of Lords★★

Richly decorated, the **House of Lords** is adorned with gold and scarlet. The throne occupied by the royal family on the day of the session's opening, topped by a large, entirely gold Gothic-style canopy, occupies the entire back of the room. Under a gilded and ribbed ceiling are red leather benches and the curious *woolsack*, seat of the Lord Chancellor, reminiscent of wool sacks on which the king's advisors once sat.

Westminster Abbey ★★★

E6 *Parliament Square –* ⊖ *Westminster –* ☎ *020 7222 5152 – www.westminster-abbey.org –* ♿ *– 9:30AM–3:30PM, varying hours – £29.* 🙂 *A ticket bought online grants three visits over one year: ask at reception to convert your ticket into this annual pass.* Having hosted most coronations since that of William the Conqueror (1066), royal weddings, and funerals (including that of Elizabeth II), **Westminster Abbey** is one of the most iconic buildings in London. Originally built by Edward the Confessor in the Romanesque style, it gained its Gothic appearance following its reconstruction under Henry III in 1220. He began by commissioning the **Lady Chapel** to house the shrine to Edward the Confessor, canonized in 1163. It took more than two centuries to complete the building, which was finished in 1503–1519 with the Henry VII Chapel, a masterpiece of the

Historic Funerals

On September 19, 2022, the funeral of Queen Elizabeth II, who passed away on September 8 after a 70-year reign, gathered more than 2,000 dignitaries and guests at Westminster Abbey, including 500 heads of state. This historic event was broadcast live and watched by over 4 billion viewers worldwide!

Perpendicular style (a late English Gothic movement). Additions like the western towers by **Christopher Wren** and Nicholas Hawksmoor, built between 1722–1745, were made in the same Gothic spirit.

Interior – The vaults are splendid, the carvings and engravings on the railings and arches delicate, often wonderful, sometimes humorous; the tombs in the chapels of Henry VII and St Edward, as well as the radiating chapels, are solemn and expressive. The transept and aisles are full of sculpted monuments, particularly the right crossing and its famous **Poets' Corner★**. The coronation ceremony takes place in the sanctuary beyond the choir. On the right, there's a 16th-century tapestry behind a grand 15th-century altarpiece of rare beauty.

17

WESTMINSTER WHITEHALL TRAFALGAR SQUARE

0   100 m
100 yards

DINING
The Portrait...................... 8
Cellarium Café & Terrace........ 13
The Cinnamon Club................ 23
Bancone......................... 87

GRAB A DRINK
St Stephen's Tavern.............. 7
Muriel's Kitchen................ 34

Henry VII Chapel★★★ – With its stunning fan-vaulted ceiling, this is the most beautiful of the abbey's many treasures. The heraldic banners of the Knights Grand Cross of the Order of the Bath still float above the stalls.

Chapel of Edward the Confessor★★ – *Guided tour only.* The shrine of the sainted king is surrounded by the tombs of five kings and three queens. At the center, against a stone screen (1441), stands the **coronation chair** under which the **Stone of Scone** is placed.

Chapter House★★ (1248–1253) – Octagonal, it features lierne and tierceron vaults projecting onto a central pillar with eight Purbeck "marble" columns. Medieval paintings adorn some of the walls.

Queen's Diamond Jubilee Galleries★ – *Access via Weston Tower from Poets' Corner – £5.* These galleries offer an exceptional exhibition space overlooking the nave: manuscripts, statues, furniture, and an unbeatable view of the abbey.

Tate Britain ★★★

E7 *Atterbury St. – ⊖ Pimlico – ℘ 020 7887 8888 – www.tate.org.uk – &* – *10AM–6PM – free – late night opening 1st Friday of the month ("Late at Tate," until 10PM).*

In 1891, **Henry Tate**, a sugar merchant and modern art collector, donated his collection to the nation along with £80,000 for the construction of a building. The site of the former Millbank prison was donated by the government. The Tate, whose collection also included many

---

🍴 Lunch at the Abbey

For lunch or a break, consider the excellent café-restaurant at Westminster Abbey, **Cellarium**. *𝄐 p. 116.*

---

paintings acquired by the state since the founding of the National Gallery (1824), opened in 1897 as a museum of British modern art.

Dedicated to **British art from 1500 to the present day**, the collections offer a chronological journey that showcases the evolution of painting and other media through the ages. You will discover such great British painters as Reynolds, Hogarth, Blake, Constable, Gainsborough, the Pre-Raphaelites, representatives of the contemporary period – Bacon, Freud, Hockney – and conceptual art, as well as sculptures by Henry Moore and Barbara Hepworth. The Clore Gallery houses the largest collection of **Turner**'s works anywhere in the world (over 300 oils and a large number of watercolors), some of which are exhibited in rotation.

Whitehall★ and Trafalgar Square★★

Trafalgar Square, known worldwide for its iconic statue, fountains, and view of the National Gallery, is the end point of Whitehall Avenue, which starts at the Palace of Westminster. Trafalgar Square serves as a forum for political meetings as well as Christmas gatherings around the Norwegian tree and New Year's Eve celebrations, when locals and tourists alike wait to hear Big Ben chime midnight.

▶ **Access:** ⊖ Charing Cross, Westminster, St James's Park.
Neighborhood map p. 17. Detachable map E4–5.
▶ **Tip:** Take advantage of free entry to major national museums, and avoid trying to see everything in one day.
◉ *Where to Go pp. 117 and 129.*

WHITEHALL ★

E5 ⊖ *Charing Cross or Westminster.*
The axis formed by Whitehall, formerly known as King Street, and Parliament Street is lined with official buildings. Whitehall is the seat of England's executive power.

Churchill War Rooms ★★

E5 *Clive Steps, King Charles St. –*
⊖ *Westminster or St James's Park –*
℘ *020 7416 5000 – www.iwm.org.uk –*
♿ *– 9:30AM–6PM – £32 audioguide included.*
The shelter set up to protect Winston Churchill, his **war cabinet**, and the chiefs of staff from air raids served as the headquarters of the British government during World War II. The various rooms of this underground labyrinth, where hundreds lived, have remained untouched since 1945. They now house a museum dedicated to Churchill, showcasing both the statesman and the private individual. The exhibition centers around an interactive biography detailing the five major periods of his life: his youth (1874–1900), his political rise (1900–1929), the 1930s, his role as a wartime leader (1939–1945), and his role as a statesman during the Cold War (1945–1965).

Downing Street

E5 ⊖ *Westminster.*
This famous street is lined with Georgian-style houses. **No. 10** has been, since its reconstruction by Robert Walpole in 1732, the official residence of the Prime Minister.

Banqueting House ★★

E5 *Whitehall –* ⊖ *Charing Cross or Westminster –* ℘ *020 3166 6154 – www.hrp.org.uk –* ♿ *– open during* *private events or rare occasions (dates on the website).*

This is the only vestige of the Whitehall Palace, inhabited by monarchs until 1689. Banqueting House was built by **Inigo Jones** for James I in 1619. The stunning west facade shows Italian influences with its stacked ionic and Corinthian columns, topped with balustrades; Jones added his personal touch by omitting the traditional central door, enhancing the overall grandeur. Inside, a beautiful hall is spanned by a gallery balcony. Richly decorated beams divide the ceiling into compartments adorned with magnificent paintings (1634–1635) by **Rubens**.

Horse Guards ★★★

E5 *Opposite Banqueting House – ⊖ Charing Cross or Westminster – www.householddivision.org.uk/changing-the-guard – mounted guard change: Mon., Wed., Fri., and Sun. at 11AM; Jul.–Aug.: daily (schedule on the website) – parade on the Mall between Horse Guards and Hyde Park barracks.*

The sentries on duty in front of the building highlight its role as the official entrance to Buckingham Palace. Crowds of tourists visit daily for a selfie beside these proud, helmeted, silver-armored riders and their magnificent black horses. With its central body topped with a clock tower and spanning three arches, the regiment's barracks, erected in the mid-18th century by William Kent, frame Horse Guards Parade. The **Changing of the Guard** takes place on this esplanade, behind the building, as does the

Trooping the Colour ceremony, a military parade celebrating the official birthday of the monarch on the second Saturday of June.

TRAFALGAR SQUARE ★★

E4 ⊖ *Charing Cross.*
Pedestrian-focused and dedicated to all sorts of events, this square, which has become a national symbol, remains the preferred gathering place for major occasions. Completed around 1840, when Charles Barry leveled it and constructed the National Gallery's northern terrace, it has been dominated since 1842 by the iconic **Nelson's Column**, which features a 14.76-foot statue of the illustrious admiral who lost his life winning the Battle of Trafalgar against Napoleon's fleet.

At each of the four corners, a plinth is topped with a historical hero, except for one that remained empty due to funding constraints at the time of the square's design. This was rectified in 2005 when the **Fourth Plinth** began hosting a contemporary art sculpture, which changes every two years. Across from Whitehall stands the equestrian statue of **Charles I** created by Le Sueur in 1633. To the left of the National Gallery facade, **Canada House**, a classic building of Bath stone, was built from 1824 to 1827 by Robert Smirke.

The National Gallery ★★★

E4 *Trafalgar Square – ⊖ Charing Cross, Leicester Square, Embankment, and Piccadilly Circus – ✆ 020 7747 2885 – www.nationalgallery.org.uk –*

VWpics/hemis.fr

The National Gallery

♿ – 10AM–6PM, Fri. 10AM–9PM – free. ☃ *The museum celebrated its 200th anniversary in 2024. Refurbishments to the **Sainsbury Wing** include increasing natural light and improving visitor capacity.*

The collection's origins lie in the 38 paintings gathered by broker **John Julius Angerstein (1735–1823)** and purchased by Parliament in 1824. To house them, William Wilkins was tasked with constructing a museum adorned with a Corinthian column portico. Completed in 1838, the building quickly proved too small for the ever-growing collections: transfers and expansions continued until 1991 with the construction of the Sainsbury Wing.

Sainsbury Wing – This is dedicated to works prior to 1500 (Italian, Flemish, and German schools): Giotto, Leonardo da Vinci and his *Virgin and Child with St. Anne and St. John the Baptist*, *The Battle of San Romano* by Uccello, Masaccio, Botticelli with *Venus and Mars*, Mantegna, Piero della Francesca with *The Baptism of Christ*; Van Eyck and his famous *Arnolfini Portrait*, Bosch, Gerard David, Memling, Dürer and *The Painter's Father*.

West Wing – This houses the 16th century: Michelangelo, Titian, Tintoretto alongside Bruegel the Elder, Cranach, Holbein (*The Ambassadors*), and Altdorfer.

North Wing – The classical period (17th century) is gathered here. Vermeer (*A Young Woman Standing at a Virginal*), Ruysdael, Rubens, Rembrandt (*Self-Portrait at the Age of 34*) and Hals represent the Dutch; Velázquez (*The Rokeby Venus*), Zurbarán, Murillo, for Spain; Italy is represented by Caravaggio, Guercino, and A. Carracci; and France by Claude Lorrain, Poussin, Philippe de Champaigne (*Portrait of Cardinal Richelieu*) or the Le Nain brothers.

East Wing – This spans from 1700 to 1930, with the English (Constable, Gainsborough, Turner, Reynolds), the Italians (Canaletto, Guardi, Tiepolo), Goya's *Duke of Wellington*, and a rich French collection from the 18th (Chardin, Fragonard, Boucher, Greuze, etc.) and 19th centuries (David, Ingres, Delacroix, Daumier, Courbet, Corot, the Impressionists, Van Gogh and his *Sunflowers*, Gauguin, etc.).

National Portrait Gallery ★★

E4 *St Martin's Place –* ⊖ *Leicester Square or Charing Cross –* ✆ *020 7306 0055/12 2463 – www.npg.org.uk –* ♿ *– 10:30AM–6PM (9PM Fri.–Sat.) – free (except temporary exhibitions).*
☺ *Don't miss the restaurant on the 4th floor (◉ p. 117).*
Founded in 1856, then established in 1896 in a beautiful Renaissance building behind the National Gallery, the National Portrait Gallery reopened in 2023 after three years of renovation and expansion. Its extraordinary collection gathers over 12,000 portraits of famous Britons, exhibited on a rotating basis. The museum is arranged chronologically. The visit begins on the 3rd floor with Tudor-era portraits. While some works were created by the greatest British artists, such as Hogarth, Reynolds, Gainsborough, or Watts, the NPG is also worth visiting for its historical interest. Paintings, drawings, caricatures, photographs, sculptures, and videos reveal the faces of the personalities who shaped the country's history and culture, from the Tudor era to the present day. Fascinating!

St Martin-in-the-Fields Church ★

E4 *Trafalgar Square –* ⊖ *Charing Cross –* ✆ *020 7766 1100 – www. stmartin-in-the-fields.org –* ♿ *– 9AM–5PM.*
☺ *Cafeteria in the crypt. Baroque music lovers, be sure to check out the concert schedule at St Martin-in-the-Fields!*
Built by **James Gibbs** between 1722 and 1726, the fourth church erected on this site since the Middle Ages, St Martin-in-the-Fields is adorned with a Corinthian portico and an elegant spire. It boasts excellent acoustics and a long musical tradition, notably highlighted by the creation in 1959 of the famous Academy of St Martin-in-the-Fields, a chamber orchestra founded on the initiative of violinist Neville Mariner, pivotal in the revival of Baroque music.

St James's ★★

Besides housing a royal palace, the prestigious St James's district is home to venerable houses that serve as royal residences, official buildings, members' clubs, specialty stores, and theaters. At the edge of St James's Park stands Buckingham Palace. The official residence of the royal family in London (even though Charles III and Camilla prefer to stay at Clarence House), it is open to the public in the summer when the monarch goes on vacation. Its annexes, the Royal Mews and the King's Gallery, remain open year-round.

Access: ⊖ St James's Park, Victoria, Green Park, Charing Cross.
Neighborhood map p. 24. Detachable map CDE5–6.
Advice: Buckingham Palace opens to the public only from mid-July to the end of September; as tickets are dated, you must reserve well in advance. At all royal sites *(www.rct.uk)*, ask the reception to date and stamp your ticket to make it a year-valid pass. King's Gallery and Royal Mews: discounts for online early ticket purchases.
📍 Where to Go pp. 117, 129, 132, and 136.

St James's Palace ★

D5 ⊖ *Green Park – 📞 030 3123 7324 – www.rct.uk – palace closed to the public.*
The Tudor manor where the king and his court settled after Whitehall Palace was destroyed in 1698 was built between 1530 and 1532 at the request of Henry VIII. Its crenelated brown brick facade, dominated by an imposing medieval-style entrance pavilion, stands in stark contrast to the classical architecture buildings along **Pall Mall★** and St James's Street. **Charles III** was officially proclaimed king there on September 10, 2022. Adjacent to the palace, **Clarence House** was the residence of Elizabeth Bowes-Lyon, mother of Queen Elizabeth II, and Charles III and Camilla

Birute/Getty Images Plus

A royal guard.

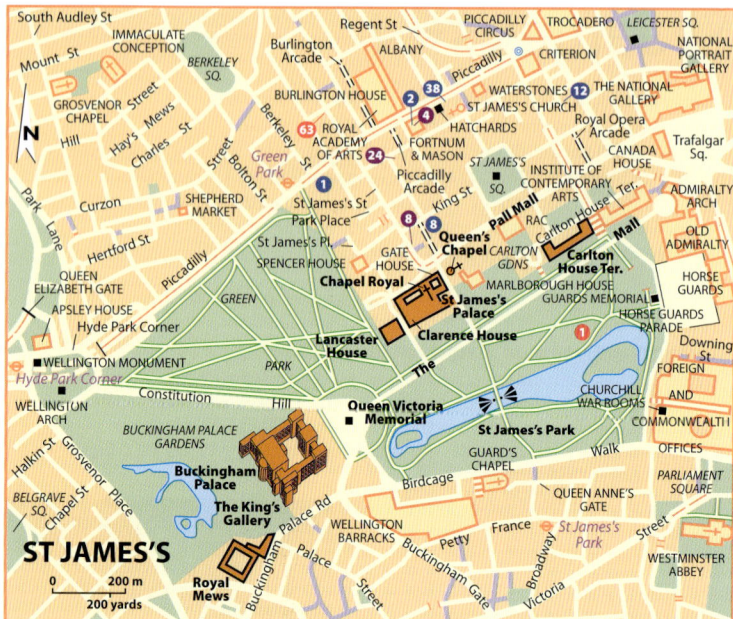

South Audley St
IMMACULATE
CONCEPTION
Mount St
BERKELEY SQ.
GROSVENOR CHAPEL
Hay's Mews
Hill
Charles St
Curzon
SHEPHERD MARKET
Hertford St
QUEEN ELIZABETH GATE
Piccadilly
APSLEY HOUSE
Hyde Park Corner
WELLINGTON MONUMENT
Hyde Park Corner
WELLINGTON ARCH
Constitution
Hill
BUCKINGHAM PALACE GARDENS
BELGRAVE SQ.
Halkin St
Grosvenor Place
Chapel St
ST JAMES'S
0   200 m
200 yards
Royal Mews
Buckingham Palace
The King's Gallery
WELLINGTON BARRACKS
Buckingham Palace Rd
Palace
Street
Buckingham Gate
Petty
France
Broadway
Victoria

Regent St
Burlington Arcade
ALBANY
BURLINGTON HOUSE
Berkeley St
ROYAL ACADEMY OF ARTS
Green Park
St Bolton St
St James's St
Park Place
St James's Pl.
SPENCER HOUSE
GATE HOUSE
Chapel Royal
Queen's Chapel
CARLTON GDNS
GREEN
PARK
Lancaster House
Clarence House
The
Queen Victoria Memorial
St James's Park
Birdcage
GUARD'S CHAPEL
QUEEN ANNE'S GATE
St James's Park
PICCADILLY CIRCUS
TROCADERO
LEICESTER SQ.
CRITERION
NATIONAL PORTRAIT GALLERY
Piccadilly
WATERSTONES
ST JAMES'S CHURCH
THE NATIONAL GALLERY
HATCHARDS
FORTNUM & MASON
Royal Opera Arcade
CANADA HOUSE
Trafalgar Sq.
ST JAMES'S
Piccadilly Arcade
King St
ST JAMES'S SQ.
INSTITUTE OF CONTEMPORARY ARTS
Pall Mall
RAC
Carlton House Ter.
MARLBOROUGH HOUSE
St James's Palace
CARLTON HOUSE TER.
Mall
GUARDS MEMORIAL
HORSE GUARDS PARADE
ADMIRALTY ARCH
OLD ADMIRALTY
HORSE GUARDS
Downing St
FOREIGN AND COMMONWEALTH OFFICES
CHURCHILL WAR ROOMS
Walk
PARLIAMENT SQUARE
WESTMINSTER ABBEY

24

DINING		SHOPPING
St James's Café..............1	Fortnum & Mason's Restaurants........2	Fortnum & Mason..............4
Gymkhana..............63	Golden Lion..............8	Lock & Co. Hatters..............8
GRAB A DRINK	Ole and Steen..............12	Hilditch & Key..............24
The Ritz London..............1	Maison Assouline..............38	

---

have resided there since 2003. The royal couple plans to continue living there until renovations at Buckingham Palace, scheduled to be finished by 2027, are completed.
Distinguished guests are accommodated at **Lancaster House**, a nearby mansion used for some official receptions.

During services, access may occasionally be granted to the **Chapel Royal** (*Ambassadors Court – Sundays, Oct.-Easter*) or the **Queen's Chapel** (*Marlborough Rd – Sundays, Easter-July*). It was in the latter that the coffins of Diana and Elizabeth Bowes-Lyon were displayed before their funerals.

The Mall ★★

DE5 ⊖ *Charing Cross.*
This beautiful tree-lined avenue, which hosts grand royal parades, runs along St James's Park to the north and connects Admiralty Arch to the **Queen Victoria Memorial**, which stands before Buckingham Palace. The route is flanked by the neoclassical facades of **Carlton House Terrace**, two sprawling residences designed in 1829 by **John Nash.**

St James's Park ★★

D5 ⊖ *St James's Park – ℘ 030 0061 2350 – www.royalparks.org.uk – 5AM–12AM.*
This 57-acre royal park, created by Henry VIII in 1532 to enhance the marshy environs of his newly built manor (**𝒞** *p. 23*), was redesigned in the 17th century and later remodeled in the 19th century by John Nash, King George IV's favored architect. Its flower-lined paths and small **lake**, where an unexpected colony of pelicans live (fed daily between 2:30PM and 3:00PM), provide a delightful place to stroll. The **bridge** over the lake offers a lovely view of Buckingham Palace and Whitehall.

> 🥤 **Before or after the Changing of the Guard**
> Take a break in the park at **St James's Café** (**𝒞** *p. 117*). If it rains, warm up at the **Golden Lion** (**𝒞** *p. 132*).

The Changing of the Guard ★★★ at Buckingham Palace

The changing of the guard is one of London's main attractions. It usually takes place every other day *(schedule available on www.householddivision.org.uk)*. Starting at 11AM, the detachment responsible for Buckingham Palace is inspected, joined 15 minutes later by the one from St James's Palace. Together they form the "old guard," as opposed to the "new guard" that will take over. Departing from the Wellington Barracks with the regimental band and drum corps, the new guard arrives at 11:30AM. They salute the "old guard" before being symbolically handed the palace keys. The sentinels are then replaced. 35 minutes later, the "old guard" leaves Buckingham Palace's courtyard to return to Wellington Barracks, while the "new guard" splits into two, with one detachment heading to St James's Palace. The guard is made up of five foot regiments. They wear a red tunic with a dark blue collar and a bearskin and are distinguished by the color of their plume and the arrangement of buttons: the **Grenadiers** (1656) have a white plume on the left and evenly spaced buttons; the **Coldstream** (1650), a red plume on the right and buttons grouped in pairs; the **Scots** (1642), no plume and buttons in groups of three; the **Irish** (1900), a blue plume on the right and buttons in groups of four; the **Welsh** (1915), a green and white plume on the left and buttons in groups of five.

Buckingham Palace ★★

D5 *Buckingham Palace Rd –*
⊖ Victoria – ☎ 020 7766 7300 –
www.rct.uk – ♿ – mid-Jul. to late Sep.:
9:30AM–7:30PM (6:30PM in Sep.); last
entry 2h15 before closing – State Rooms
closed Tue.–Wed. – £35, audioguide
included – online reservations. Guided
tours, special tours (including gardens):
see website.

The palace we see today originated
from the brick house built in 1702 for the
first Duke of Buckingham, purchased in
1762 by King **George III** for the pleasure
of his wife, Queen Charlotte. Significant
changes were made over the following
century, but much of the work was led
by the architect **John Nash** in the late
18th century.

Victoria was the first monarch to settle
in Buckingham in 1837, and the royal
standard has flown there ever since
when the monarch is at the palace.
Of the 660 rooms within the palace,
only the 19 **State Rooms** are open to
the public. These are grand ceremonial
rooms used for official banquets and
receptions. Guests enter the Guard
Room via the Grand Hall and the
majestic **Grand Staircase**. Highlights
include the Green Drawing Room,
Dining Room, Blue Drawing Room,
Music Room, and White Drawing
Room, but the centerpiece remains the
Throne Room and the **Portrait Gallery**
featuring masterpieces by Van Dyck,
Rubens, Rembrandt, Vermeer, and
Canaletto, among others.

The King's Gallery ★★

D5 *Buckingham Palace Rd –*
⊖ Victoria – ☎ 030 3123 7324 –
www.rct.uk – ♿ – Thu.–Mon.

10AM–5:30PM (last entry 4:15PM) – £19.
Built on the site of an old private chapel,
this gallery showcases temporary
exhibitions of artworks from the
magnificent royal collection.

Royal Mews ★★

D6 *Buckingham Palace Rd –*
⊖ Victoria – ☎ 030 3123 7324 –
www.rct.uk – ♿ – Mar.–Oct.: Thu.–
Mon. 10AM–5PM (last entry 1h before
closing) – £19.

A visit to Buckingham Palace would
be incomplete without touring the
Royal Mews, which house the royal
carriages and vehicles used by the
royal family during official events.
Reconfigured by architect **John Nash**,
they were moved here in 1825 on King
George IV's orders. The "star" of this
remarkable collection is undoubtedly
the **Gold State Coach** made in 1762 at
the request of **George III** and used for
every coronation. Designed by **William
Chambers**, with contributions from
renowned artists like sculptor Joseph
Wilton and Florentine painter G.B.
Cipriani, it weighs 4 tons and requires a
team of eight horses to draw it.
Since the first car was introduced to
the stables by **King Edward VII** in
1901, eight official cars, including three
Rolls-Royces and two Bentleys, are
also parked here. Only one car, a 1907
Rolls-Royce Silver Ghost, one of the
most beautiful and prestigious cars
ever built, is on permanent display.
Finally, visitors can see the
immaculately kept stalls of the royal
horses, the Windsor Greys and
Cleveland Bays, along with a fine
collection of saddlery items.

Mayfair★
and Piccadilly ★

Just the name Mayfair evokes elegance and luxury, symbolized by the beautiful store windows on Bond Street. To the south, the neighborhood is bordered by Piccadilly. At its eastern end lies Piccadilly Circus, with its statue of Eros and giant neon signs, making it one of London's bustling districts and a must-see for visitors.

▶ **Access:** ⊖ Bond Street, Green Park, Piccadilly Circus, Marble Arch, Hyde Park Corner.

Neighborhood map pp. 28–29. Detachable map CD4–5.

☉ *Where to Go pp. 118, 135 and 136.*

MAYFAIR ★

Shepherd Market ★

C5 ⊖ *Green Park –*
www.shepherdmarket.com.
This **market** is made up of a labyrinth of lanes and courtyards connected by vaulted alleys. The Victorian and Edwardian period pubs, the small houses with their stores (watchmakers, barbers, art galleries) on the ground floor, cafés with terraces, and restaurants serving international fare give the area a cosmopolitan village feel.

Berkeley Square

C4 ⊖ *Green Park.*
The memory of Berkeley's garden endures thanks to the plane trees planted in 1789. The square was laid out in 1737. From the original architectural setting, a few 18th-century houses remain on the western side with their wrought-iron balconies, carriage lights, and torch extinguishers.

Chrispictures/Shutterstock

Shepherd Market in Mayfair.

Mount Street

C4 ⊖ *Marble Arch or Hyde Park Corner.*

A serene atmosphere, with discreet opulence, reigns on Mount Street, which stretches to the northwest corner of Berkeley Square, passing in front of the **Connaught**, symbolic of the luxurious hotels of the late 19th century. Flanked by tall brick houses with irregular gables adorned with terracotta, this street is home to a succession of boutiques featuring renowned trunk makers, shoemakers, fashion designers, galleries, etc.

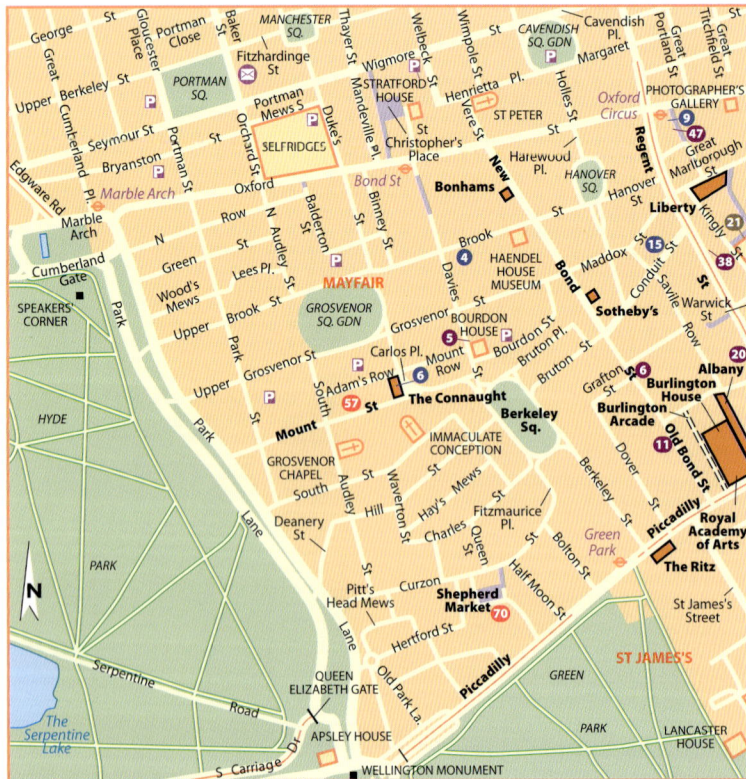

Bond Street ★

CD4 ⊖ *Bond Street.*
An old Tudor-era lane, Bond Street runs through Mayfair from north to south. **New Bond Street**, built in 1720, was home to London's elite, who hired the area's bespoke tailors and perfumers. Since then, it is a symbol of elegance, lined with luxury leather goods, top fashion houses, chic stationery stores, and art dealers. At Nos. 35 and 77–78 is **Sotheby's**, the world's largest auction house since its inception in 1744. Its great rival, **Bonhams**, is located in the same area *(Nos. 101 and 107 New Bond St.)*. Beyond the bronze sculpture honoring Churchill and Roosevelt stretches **Old Bond Street★**, flanked by luxury stores

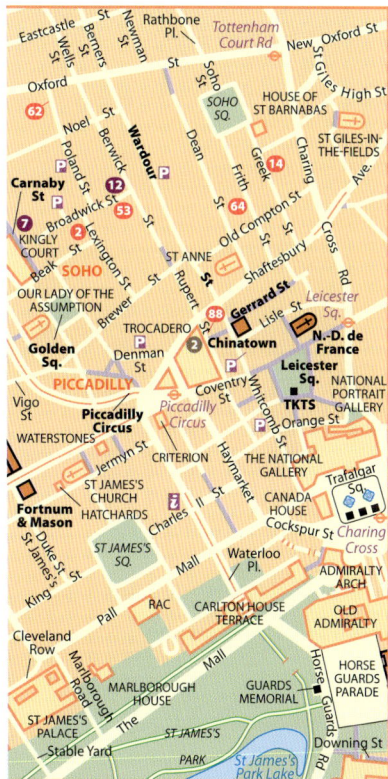

MAYFAIR PICCADILLY SOHO

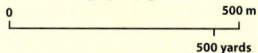

0   500 m

500 yards

DINING

BAO	2
10 Greek Street	14
Yauatcha Soho	53
Scott's	57
Golden Union	62
Koya Bar	64
L'Autre	70
The Palomar	88

GRAB A DRINK

Claridge's	4
The Connaught Bar	6
Argyll Arms	9
Sketch	15

SHOPPING

Vivienne Westwood	5
Stella McCartney	6
The Rolling Stones Store	7
Charbonnel et Walker	11
Berwick Street	12
Penhaligon's	20
Hamleys	38
Beyond Retro	47

GOING OUT

Bar Rumba	2
Cirque le Soir	21

with a well-established reputation. Not far from here is the Regency passage of **Burlington Arcade**.

Burlington House ★

D4 ⊖ *Piccadilly Circus.*
In 1664, the first Earl of Burlington acquired this property. His descendant began rebuilding the residence in the Palladian style in 1715. Restored in the 19ᵗʰ century, the building was altered once more between 1867–1873 in the Neo-Renaissance style. In 1869, the rear of Burlington House was transformed in the Neo-Gothic style. Decorated with towers, a portico, and a grand porch, this wing of the building features about twenty statues of magistrates.
Royal Academy of Arts – *Accessible via Burlington House or Burlington Gardens* – 📞*020 7300 8090 – www. royalacademy.org.uk* – ♿ *– Tue.–Sun. 10AM–6PM (9PM on Fri.).* Burlington House homes the headquarters of the School of Fine Arts, which supports contemporary creation and organizes numerous exhibitions.

PICCADILLY ★

CD4–5 ⊖ *Piccadilly Circus or Hyde Park Corner.*
This famous artery stretches from Piccadilly Circus to Hyde Park Corner, separating the St James's (*ⓒ p. 23*) and Mayfair districts. It is lined with elegant buildings, elite clubs, luxury stores, and prestigious hotels like the **Ritz**. Since its opening in 1906, this building, inspired by French classicism and decorated in Louis XVI style, has hosted the world's greats.
Founded in 1707, **Fortnum & Mason** *(181 Piccadilly)* is an internationally renowned fine grocery store. It is also known for the musical clock that can

be seen on the side of the building, which automates a bow between the founders of the store at the top of every hour (*ⓒ p. 136*).

Piccadilly Circus ★

D4 ⊖ *Piccadilly Circus.*
Once considered the center of the British Empire, this bustling intersection is at the crossroads of three major avenues: Piccadilly, Haymarket, and Shaftesbury Avenue. Its beautiful **fountain** was erected in 1893 in homage to Lord Shaftesbury (1801–1885), a famous British philanthropist. The golden bronze *Angel of Christian Charity* surmounting it, commonly associated with Eros, has become one of the city's emblems, much like the square's illuminated signs.

> **For a Chic Afternoon Tea**
>
> Around Piccadilly and Mayfair, prestigious places serve exceptional afternoon teas in a refined setting: Harrods, Claridge's, Ritz, Fortnum & Mason's... *ⓒ p. 130.*

Soho★

A bohemian and trendy district, Soho is the playground of advertisers and the fashion and film industries. It's also the stronghold of London's LGBTQ+ community. At night, the parade of night owls brings life to the pubs and French, Italian, Greek, Chinese, and Caribbean restaurants, while crowds gather around theaters, cinemas, jazz clubs, and nightclubs.

▶**Access:** ⊖ Oxford Circus, Tottenham Court Road, Leicester Square, Piccadilly Circus.
Neighborhood map pp. 28–29. Detachable map DE3–4.
▶**Tip:** It's best to visit on weekend evenings, when the neighborhood's festive atmosphere can be most strongly felt.
⦿ Where to Go pp. 118, 132, 137, and 143.

Regent Street ★★

D4 ⊖ *Oxford Circus or Piccadilly Circus.*
This elegant avenue designed by John Nash (1812) remains the shopping kingdom. You can find major British and international brands here, including the massive Hamley's toy store (⦿ p. 138)... not to mention the famous and luxurious Café Royal hotel.

Liberty ★★

D4 *Great Marlborough St. –* ⊖ *Oxford Circus.*
This "emporium," founded in 1875 by Arthur Liberty, offered a vast array of items imported from the British Empire, complemented by furniture made in Soho workshops. The store created its own product lines, inspired by traditional Indian models or commissioned from leading designers whose work nodded to the Arts & Crafts movement. Art Nouveau-style jewelry was generally imported from Europe. But the Liberty brand is mainly famous for its lightweight cotton fabrics with characteristic floral patterns, popularized in France in the 1960s by the house of Cacharel. Note the magnificent colonnade of the former facade on Regent Street, dominated by the monumental statue of *Britannia* surrounded by three stone figures. The **Tudor facade** (1924) facing Great Marlborough Street was designed by Edwin T. and Stanley Hall, then built with oak and teak from the last two Royal Navy schooners.

Carnaby

D4 ⊖ *Oxford Circus.*
This largely pedestrian area around **Carnaby Street** was a hotspot of Swinging London in the 1960s (⦿ p. 180). It now houses sophisticated stores, trendy bars, restaurants, and clubs. Explore the surrounding alleys and courtyards, such as the pretty **Kingly Court**, whose walkways are home to cafés and restaurants.

Golden Square

D4 Piccadilly Circus.
This beautiful square, featuring a garden enclosed by railings, is the preserve of the fashion and media industries. The calm that reigns there contrasts with the hustle and bustle of the neighborhood.

Wardour Street

D3–4 Leicester Square.
A symbol of the film industry in the 1930s, the street remains home to several film production companies. In the evening, the action is in full swing in its bars and restaurants.

Chinatown ★

D4 Leicester Square.
Guarded by tall pagoda-style gates, **Gerrard Street** is the center of this colorful neighborhood, filled with East Asian restaurants, medicine centers, and red-and-gold lanterns. It's here that Chinese New Year is celebrated every year (Jan.–Feb.).

Leicester Square ★

DE4 Leicester Square.
This vast square was long the heart of London's entertainment world, as evidenced by the Empire Theatre building (1884) on the north side. Today lined with stores, restaurants, and cinemas, Leicester Square is a bustling passing place where a small break can be enjoyed in front of the Shakespeare Memorial Fountain, erected in 1874.

PurpleImages/Getty Images Plus

Chinese New Year in Chinatown.

On the south side, the **TKTS booth** (☎ p. 144) sells same-day theater tickets at half price.
Northeast of the square, the **Notre-Dame-de-France Church** features frescoes by **Jean Cocteau** (1959) and an Aubusson tapestry by Dom Robert (1954). 5 Leicester Pl. – www.ndfchurch.org – Mon. and Wed.–Sat. 9:30AM–9PM, Sun. 12PM–6PM.

Covent Garden ★

Covent Garden serves as the lively heart of London's tourist center. The pedestrians strolling around the Piazza have taken the place of the merchants who used to line the market's edges. In the evening, pub patrons spill onto the sidewalks, and theater-goers hurry into restaurants before attending one of the many shows staged in the area.

▶ **Access:** ⊖ Covent Garden.
Neighborhood map p. 34. Detachable map E4.
◉ *Where to Go pp. 119, 129, 132, 138, and 147.*

The Piazza ★

E4 Built on the site of a garden in a convent (actually Westminster Abbey), this square was designed in 1631 by **Inigo Jones** at the request of Francis Russell, the 4th Earl of Bedford, who became the owner of the estate after the Reformation. The distinguished architect (◉ *p. 174*) drew inspiration from the Place Royale in Paris (now Place des Vosges) and the Piazza Grande in Livorno (Italy), which he had admired a few years earlier. Today, only the houses to the west of Russell Street remain from Inigo Jones' original design, although they have been rebuilt since.

St Paul's Church ★

E4 *Entrance via the Piazza or Bedford St. –* ☎ *020 7836 5221 – actorschurch.org –* ♿ *– 8:30AM–5:30PM, Sun. 9AM–1PM.* This graceful Tuscan-style pink brick church, built by Jones in 1633, was faithfully reconstructed after a fire damaged it in 1795. It is also known as the Actors' Church, because its crypts and graveyard house several celebrities, including actress Edith Evans (1888–1976) and sculptor **Grinling Gibbons** (1648–1721), whose works embellish the church.

Covent Garden Market

E4 This flower, fruit, and vegetable market founded in the 16th century (made famous by G. B. Shaw's Eliza Doolittle) was moved to Nine Elms (close to Battersea) in 1974 and replaced by a crafts market. Stores, cafés, and restaurants have been set up in the former warehouses, designed in 1832 by Charles Fowler and connected by glass roofs in 1872.

Jubilee Market Hall

E4 The hall is occupied by souvenir merchants from Tuesday to Friday *(10:30AM–6PM)*, followed by artists and craftspeople on Saturday and Sunday *(10AM–6PM)*, and antique dealers on Monday *(10AM–4PM)*. The **Jubilee Hall** (1904) houses a sports center.

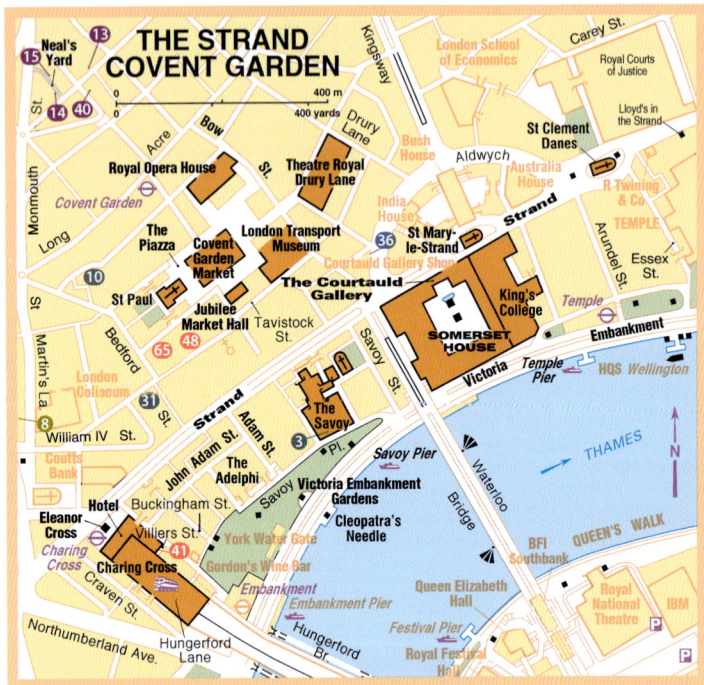

THE STRAND COVENT GARDEN

Neal's Yard

Royal Opera House

Theatre Royal Drury Lane

Covent Garden

The Piazza

Covent Garden Market

London Transport Museum

St Paul

Jubilee Market Hall

Tavistock St.

St Mary-le-Strand

Courtauld Gallery Shop

The Courtauld Gallery

King's College

SOMERSET HOUSE

Kingsway

London School of Economics

Carey St.

Royal Courts of Justice

Lloyd's in the Strand

St Clement Danes

Aldwych

Australia House

R Twining & Co

TEMPLE

Arundel St.

Essex St.

Temple

Embankment

Drury Lane

Bush House

India House

Strand

Acre

Bow

Long

Monmouth St.

Neal's Yard

London Coliseum

William IV St.

Coutts Bank

Bedford St.

Martin's La.

St Martin's

The Adelphi

John Adam St.

Adam St.

Strand

Victoria

Temple Pier

HQS Wellington

THAMES

Savoy St.

The Savoy

Pl.

Savoy Pier

The Adelphi

Buckingham St.

Hotel

Eleanor Cross

Charing Cross

Villiers St.

York Water Gate

Gordon's Wine Bar

Victoria Embankment Gardens

Cleopatra's Needle

Savoy

Waterloo Bridge

BFI Southbank

QUEEN'S WALK

Craven St.

Northumberland Ave.

Hungerford Lane

Embankment

Embankment Pier

Hungerford Br.

Queen Elizabeth Hall

Festival Pier

Royal Festival Hall

Royal National Theatre

IBM

400 m
400 yards

N

DINING

MOC Kitchen 41
Rules 48
Flat Iron 65

GRAB A DRINK

The Savoy 3

Lamb & Flag 10
Brigit's Bakery 31
One Aldwich 36

SHOPPING

Magma 13

Neal's Yard Dairy 14
Neal's Yard Remedies 15
Tatty Devine 40

ACCOMMODATION
Hub by Premier Inn
    Covent Garden 8

London Transport Museum ★

E4 *Covent Garden Piazza – 📞 020 7379 6344 – www.ltmuseum.co.uk – ♿ – 10AM–5PM – £24.50, ticket valid for 1 year.*

Highly popular with families, this interactive museum tracks 200 years of history and technology. Established in the 1920s and 1930s by the London General Omnibus Company, the collection was moved in 1980 to this building, the former flower market. The exhibits showcase the development and impact of London's urban transport network, one of the largest in the world. On show are vehicles like the Shillibeer horse omnibus (1829–1834), an 1866 subway unit, and the first bus from 1910.

Theatre Royal Drury Lane

E4 *Catherine St. – 📞 020 7557 7300 – www.lwtheatres.co.uk – guided tour (1h) daily except Tue. – £18.50/22.50.*

Founded in 1663, this is the fourth theater built on the site of an original structure from the Restoration. The current building is the contribution of Benjamin Wyatt (1812). It was here that King Charles II met the English actress Nell Gwyn (1650–1687), his most famous mistress, with whom he had two children.

Royal Opera House ★

E4 *Bow St. – 📞 020 7304 4000 – www.roh.org.uk – ♿ – guided tour (1h30) – £20 – reservation required.*

The **Royal Opera** was founded in 1732. The current building (1856) expanded with a beautiful and bright contemporary wing (2000) housing a hall with over 2,200 seats, host to the Royal Opera, the Royal Ballet, and the Royal Orchestra. Use the escalators to discover the view of the Piazza from the loggia on the upper level.

Neal's Yard ★

E4 *Between Shorts Gardens St. and Monmouth St.*

Vegetarian restaurants, a lovely cheese shop (◉ *"Shopping" p. 138*), and stores offering organic products and alternative medicine have set up in this picturesque, colorful courtyard, which has retained the old-world charm of its pulley systems, dovecotes, flower boxes, and potted trees.

> ### Members' Pubs and Clubs
>
> The southwest part of Covent Garden is famous for its members' clubs. The **Garrick Club** (1831; *15 Garrick St.*) and the **Beefsteak Club** (1867; *9 Irving St.*) carry on this tradition. The **Rules** (*34–35 Maiden Lane*), the oldest restaurant in London (1798), still attracts a fashionable crowd (◉ *p. 119*). The **Lamb & Flag** is the oldest restaurant in the area and has been open since 1623 (◉ *p. 132*).

The Strand ★

Situated at the edge of Covent Garden and the City, the Strand neighborhood is full of charm, despite the constant traffic that clutters it. Flanked by beautiful buildings from its aristocratic past, it features elegant hotels, lively theaters, and at Somerset House, the magnificent art collections of the Courtauld Gallery, all the while maintaining its reputation as a go-to neighborhood.

▶**Access:** ⊖ Temple, Charing Cross, Embankment.
Neighborhood map p. 34. Detachable map EF4–5.
⊙ Where to Go p. 119.

Charing Cross Station

E4–5 ⊖ *Charing Cross or Embankment.*
Serving the south of England, along with Victoria Station, Charing Cross Station was built in 1863.
Right next to it, the neo-Gothic **Charing Cross Hotel** (1864), with two upper floors added later, is the work of E. M. Barry. The 1990-built edifices behind it are notable for the large white arch that partially covers the railroad viaduct by Sir Terry Farrell.
Charing Cross Collectors Market is held on Saturdays (9AM–5PM) at the end of Villiers Street, under the viaduct.

Victoria Embankment Gardens ★

E4 ⊖ *Embankment.*
The gardens on the **Victoria Embankment** were planted in 1864; concerts are held there in summer. On the opposite riverbank stands **Cleopatra's Needle**, an Egyptian obelisk in pink granite gifted to George IV by Muhammad Ali, Viceroy of Egypt, in 1878. However, this is not the original needle, which is now located in Central Park, New York. Without its pedestal, the obelisk stands 69 feet high (the one in New York is 77 feet; the one in Rome, 82 feet) and weighs 201 tons.

The Adelphi

E4 ⊖ *Charing Cross or Embankment.*
This sheltered neighborhood nestles between the Strand and the Thames, from Villiers Street to Adam Street. In the 18th and 19th centuries, it was a sort of little Athens favored by artists. Starting in 1768, the **Adam brothers**, all three architects, developed the Adelphi district, creating a planned urban ensemble with streets lined with similar, antique-style facades. Unfortunately, nearly all the residences were demolished in the 1930s. At least two beautiful examples remain, typical of the Adam style. On **John Adam Street**, at No. 8, stands the **Royal Society of Arts**. There's a lovely view

of the RSA from the top of the small stairway that connects Durham House Street to the Strand. A bit further, at No. 7, a house features pilasters carved with honeysuckle.

The Savoy ★

E4 ⊖ *Charing Cross.*
The Savoy is a complex including a chapel, a **theater** built by Richard d'Oyly Carte in 1881 that was the first London building lit by electricity, and an exceptional **hotel** by the same architect. Typically British, the Savoy Hotel, one of London's most renowned, occupies the site of the Savoy Palace built in 1246 by Henry III for Peter, Count of Savoy.

> **Afternoon Tea**
>
> Taking afternoon tea at the **Savoy** is a delightful way to experience the interior of this exceptional hotel. ☉ *p. 130.*

Somerset House ★★

E4 *Access via the Strand and Victoria Embankment –* ⊖ *Temple –* ☎ *020 7848 2323 – www.somersethouse. org.uk –* ♿ *– 8AM–11PM – guided tours (free – 1hr – reservation required, times on the website) – lectures, screenings, concerts.*
This stunning Portland stone building, stretching between the Strand and the Thames, was designed by the architect **William Chambers** (☉ *p. 175*). It was erected at the end of the 18th century on the site of a former royal palace commissioned by the Lord Protector

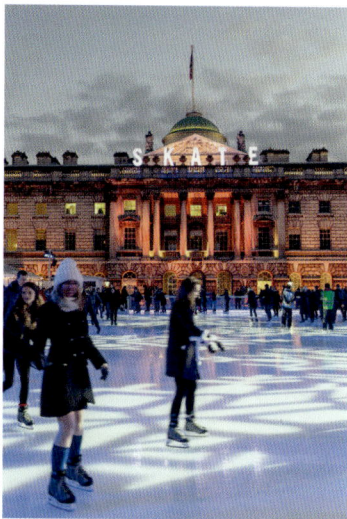

The seasonal ice rink in front of Somerset House.

ultraforma/Getty Images Plus

37

Somerset in 1547. Its narrow facade doesn't impress much, but the beauty of the place is fully revealed upon crossing the portico. A vast courtyard is dotted with elegant water jets that are a delight for young and old in summer. Numerous events (concerts, sound and light shows, etc.) are organized on the piazza of Somerset House throughout the year.

The Courtauld Gallery ★★

E4 *Somerset House – ⊖ Temple – ☎ 020 3947 7777 – www. courtauld. ac.uk – ♿ – 10AM–6PM – £10 weekdays, £12 weekends.*

Set in the salons of Somerset House, overlooking the Strand, admirable for its elegant stucco ceilings, this gallery was renovated in 2021. On three levels, it houses the exceptional collections of the Courtauld Institute of Art, founded in 1932 by English industrialist and patron Samuel Courtauld.

1st floor – Dedicated to **medieval art**, with the remarkable *Seilern Triptych* by Robert Campin.

2nd floor – The **Blavatnik Fine Rooms** highlight masterpieces from the Renaissance to the 18th century, notably from Italian and Northern schools. Must-sees include *The Holy Trinity* (or *Pala delle Convertite*) by Botticelli, *Adam and Eve* by Cranach the Elder, *Landscape with the Flight into Egypt* by Bruegel the Elder, and Rubens' oils, including *The Descent from the Cross* and *The Family of Jan Bruegel the Elder.*

3rd floor – Here you'll see the jewel of the Courtauld Gallery, its extraordinary **collection of Impressionist** and Post-Impressionist works, exhibited in the **LVMH Great Room:** Manet (*A Bar at the Folies-Bergère*), **Van Gogh** (*Self-Portrait with Bandaged Ear*), Cézanne (*The Card Players*), Monet, Seurat, Renoir, Degas, Gauguin, and Modigliani are among the artists represented. On the same floor, a room showcases some works by artists of the **Bloomsbury Group** on rotation. Temporary exhibitions are organized from the gallery's incredible reserves.

St Mary le Strand

E4 *The Strand – ⊖ Temple – www. stmarylestrand.com – Mon–Fri 12PM–4PM.*

Built by **James Gibbs** between 1714 and 1724, this baroque-style church features a rotunda porch, terrace roof, and tiered bell tower marked by a lantern. Inside, its coffered ceiling is carved with flower or cherub motifs. If one disregards the tower, the building resembles a small palace. Taxi drivers call it "St Mary-in-the-Way," because it splits the street!

St Clement Danes ★

F4 *St Clement Danes Church – Strand – ⊖ Temple – ☎ 020 7242 2380 – stclementdanesraf.org – ♿ – 10AM–12PM, 1PM–4PM, weekends 10AM–3PM.*

The Danes who settled between London and Westminster in the 9th century had established their burial grounds where **Christopher Wren** built the current structure in 1682. The bell tower, redone by Gibbs in 1719, has several similarities with that of St Mary. The church, burned down in 1941 during the Blitz, was restored between 1955 and 1958 under the patronage of the Royal Air Force and later became its shrine: 735 unit shields are inlaid in the floor. The interior is very harmonious and features the pews and galleries beloved by Wren; their dark tones contrast with the light tones of the pillars and the white stucco vaults standing out against gray backgrounds. The pulpit was crafted by **Grinling Gibbons**.

Temple★
and Chancery Lane★

The grand stone vessel of the Royal Courts of Justice stands at the heart of London's legal district. Surrounding it are the prestigious Inns of Court, the four law schools that oversee the profession and prepare students for the bar: Gray's Inn and Lincoln's Inn in the Chancery Lane area, north of the courthouse; and Inner Temple and Middle Temple in the former Templar district, near the Thames. Wander through this maze of old buildings, courtyards, and squares. The atmosphere is peaceful and studious, even tinged with a bit of mystery. To extend this journey through time, get lost in the nooks and crannies of the Sir John Soane's Museum, an indescribable cabinet of curiosities.

▶ **Access:** ⊖ Temple, Holborn, Chancery Lane.
Neighborhood map p. 41. Detachable map EF3–4.
▶ **Tip:** Since most of these visits are outdoors, choose a day without too much rain.
𝒞 *Where to Go pp. 132, 133, and 139.*

Royal Courts of Justice ★

F4 *The Strand* – ⊖ *Temple* – *www.theroyalcourtsofjustice.com* – ♿ – *Mon.–Fri. 9:30AM–4:30PM by reservation – guided tour in English (1h) £20.*
Built between 1874 and 1882, the neo-Gothic **Palace of Justice** is undeniably impressive: 3 miles of corridors, over 1,000 rooms, 35 million stone blocks, and a **Great Hall** of intimidating dimensions resembling the nave of a cathedral. This is where civil hearings and appeal trials take place (criminal cases are judged at the Old Bailey). Except for closed-door trials, hearings are open to the public; the last two rows of benches are thus reserved. Outside each court, a sheet lists the parties' names and specifies whether the trial will be *robed* or *unrobed*. For formal hearings, judges wear robes and sometimes long wigs. Lawyers, recognizable by their starched collars with ribbons, sport a more modest wig.
On the 1st floor of the building, you can see a small exhibition of old costumes (room 10, known as the robe room).

Temple ★

F4 *Access via Inner Temple Gateway (between Nos. 16 and 17 Fleet St.).*
A surprising maze of courtyards, arches, passages, and small gardens leads down to the banks of the Thames. These grounds owe their name to the Knights Templar, established here in the 12th century before giving way to the Order

of Malta, and were occupied by schools and law offices. Still dedicated to legal activities, this is a haven of peace, housing buildings from the 17th and 18th centuries.

Temple Church★★

King's Bench Walk – ✆ 020 7353 8559 – www.templechurch.com – ♿ – Mon.–Fri. 10AM–4PM (for exceptions, see website calendar) – £5 – concerts (some free).

This church is well known to fans of Dan Brown's *Da Vinci Code*, as it is one of the key locations in the novel and film. Built in the 12th century on a circular plan typical of the Order of Malta churches, it features a Romanesque porch. The rotunda, in the Romanesque-Gothic transition style, holds some knightly effigies (12th–13th centuries), while the choir offers a fine example of Early English style.

St Bride's Church ★

F4 *Fleet St. – ⊖ Blackfriars – ✆ 020 7427 0133 – www.stbrides.com – 8AM–5PM, Sat. 10AM–3:30PM, Sun. 10AM–6:30PM – free – concerts.*

The famous white **spire★★** of St Bride's,

Fleet Street

F4 This street was once considered to be the home of British journalism until technology transformed the production of major newspapers, whose offices gradually moved to the Docklands in the 1980s. This grand thoroughfare, also a royal route, is lined with imposing buildings in various architectural styles.

designed by **Christopher Wren**, was set on fire in 1940; only the shell and the tower remained standing. The building's exterior has been restored following Wren's original design, with large rounded bays between the pedimented doors, topped with circular windows. Inside, a neoclassical altarpiece closes the nave and seals the apse.

Lincoln's Inn ★★

F3 ⊖ *Chancery Lane – ✆ 020 7405 1393 – www.lincolnsinn.org.uk – park: Mon.–Fri. 8AM–7PM – chapel: Mon.–Fri. 9AM–7PM – guided tour of the buildings at 11AM – £15 (online reservation).*

This site belonged to the Dominicans until 1276 and was then acquired by the Earl of Lincoln, who built a large house that became a residence for law students.

A main gate gives access to a tangle of courtyards and buildings surrounded by gardens and sheds. 17th-century constructions, mostly occupied by law offices, frame **New Square**.

The southern part is marked by brick gabled buildings in Tudor style (rebuilt in 1609), called the **Old Buildings**. The oldest Lincoln's Inn building, the **Old Hall**, dates from 1490.

The **chapel** (*access via the staircase to the left of the Old Hall*) is in Gothic style, although rebuilt between 1619 and 1623. The stained-glass windows, from the same period, are by Flemish artists, the Van Linge brothers. In the past, lawyers received their clients in the lower gallery. The treasurers left their names and coats of arms here: Thomas More, Richard Cromwell, Horace Walpole, William

40

N

Emerald Street
Theobalds
Red Lion Street
Princeton St
RED LION SQUARE GARDENS
Eagle St
High 37
Bedford Row
Sandland St
Whetstone Park
Jockey's Fields
Road
Jockey's Fields
Gray's
Gray's Inn
South Square
GATEHOUSE
Portpool La.
Baldwin's Gardens
Chancery Lane

27
Leather Lane
Hatton
Cross Kirby Street
Saffron St.
Farringdon Street
Turnmill St.
Farringdon 🚇

Greville St
Ely Place
ST ETHELDREDA
Hill
Charterhouse
Farringdon
Road
St

Brooke St
Prudential Assurance Building
Holborn
Garden
Holborn Circus
Holborn
ST ANDREW HOLBORN
Viaduct

Holborn
Stone Buildings
Lincoln's Inn
Chancery
Staple Inn
LONDON SILVER VAULT
PATENT OFFICE
Barnard's Inn

Lane
New Fetter La.
Shoe Lane
Stonecutter Street
ST BRIDE St.

Sir John Soane's Museum
Lincoln's Inn Fields
Powis House
Lindsey House
Lincoln's Inn Fields
Chapel
Old Hall
New Hall and Library
New Square
Old Buildings
Gatehouse
Cursitor St
Bream's Buildings
DR JOHNSON'S HOUSE
Fetter Lane
Fleet Street
Ludgate Circus

Kingsway
ROYAL COLLEGE OF SURGEONS
Portugal St
Carey Street
Street
Bell Yard
ST DUSTAN-IN-THE-WEST
REUTERS
St Bride's

Kean St
LONDON SCHOOL OF ECONOMICS
Royal Courts of Justice
TEMPLE BAR
ST CLEMENT DANES
16
Fleet
Temple Church
Whitefriars St.
Bouverie Street
ST BRIDE PRINTING LIBRARY

Drury La.
Aldwych
BUSH HOUSE
Strand
Middle Temple La.
Temple
Carmelite St.
Tudor Street
UNILEVER HOUSE

ST MARY LE STRAND
COURTAULD GALLERY
KING'S COLLEGE
SOMERSET HOUSE
Temple
Arundel Street
Essex St.
Surrey St
Temple Place
Temple Ave.
INNER TEMPLE GARDENS
Embankment

Lancaster Place
Victoria
Temple Pier
Waterloo Bridge
HQS Wellington
Thames
River
Blackfriars Bridge

41

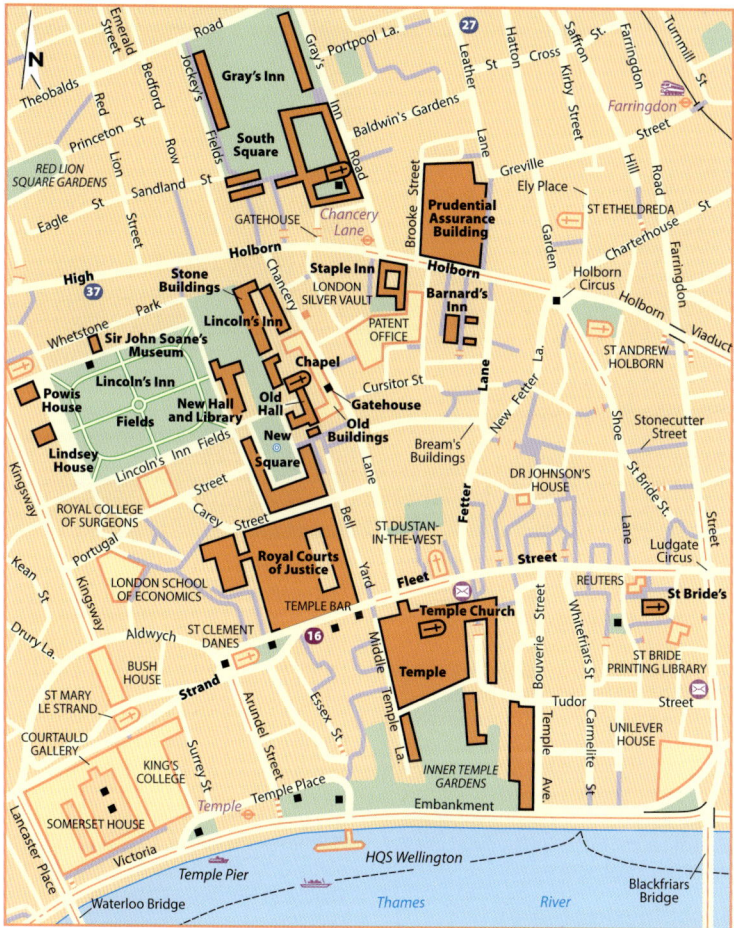

TEMPLE CHANCERY LANE

0   200 m
200 yards

GRAB A DRINK
Craft Beer Co...................... 27
Rosewood Hotel...................... 37

SHOPPING
Twinings...................... 16

New Square, Lincoln's Inn.

Pitt, Lord Brougham, Disraeli, etc.
The **Stone Buildings** were erected around 1775 in classical style.
The **New Hall** and the **Library** occupy a large Tudor-style building (1845–1873).
The **Gatehouse**, the entrance pavilion with brick and corner turrets, dates from 1518. The massive oak doors concealing the four-centered arch are original. The arms of Henry VIII, the Earl of Lincoln, and Sir Thomas Lovell are shown just above.

Lincoln's Inn Fields

E3 ⊖ *Holborn.*
Around 1650, a developer who had acquired the lands stretching west of Lincoln's Inn built houses on three sides of the garden, a sanctuary in the heart of a lively neighborhood.
One of them, **Lindsey House**, probably designed by Inigo Jones, still exists, though it is now divided (Nos. 59 and 60).
Several houses date from the 18th century, like Nos. 57 and 58, built in 1730 in the Palladian style, and **Powis House** (1777) at No.66, with the central bay topped by a pediment.
On the north side, Nos. 1–2 are from the early 18th century; Nos. 5–9, Georgian style; and No. 15, from the mid-18th century.
To the south rise the former **Land Registry** (now London School of Economics), in James I style, the neo-Georgian Nuffield College of Surgery (1956–1958), and the Royal College of

Surgeons (late 19th to early 20th centuries). At the corner, on Portsmouth Street, a half-timbered building displays the date 1567. Named **The Old Curiosity Shop** after the title of a novel by Charles Dickens, it attracts literature fans to the neighborhood.

Sir John Soane's Museum ★★

E3 *13 Lincoln's Inn Fields –* ⊖ *Holborn –* ☎ *020 7405 2107 – www.soane.org –* ♿ *– Wed.–Sun. 10AM–4:30PM – free.* 😊 *Candlelit Tour (Soane Late) one evening per month (by reservation, £25).* Between 1792 and 1823, the **architect John Soane**, who conceived the original designs for the Bank of England, acquired, remodeled, and combined Nos. 12, 13, and 14 of Lincoln's Inn Fields to create his family residence, his offices, and a museum. In 1833, the British Parliament passed a resolution to ensure the museum's preservation after his death. Thus, the collections allow a breathtaking glimpse into the world of a great collector of that era.

The rooms are small, the corridors narrow, the staircases modest, but the ingenious arrangement of mirrors, moving partitions, lighting, and windows on inner courtyards, as well as the decoration, enhance depth, surfaces, and perspectives. Fragments, casts, and models are displayed along the galleries, while in the **basement** are the crypt (urns and funerary vases), the monk's parlor, and the sepulchral chamber containing the sarcophagus of Seti I (around 1300 BC), carved from a monolithic block of calcite.

The **ground floor**, the dining room, the office, the cupola room for breakfast, and the portrait of Soane at 75 years old, painted by Lawrence, are very evocative. The **painting collection** (painting room) includes original drawings by Piranesi, satirical scenes by **Hogarth**, and also paintings by Canaletto, Reynolds, and Turner.

The **1st floor** contains prints, architectural plans, and rare books. The south drawing room contains a painting by Turner, hung opposite the fireplace. **The 2nd floor** is accessible only during guided tours. There, you can discover no fewer than 40 models that give insight into the extent of the architect's work. The room of the architect's wife, Eliza Sloane, the bathroom, and several living rooms have also been reconstructed precisely.

Gray's Inn ★

EF3 *South Square –* ⊖ *Chancery Lane.* The foundations of this law school date back to the 14th century, while the buildings are from the 16th century. The main entrance is marked by an elegant guardhouse from 1688.

Inside the enclosure, **South Square**, entirely rebuilt (except for No. 1, which dates back to 1685), is adorned with a beautiful bronze statue of the philosopher **Francis Bacon**, the most illustrious member of Gray's Inn. The gardens were once one of Londoners' favorite promenades. Magnificent wrought-iron gates from the early 18th century close them to the south.

Staple Inn ★

F3 Chancery Lane.

At the edge of the City, Staple Inn, originally attached to Gray's Inn, is one of the nine chancery schools where law students spent their first year. Partly built of wood, it represents one of the rare views of medieval London.

The facade on Holborn, with jettied gables and balconies, dates back to the years 1586–1596 and is the only surviving example of Elizabethan urban architecture in London.

A vaulted passage gives access to a charming courtyard surrounded by 18th-century buildings, beyond which stretches a garden.

High Holborn

F3 Chancery Lane.

On the way to Holborn Circus stands the massive red-brick facade of the **Prudential Assurance Building**, also known as Holborn Bars, designed by A. Waterhouse (early 20th century).

Just opposite, **Barnard's Inn** now houses **Gresham College**, the first free university in London. Founded in 1597 by Sir Thomas Gresham at his Bishopsgate residence in the heart of the City, the institution moved into these buildings in 1843.

Sir John Soane's Museum.

Bloomsbury★

Bloomsbury boasts beautiful squares from the 18th and 19th centuries, lined with Georgian and Victorian homes.
Once favored by artists and writers, this residential area was, at the start of the 20th century, the birthplace of the Bloomsbury Group, which included Virginia Woolf. Major institutions like the British Museum and the University of London continue this artistic and intellectual tradition.

▶ **Access:** ⊖ Tottenham Court Road, Goodge Street, Russell Square.

Detachable map DE2–3.

▶ **Tips:** The British Museum is vast: don't plan an overly ambitious itinerary. A good approach is to join one of the many free themed guided tours offered daily.
ⓒ *Where to Go pp. 120, 139, and 147.*

Bedford Square ★★

DE3 ⊖ *Tottenham Court Road.*
The most beautiful and best-preserved square in Bloomsbury was laid out starting in 1775 by architect Thomas Leverton. The three-floor brick houses have rounded doors topped by elegant half-moon windows, and balconies enhanced by a central stucco pediment.

The British Museum ★★★

E3 *Great Russell St. –* ⊖ *Tottenham Court Road or Holborn –* ✆ *020 7323 8000 – www.britishmuseum.org – &. – 10AM–5PM (Fri. 8:30PM) – closed Dec. 24–26 – free (except for temporary exhibits).*
☺ *Many free guided tours are organized daily (schedule available at reception and online). Hands-on sessions allow you to handle and learn more about some objects.*
The British Museum is the world's oldest national museum (1759).

Known primarily for its ancient and ethnographic collections, it spans over two million years of human history across five continents through about sixty galleries.

Great Court – Covered by Norman Foster with a large glass canopy and steel framework, this vast atrium forms the heart of the museum. Surrounding the round reading room of the former British Library, it houses the museum's bookstore and shops, cafés, and sculptures, offering a taste of the place's treasures.

Antiquity – This is the best-represented period. Don't miss the Egyptian collections, including the famous **Rosetta Stone**, which enabled Champollion to decipher hieroglyphs, and the six rooms dedicated to funeral rites. The richly endowed **Assyrian and Babylonian section** presents reliefs from King Ashurbanipal's palace at **Nineveh**. Large rooms are devoted to the sculptures from the Parthenon, brought back from Athens by Lord Elgin at the beginning of the 19th century, which the Greek government has been demanding back since the 1980s without success. Also admire the statues retrieved from the site of the **Mausoleum of Halicarnassus**, one of the seven wonders of the ancient world, and the **Portland Vase** (1st century), a prime example of Roman cameo glass art.

The well-stocked rooms on Europe illustrate, among other things, the **archaeology of the British Isles**, from prehistory (Lindow Man, 1st century) to the Middle Ages (Saxon ship from Sutton Hoo, 7th century; Lewis Chessmen, 12th century).

Ethnography – The collections of Islamic art and works from pre-Columbian America, Asia, and Africa complete the visit.

Don't leave without exploring the reconstructed **cabinet of curiosities** typical of the Enlightenment period on the ground floor and the gallery **Living and Dying**, showcasing the importance and nature of rituals worldwide.

Russell Square

E2–3 ⊖ *Russell Square.*
Created in 1800, Russell Square is bordered by beautiful Victorian houses. The garden, occupying nearly the entire square, lends it a country air.

Charles Dickens Museum

E2 *48 Doughty St.* – ⊖ Russell Square – ✆ *020 7405 2127 – www.*

Dennis Diatel/Shutterstock

47

Egyptian Antiquities Hall, British Museum.

dickensmuseum.com – ♿ – *Wed.–Sun. 10AM–5PM – £12.50.*

🙂 *A pleasant café open to all is located in the garden of the museum.*

The museum is housed in the 18th-century home where the most famous British novelist lived with his family from 1837 to 1839. It is the only one of his London residences still in existence today. It was here that Dickens wrote some of his most important works: *The Pickwick Papers*, *Nicholas Nickleby*, and *Oliver Twist*. Portraits, furniture, personal effects, manuscripts, the first bound editions of his novels, and the notes he used for public readings are displayed in the various rooms of the house.

The City★★★

Also known as the "Square Mile," the City is bounded by the outline of the old London wall that defined the area in Roman and medieval times. As the financial district of the capital and a major global stock exchange, the City has successfully evolved and features numerous architectural achievements, juxtaposed here and there with churches and passages from a distant past. The whole is undeniably charming and full of surprises.

▶**Access:** ⊖ St Paul's, Mansion House, Bank, Cannon Street, Monument, Aldgate, Barbican, Liverpool Street.

Neighborhood map pp. 50–51. Detachable map FGH3–4.

▶**Tip:** Visit this area during the weekdays and daytime when it's buzzing with activity (lots of bars, restaurants, stores): the City empties out in the late evening and on weekends.

◉ *Where to Go pp. 120, 133, 135 and 143.*

St Paul's Cathedral ★★★

G4 *St Paul's Churchyard –* ⊖ *St Paul's –* ✆ *020 7246 8350 – www. stpauls.co.uk –* ♿ *– Mon., Tue. and Thu.–Sat. 8:30AM–4:30PM, Wed. 10AM–4:30PM – £25, includes audioguide or guided tour (discounts online).*

Crowning the City with its gigantic dome, St Paul's Cathedral, a masterpiece by **Christopher Wren** (◉ *p. 174*), stands on Ludgate Hill. The first stone of the cathedral, designed after the Great Fire (1666), was laid on June 21, 1675. Thirty-three years later, the architect's son placed the final stone atop the structure's lantern.

Exterior

Unlike the dome of St Peter's in Rome that influenced Wren, the **dome★★★** of St Paul's doesn't have a true hemispherical shape. Its drum has two levels: the lower level is encircled by a colonnade topped with a balustrade, while the upper level forms a circular panoramic gallery, the **Stone Gallery**. The lantern at the top of the dome is crafted in a restrained English Baroque style, with columns on all four sides and a small dome serving as a base for the 6-foot, 7-inch golden cap. The **western end**, preceded by two broad flights of stairs, has a two-level portico with columns under a decorated pediment, topped with a portrait of St Paul.

On the other side rise the most Baroque towers ever created by Wren, as if to enhance the dome. Admire the external sculptures, some created by **Grinling Gibbons**.

Mauro_Repossini/Getty Images Plus

St Paul's Cathedral in the heart of the City.

Interior

Rich and imposing, the interior is noteworthy for the breathtaking surge of its massive dome, as wide as the nave and aisles combined and decorated with grisaille paintings by **James Thornhill**. In the nave, notice the imposing mausoleum of the Duke of Wellington, victor over Napoleon at Waterloo; opposite, in the north transept, hangs *The Light of the World* by **W. Holman Hunt** (1900). Stunning views of the dome and transept can be seen from the **Whispering Gallery** 259 steps below. Note the curious acoustic effect that gives the gallery its name.

The **panorama★★★** from the **Golden Gallery** at the very top of the dome *(543 steps)* provides an extensive **view** of London.

The transept arms are shallow; the left arm contains baptismal fonts sculpted in 1727 by **Francis Bird**, while the right houses **Flaxman**'s splendid monument to Lord Nelson.

In the choir, the magnificent **stalls★★** are also the work of Gibbons. The graceful sculpture of the Virgin and Child placed in the north aisle is by **Henry Moore** (1984). In the right ambulatory, see the astonishing statue of the poet John Donne, dean of St Paul's between 1621 and 1631, the temporary exhibitions in the south wing, and a Pietà, opposite.

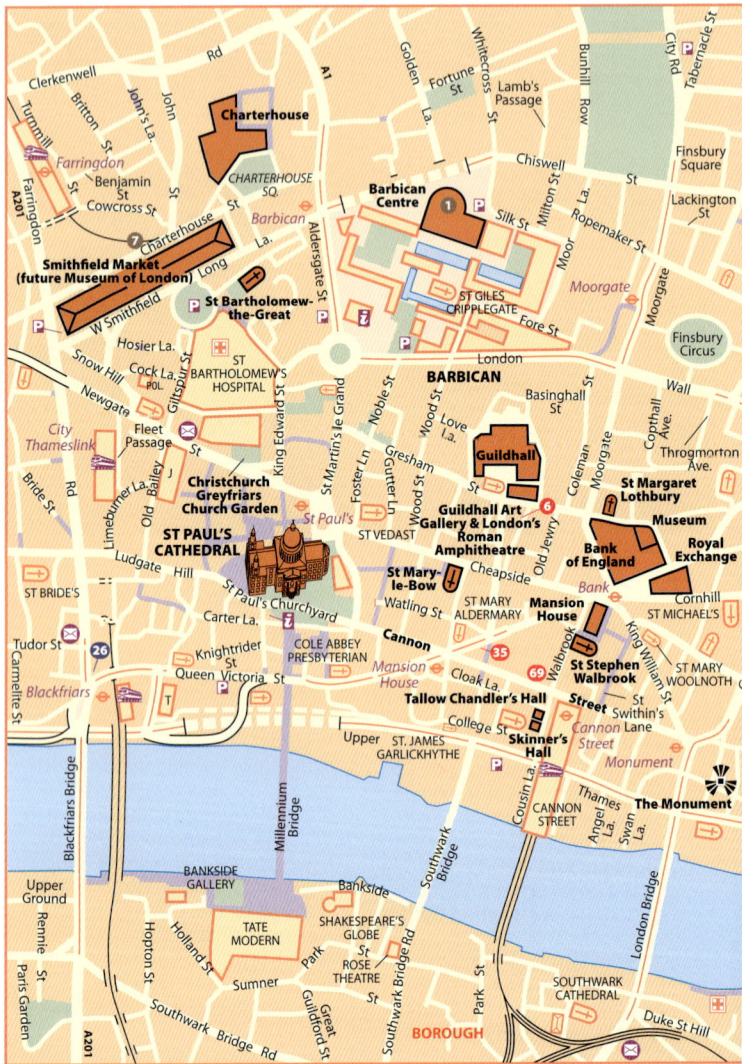

Clerkenwell Rd

Turnmill St

Britton St

John's La.

John St

Farringdon

Farringdon Rd

A201

Benjamin St

Cowcross St

Charterhouse St

Charterhouse

CHARTERHOUSE SQ.

Barbican

Charterhouse La.

A1

Golden La.

Fortune St

Whitecross St

Lamb's Passage

Bunhill Row

City Rd

Tabernacle St

Chiswell St

Finsbury Square

Lackington St

Barbican Centre

1

Silk St

Milton St

Ropemaker St

Moor La.

Moorgate

Moorgate

Aldersgate St

ST GILES CRIPPLEGATE

Fore St

Finsbury Circus

50

Smithfield Market (future Museum of London)

Long La.

Long La.

W Smithfield

7

St Bartholomew-the-Great

Hosier La.

Snow Hill

Cock La.

POL.

Giltspur St

ST BARTHOLOMEW'S HOSPITAL

King Edward St

BARBICAN

London Wall

Basinghall St

Coleman St

Copthall Ave.

Wall

Throgmorton Ave.

Throgmorton St

Newgate St

Fleet Passage

City Thameslink

Bride St

Old Bailey

Limeburner La.

Christchurch Greyfriars Church Garden

St Martin's le Grand

Foster La.

Gutter La.

Noble St

Wood St

Wood St

Love La.

Gresham St

Guildhall

Guildhall Art Gallery & London's Roman Amphitheatre

Old Jewry

6

St Margaret Lothbury

Museum

Bank of England

Royal Exchange

ST BRIDE'S

Ludgate Hill

St Paul's

ST VEDAST

Foster La.

ST PAUL'S CATHEDRAL

St Paul's Churchyard

Carter La.

Cheapside

St Mary-le-Bow

Watling St

ST MARY ALDERMARY

Bread St

Bank

Cornhill

ST MICHAEL'S

King William St

ST MARY WOOLNOTH

Tudor St

26

Carmelite St

Blackfriars

Knightrider St

Queen Victoria St

St Paul's

COLE ABBEY PRESBYTERIAN

Mansion House

Cannon

Mansion House

35

Walbrook

69

St Stephen Walbrook

Cloak La.

Tallow Chandler's Hall

Street

Cannon Street

St Swithin's Lane

Monument

Skinner's Hall

College St

Upper Thames St

ST JAMES GARLICKHYTHE

Cousin La.

CANNON STREET

Thames St

Angel La.

Swan La.

The Monument

Blackfriars Bridge

Millennium Bridge

Southwark Bridge

London Bridge

Upper Ground

Rennie St

Paris Garden

BANKSIDE GALLERY

Hopton St

Holland St

TATE MODERN

Sumner St

Park St

SHAKESPEARE'S GLOBE

Bankside

St Guildford St

ROSE THEATRE

Southwark Bridge Rd

Park St

SOUTHWARK CATHEDRAL

Duke St Hill

A201

Southwark Bridge Rd

Great Guildford St

BOROUGH

Map Labels

Epworth St

SHOREDITCH

Worship St

Wilson St

Earl St

Clifton St

Sun St

Appold St

Primrose St

Curtain Rd

Shoreditch High

Broadgate Plaza

Bishopsgate

Folgate St

Elder St

Commercial St

Brick La

Eagle St

OLD TRUMAN'S BREWERY

Lamb St

Buxton St

Grey

Princelet St

DENNIS SEVERS HOUSE

Fournier St

Brushfield St

Fashion St

Broadgate Circle

LIVERPOOL STREET

Artillery La.

Middlesex St

Bishopsgate

Liverpool Street

Liverpool St

New St

Bell La.

Toynbee St

Wentworth

Gunthorpe St

La.

Wormwood St

Old Broad St

Heron Tower

Devonshire Square

Harrow Pl.

Houndsditch

Goulston St

WHITECHAPEL GALLERY

18

Tower 42

St Helen's Bishopsgate

Bevis Marks

Botolph St

Aldgate East

Whitechapel High St

Twentytwo

St Mary Axe

The Gherkin

Aldgate

Leman St

Leadenhall Building (Cheesegrater)

Duke's Pl.

Aldgate High St

Leadenhall St

Vine St

Alie St

The Scalpel

Billiter St

Mansell St

Gracechurch

Lloyd's Building

Willis Building

FENCHURCH STREET

Minories

Portsoken St

S Tenter St

Prescot St

Leadenhall Market

Gracechurch

The Walkie Talkie

ST OLAVE

St

Chamber St

Hill

Fish St

St Mary-at-Hill

Mincing Ln

Pepys St

Seething La.

Tower Hill

Pudding Ln

ALL HALLOWS-BY-THE-TOWER

TOWER GATEWAY

Cartwright St

St

ST DUNSTAN-IN-THE-EAST

Tower Thames St

Petty Wales

TOWER OF LONDON

E Smithfield

THAMES

St Katharine's & Wapping

St Katharine's Way

HMS BELFAST

English Grounds

Hay's La.

HAY'S GALLERIA

Tower Bridge

N

THE CITY

0 — 200 m

0 — 200 yards

Christchurch Greyfriars Church Garden

FG3 *King Edward St. – ⊖ St Paul's – www.cityoflondon.gov.uk – free access.*

This **church** dating from the 13th century is the sole remnant of a Franciscan monastery. Rebuilt by Christopher Wren at the end of the 17th century after the Great Fire of London, it was devastated by Blitz bombings in 1940. Within its ruins, preserved as a memorial after the war, a **public garden** dominated by roses has been created. An unexpected and charming spot.

Barbican ★

G3 ⊖ *Barbican.*

Devastated by World War II bombings, this neighborhood was completely rebuilt, starting in 1958, as a closed and austere architectural utopia, where pedestrians circulate on the upper level while car traffic is separated on the lower level. This is a kind of concrete universe, where fans of brutalist architecture can wander between massive residential complexes, water features, gardens, and terraces before reaching the **Barbican Centre** *(www.barbican.org.uk)*, a major venue for cultural life in London (theater, concert hall, art gallery, library, restaurants, etc.).

St Bartholomew– the-Great ★★

G3 *West Smithfield – ⊖ Barbican – ✆ 020 7600 0440 – www.greatstbarts.com – ♿ – 10AM–5PM, Sun. 1PM–5PM – free.*

This church, undoubtedly the most charming in London, is the last remnant of an Augustinian priory dissolved in 1539. Built in 1123, it captivates with its eclecticism, blending Romanesque and Gothic architecture.

The simplicity of the **choir** (12th century) is enhanced by a beautiful sculpted loggia. Notice the **baptismal font** (15th century), among the few that survived the Reformation in London, where the painter William Hogarth was baptized in 1697. The church appears in scenes from the films *Four Weddings and a Funeral* and *Shakespeare in Love*. It also houses contemporary artworks.

Smithfield Market

F3 *201–232 Charterhouse St. ⊖ Barbican, Farringdon.*

The new Museum of London (*www.museumoflondon.org.uk*) is scheduled to open in stages between 2026 and 2028 in the disused buildings of this former Victorian meat market. Having previously been located near the Barbican, the museum closed its doors at the end of 2022. The red brick buildings, flanked by towers at each end, were constructed (starting in 1868) on more than 3 acres. The new buildings are designed by the architects Stanton Williams (known for the transformation of the Royal Opera House) and Asif Khan.

Charterhouse ★

FG3 *Charterhouse Square – ⊖ Barbican – ✆ 020 7253 9503 – www.thecharterhouse.org – Tue.–Sat. 10:30AM–4:30PM – closed Dec. 25–27 and Dec. 31 – Jan. 2 – free – guided tours at 11AM and 2:15PM–£8/£18.*

Founded in 1371, this former Carthusian monastery was transformed into a Tudor mansion when Henry VIII dissolved the community and confiscated its buildings in 1537. In 1611, the building was purchased by **Thomas Sutton** (1532–1611), who established a charitable hospice and school for boys there.

The charterhouse has been remodeled over the centuries, but you can still admire the splendid **Great Hall**, a Tudor hall with diaphragm timbering, wood paneling, and galleries from the 16th century; the **Great Chamber** in Elizabethan style, adorned with a monumental painted fireplace, gilded ceilings, and leaded windows; and the **chapel**, which has occupied the former chapter house since 1614. The **museum** offers a detailed retrospective of the history with period documents and even a skeleton of a victim of the Great Plague.

Guildhall ★

G3 *Gresham St. – ⊖ St Paul's – 𝒫 020 7332 1313 – www.guildhall. cityoflondon.gov.uk – 10AM–5PM subject to events – free – guided tours on the 1st Thursday of each month, when the Common Council meeting is held, £12 – info www. cityoflondonguides.com.*

The City Hall (not to be confused with the City of London's city hall) is the seat of the Corporation of London, responsible for administering this district. It provides a majestic setting for lavish corporate seminars. This building from the early 15th century miraculously survived the Great Fire of 1666 but has undergone numerous restorations following the Blitz of 1940. The **Great Hall** impresses with its vast proportions and stunning oak ceiling supported by stone arches. It is highlighted by a colorful frieze bearing the arms of England and the City, above which float the banners of the twelve principal livery companies (Great Livery Companies) of the city. The hall retains some original features, such as the exterior porch and the stained glass of the south wall (the first window to the right of the entrance). Among the monuments erected in honor of national figures, note the tall wooden effigies of **Gog** (to the north) and **Magog** (to the south) flanking the west gallery (known as the "Musicians' Gallery"). These two legendary giants are said to have intervened around 1000 BC in the conflict between the Britons and the Trojan invaders. Housed in the west wing built in 1974, the **library** preserves over 14,000 books, documents, and archives related to London.

Guildhall Art Gallery and London's Roman Amphitheatre★

𝒫 020 7332 3700 – www.cityoflondon. gov.uk – 10:30AM–4PM – free – reservations recommended at www. guildhall-art-gallery.myshopify.com. This gallery, located in the wing to the east of the courtyard, exhibits around 250 works from the important art collection amassed by the Corporation of London since the 17th century. This collection comprises nearly 4,000 works. In the basement, part of the remains of a **Roman amphitheater** is on display.

St Mary-le-Bow ★★

G4 *Cheapside – ⊖ Mansion House – ☎ 020 7248 5139 – www.stmarylebow. co.uk – Mon.–Fri. 7:30AM–6PM – numerous concerts*

☺ Take a break for lunch at Café Below, located in the crypt (www. cafebelow.co.uk).

The projecting tower on Cheapside houses the famous **Bow Bells** and supports the majestic **bell tower★★** (1671–1680) where Christopher Wren drew on the five classical orders inspired by Greco-Roman architecture. The distinctive copper dragon mounted on the roof is often mistaken for a weather vane, as it can move incrementally on its axis. Completed in 1673, this Portland stone building designed by Wren, inspired by the Basilica of Constantine in Rome, was bombed in 1941. The exterior was restored to match the original, but the interior decoration was altered. The Romanesque **crypt**, built in 1087 on the ruins of a Saxon church, houses the original columns.

St Margaret Lothbury ★

G3 ⊖ *Bank – ☎ 020 7726 4878 – stml. org.uk – ♿ – Mon.–Fri. 7AM–6PM.*

The parish church of the Bank of England, St Margaret, was built (1686–1690) to the designs of Christopher Wren. Its square tower is topped with a **spire★** crowned by a golden ball and a weather vane. Inside, admire the beautiful **woodwork★**, including panels, benches, an oak screen, a pulpit, and an altarpiece. The elegant **screen★** comes from All Hallows Church *(Upper Thames St.)*. The marble **baptismal font★** is attributed to Grinling Gibbons.

Bank of England

G4 ⊖ *Bank (Lombard St. exit).*

Founded in 1694, the Bank of England marks the heart of the City. The current building was constructed between 1924 and 1939 by Sir Herbert Baker to replace an older structure designed by Sir John Soane.

Bank of England Museum★

Bartholomew Lane – ☎ 020 3461 5545 – www.bankofengland.co.uk/ museum – ♿ – Mon.–Fri. 10AM–5PM (Until 8PM on the 3rd Thursday of the month).

The museum traces 1,500 years of economic exchange history as well as the history of the Bank of England, from its foundation in 1694 to the present day, through numerous objects and works of art.

Mansion House ★

G4 ⊖ *Bank – ☎ 020 7626 2500 – www.cityoflondon.gov.uk (Under "About Us/About the City of London Corporation") – guided tours by reservation only: Tue. at 2PM – £9.50.*

This is the official residence of the city's chief magistrate, the Lord Mayor of London. Built between 1739 and 1752, it features a Palladian facade with six Corinthian columns topped by a large triangular pediment.

Jon Arnold Images/hemis.fr

The City and St Paul's Cathedral from the Thames.

St Stephen Walbrook ★

G4 *39 Walbrook –* 🚇 *Bank or Cannon St. –* ☎ *020 7626 9000 – ststephenwalbrook.net – Mon.–Fri. 10 AM–3:30PM – concerts.*
This bold work (1672–1677) by Wren features a verdigris **dome★**. To the west, the square **tower** of rough stone is topped with an elegant balustrade. The **bell tower★**, made of Portland stone, was added in 1717. Inside, the slightly off-center dome rests on a ring of eight arches. The bays are marked by Corinthian columns arranged to create contrasts between the dark oak paneling and the light-colored sculpted furniture. The monumental travertine altar located under the dome is the work (1986) of **Henry Moore**.

Royal Exchange ★

G4 *Angle Threadneedle St. and Cornhill –* 🚇 *Bank.*
The former London Stock Exchange ceased operations in 1939. The neoclassical building now houses luxury restaurants and boutiques.
In front of the Corinthian portico of the facade stands an equestrian statue of **Wellington**.

Decipher the City Skyline

H3–4 ⊖ *Bank, Monument, or Aldgate.*

At the southern end of Lime Street stands the massive flared silhouette of the **Walkie-Talkie★** *(20 Fenchurch St.)*, a 525-foot building designed by Rafael Viñoly (2014). A garden with a panoramic terrace, the **Sky Garden★★**, complete with a bar and restaurant, is accessible on the 35th floor *(skygarden.london – 8:30AM.–10PM. (10:30PM. Fri.–Sat.) – free – reserve online a few days in advance)*.

Further north, the **Lloyd's Building★★** *(1 Lime St.)*, headquarters of the famous insurance group, bears similarities to the Centre Georges-Pompidou in Paris, which isn't surprising since it was designed by Richard Rogers, one of the two architects behind Beaubourg. The avant-garde style of this concrete tower clad in stainless steel, showcasing its ducts and elevators on the exterior to free up interior space, stirred much controversy at its inauguration in 1986.

Opposite the Lloyd's Building, the **Willis Building** *(51 Lime St.)* presents its broad, three-tiered concave profile reminiscent of a crustacean shell. This 410-foot glass tower was designed by Norman Foster.

Right next to it rises a 623-foot skyscraper nicknamed the **Scalpel** *(52–54 Lime St.)* due to its angular shape, designed by Kohn Pedersen Fox.

Across the intersection towers the imposing silhouette of the **Leadenhall Building** *(122 Leadenhall St.)*, nicknamed the "cheesegrater" for its tapered prism shape. This creation by Richard Rogers, Graham Stirk, and Ivan Harbour reaches a height of 738 feet.

The **Gherkin★★** *(30 St Mary Axe)*, affectionately called the "cucumber" by Londoners, is the building of the reinsurer Swiss Re and one of the great architectural successes of the London skyline. It was completed in May 2004 based on designs by Norman Foster.

Further west, the **Horizon 22** *(a.k.a. Bishopsgate Tower, The Pinnacle, or Twentytwo, 22 Bishopsgate)* emerged in 2021 as the tallest skyscraper in the City (62 floors, 912 feet). Just north of Horizon 22, the **Heron Tower** *(110 Bishopsgate)* reaches a height of 755 feet. Designed by Kohn Pedersen Fox (2011), it uses solar panels for energy production. Two restaurants and a bar occupy the top. The more classical **Tower 42** *(25 Old Broad St.)*, designed by Richard Seifert (1980), already seems a bit outdated.

The City skyline continues to transform, becoming ever taller and denser. Indeed, the area is expected to welcome about a dozen new skyscrapers by 2030. Some are already under construction, notably on Bishopsgate, and are scheduled for completion in 2026 and 2027. **1 Undershaft** *(1 Great St Helen's)*, at 951 feet and 73 floors, is also expected to challenge height records once completed in 2029.

Leadenhall Market ★

H4 *Leadenhall St., Gracechurch St. and Lime St. – ⊖ Bank – ☎ 020 7332 1523 – www.leadenhallmarket.co.uk – free access.*

This beautiful glass and wrought-iron hall, showcasing Victorian architecture, seems to stand resiliently against the neighboring skyscrapers. Featured in the first **Harry Potter** film, it is lined with stores, restaurants, and pubs that fill up every Friday afternoon.

St Helen's Bishopsgate ★

H3 *Great St Helen's – ⊖ Liverpool Street or Aldgate – ☎ 020 7283 2231 – www.st-helens.org.uk – ♿– Mon.–Fri. 9AM–5PM, Sun. 9:30AM–7:30PM.*

The stone facade features a double gabled front; it is topped by a square turret with a lantern (17th century), which is crowned with a weather vane. Inside, the **funerary monuments★**, elaborate tombs of notable figures, have earned it the nickname "Westminster of the City."

Cannon Street

G4 ⊖ *Mansion House or Cannon St.*

This street was known in the Middle Ages as "Candelwrichstrete" because it housed candle and wick makers. This explains the presence on Dowgate Hill of **Tallow Chandlers' Hall** and **Skinners' Hall**, built in the late 18th century. At No. 111, the **London Stone**, a block of limestone set into the wall of a modern building, is said (according to legend) to have come from the altar erected in 800 BC by Trojan, the mythical founder of Insular Britain.

The Monument ★

G4 *Fish St. Hill – ⊖ Monument – ☎ 020 7403 3761 – www.themonument.org. 9:30AM–12:30PM, 2PM–5:30PM – Closed Dec. 24–26 – £6.*

In 1667, Christopher Wren was commissioned to erect a massive **Doric column** commemorating the Great Fire of London that had occurred a year earlier. Its height (203 feet) represents the column's distance from where the fire started, in Pudding Lane. Dubbed "the Monument" by Londoners, it offers a remarkable **view★** of the City (311 steps).

St Mary-at-Hill ★★

H4 *The Rectory – ⊖ Monument – ☎ 020 7626 4184 – Mon.–Thu. 10AM–4PM – Closed in August – concerts.*

The austere facade of this church, with its bracket clock and Venetian window, was built between 1670 and 1676 by Christopher Wren and conceals an interesting internal architecture. Its **foundation★** in the shape of a Greek cross is topped by a low dome supported by four Corinthian columns; the Adam-style decoration is in pastel blue and gold. Restored in 1843 but damaged by a fire in 1988, the church was known for its woodwork. Notice the pulpit, decorated with fruits and flowers beneath a massive sounding board, accessed by a curved staircase (19th century) designed by William Gibbs Rogers.

Tower of London★★★

The "romantic" silhouette of the Tower of London, forever tied to the country's history, has been the backdrop for horror as much as royal pomp. A visit to this fortress is a must for those hoping to feel the shivers from the dark tales of the "Yeomen Warders," ceremonial guardians in Tudor attire, and to admire the sparkling Crown Jewels.

▶ **Access:** ⊖ Tower Hill, Tower Gateway (DLR).
Neighborhood map pp. 50–51. Detachable map H4–5.
▶ **Tip:** Buy your ticket in advance to avoid waiting in line at the counters.

Tower of London ★★★

H4 *Entrance via West Gate –* ⊖ *Tower Hill – ℘ 020 3166 6000 – www.hrp. org.uk –* ♿ *– 9AM–5:30PM, Sun.–Mon. 10AM–5:30PM (4:30PM Jan.–Feb.) (last entry 2 hours before closing) – £34.80, including a guided tour with the Yeomen Warders.*
Ravens hover over the Tower of London, but these birds are by no means a bad omen. Quite the contrary: their presence is linked to a legend that the monarchy would fall if these birds were ever to leave the Tower, which is why they are fed and cared for.
It's within these walls that some of the bloodiest chapters of London's history have been written. This is particularly evidenced by the **Bloody Tower**, where the sons of Edward IV were likely murdered in 1483. The **Beauchamp Tower★★** (13th century) was reserved for high-ranking prisoners, as shown by the graffiti carved in the main room. Nearby stand the Scaffold Site

From Crowned Heads to Crown Jewels

William the Conqueror (r. 1066–1087) built the first wooden fortress here in 1067, which was followed eleven years later by a stone building. Its location near the river allowed a view of any enemies crossing the Thames. The Norman king's successors valued this strategic advantage and expanded the fortress, which soon occupied 17.5 acres. Originally built to serve as a refuge for the royal family, it became a state prison from the 13th century onward and was the setting for famous political executions. Thanks to the defensive structures, it also took on various functions over the centuries, housing the Royal Menagerie (1235–1834) and the Royal Mint (1300–1810), and later accommodating the Royal Armouries and, since 1661, the Crown Jewels.

and the **St Peter-ad-Vincula chapel** *(accessible during guided tours)*, where some of the Tower's executed, including Anne Boleyn and Catherine Howard, unfortunate wives of King Henry VIII, are buried. The organ buffet was sculpted by Grinling Gibbons. At the center of the Upper Court, the keep, known as the **White Tower★★★**, is the most distinctive part of the Tower; it's one of the first fortresses of such dimensions built in Western Europe. Commissioned by William I in 1078 and completed twenty years later, the 102-foot-high stone walls form a quadrilateral with a round tower at one corner and three square towers at the others. The keep houses the **Royal Armouries Collection**, one of the largest in the world. On the second floor, **St John-the-Evangelist★★** is a stone chapel rising over two levels, remaining almost as it was in 1080. The highlight of the tour remains the **Jewel House** and its famous **Crown Jewels★★★**. These include the Great Star of Africa, the second-largest diamond in the world (530 carats), which adorns the royal scepter, and the renowned Koh-i-Noor diamond, mounted on the crown of Queen Mother Elizabeth Bowes-Lyon. This fabulous collection of royal jewels and symbols is mostly post-1660, as much of the previous treasure was sold or melted by Oliver Cromwell.

Don't miss a walk on the **battlements**. The ramparts offer great views of the fortress's interior, the Thames, and Tower Bridge.

Tower Bridge ★★

H5 ⊖ *Tower Hill or London Bridge River Boat to Tower Pier – ☏ 020 7403 3761 – www.towerbridge.org.uk – ♿ – 9:30AM–6PM (last entry 1 hour before closing) – £13.40.*

Built between 1886 and 1894 by John Wolfe Barry and Horace Jones, the bridge's total length reaches 2,641 feet. Connected to the banks of the Thames by two suspension bridges, the massive Gothic towers forming the structure's skeleton are joined by a drawbridge and, at the upper level, a pedestrian walkway, now equipped with a glass floor offering breathtaking **panoramic views★★★**. At 138 feet above the Thames, the walkway is a perfect spot to observe the bridge opening.

The roadway bridge has two bascules that lift to allow ships passage. The maneuver only takes one and a half minutes and occurs several times a day. The hydraulic lifting mechanism has never failed; in 1977, it was replaced by a hydroelectric system. The towers and the engine room house an **educational museum**. From the north tower, visitors are guided through an exhibition recounting the design and construction of the bridge.

Southwark★★

On the south bank of the Thames, the vibrant borough of Southwark is undergoing a renaissance. In the Bankside area, once infamous, the bustling Tate Modern, Norman Foster's Millennium Bridge, and the Globe Theatre showcase a successful blend of history and modernity.

▶**Access:** ⊖ London Bridge, Southwark.
Neighborhood map pp. 66–67. Detachable map FGH4–5–6.
▶**Tips:** Entry to the Tate Modern is free, so plan to spread your visit out and not see everything in one day. Book online and in advance for access to the view from The Shard, to ensure admission and get a better rate.
◓ *Where to Go pp. 120, 133, and 144.*

Butler's Wharf

H5 ⊖ *London Bridge.*
Luxury apartments, cafés, and restaurants line the waterfront, filling these renovated brick warehouses from the 1980s.

China Wharf

H5 ⊖ *London Bridge.*
Built in 1988 above the Thames, this striking red-orange structure earned architects CZWG several awards. Among other notable warehouse conversions: the **Conran Building** (*22 Shad Thames*), the modern **Saffron Wharf** (*18 Shad Thames*), and **Camera Press** in unfinished wood (*21–23 Queen Elizabeth St.*).

Maltby Street Market

H6 *Maltby St., Ropewalk –* ⊖ *Bermondsey – www. maltbystreetmarket.co.uk – market: Sat. 10AM–5PM, Sun. 11AM–4PM.*
Set up every weekend by the railroad arches, the small gourmet Maltby Street Market offers a tempting selection of street food. If the bites from various stalls aren't enough, there are a few permanent restaurants hidden under the arches.

The Queen's Walk★★★

On the south bank of the Thames, The Queen's Walk is a long promenade stretching from Westminster Bridge to Southwark, Tower Bridge, and beyond to Bermondsey. The **South Bank** (◓ *p. 65*) forms the first part of this walkway. On Bankside, **Shakespeare's Globe** and **Tate Modern** are two iconic institutions that bridge the past and present. To the east of London Bridge station, the vibrant London Bridge City and the beautiful shopping arcade **Hay's Galleria** contribute to the vitality of the borough of Southwark.

Bermondsey Market

H6 *At the corner of Bermondsey St. and Long Lane – ⊖ London Bridge – Fri. 6AM–2PM.*

Little Bermondsey **antiques market** delights early morning browsers and collectors. Silversmithing enthusiasts will find a fine selection of jewelry, cutlery and dishware, etc. The lion emblem indicates the piece is of English origin.

City Hall

H5 *The Queen's Walk – ⊖ Tower Hill – ☎ 020 7983 4000 – www.london.gov. uk – ♿ – limited access (security gate) to the ground floor café and, up the ramp, to the first two floors – Mon.–Thu. 8:30AM–6PM, Fri. 8:30AM–5:30PM – free.*

View the stunning silhouette of **City Hall**, an astonishing curved glass building (2002) designed by **Norman Foster**. At its base, an "arena" hosts theatrical and dance performances in good weather.

HMS Belfast

H5 *The Queen's Walk – ⊖ London Bridge – ☎ 020 7940 6300 – www. iwm.org.uk – ♿ – 10AM–5PM – £25.45, audioguide included.*

Moored upstream of Tower Bridge since 1971, this 11,500-ton cruiser distinguished itself during World War II, particularly in the 1944 Normandy landings.

Hay's Galleria

H5 *Tooley St. – ⊖ London Bridge.*

Adorned with contemporary sculptures, this elegantly curved former warehouse is home to stores

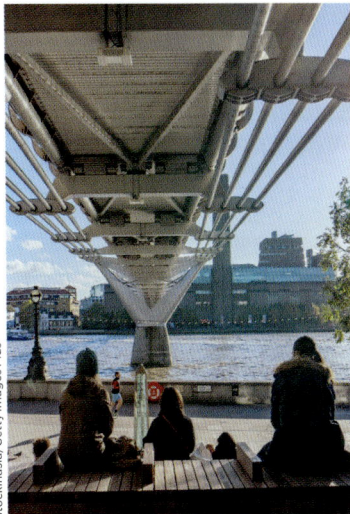

The Millennium Bridge (Foster+ Partners) and Tate Modern (Herzog & de Meuron).

and cafés. Passing through it leads directly to London Bridge station.

The Shard ★★

G5 *Joiner St. – ⊖ London Bridge – ☎ 084 4499 7111 – www. theviewfromtheshard.com – ♿ – summer: 10AM/12PM–7PM/10PM (varying hours depending on the month) – access to the terrace: £28.50 by reservation, £37 on the day.*

Designed by architect Renzo Piano, The Shard (2012) stands 1,016 feet tall, making it the highest building in London and Western Europe. Visitors can access a **panoramic terrace★★★** on the 72nd floor at 801 feet *(The View)*. The glass structure also includes offices, a hotel, bars, restaurants, and private apartments.

Courts and Inns of Southwark

G5 ⊖ *London Bridge.*
An array of alleyways and yards that once hosted inns for travelers arriving in London after the City gates had closed. By walking along Borough High Street (facing away from Tower Bridge), you'll encounter **King's Head Yard**, **White Hart Yard**, **George Inn★**, a picturesque inn referenced by Dickens in *Little Dorrit*, **Talbot Yard**, and **Queen's Head Yard**

Borough Market

G5 *8 Southwark St. –* ⊖ *London Bridge –* ☎ *020 7407 1002 – www. boroughmarket.org.uk –* ♿ *– Tue.– Fri. 10AM–5PM, Sat. 9AM–5PM, Sun. 10AM–4PM.*
Nestled under the triangle formed by three railroad bridges, Borough market is lively and flanked by pubs and small eateries. The capital's oldest food market specializes in high-quality, organic products, seasonal fruits and vegetables, and British and international cheeses, as well as artisanal baked goods... A must for its atmosphere and for your taste buds!

> 🍴 **Where to Have Lunch in Bankside?**
>
> Chic restaurants with a view, world cuisine, or quick bites at the markets: there's something for everyone!
> ⌖ *p. 121.*

Southwark Cathedral ★★

G5 *London Bridge –* ⊖ *London Bridge –* ☎ *020 7367 6700 – www. cathedral.southwark.anglican.org –* ♿ *– 9AM–6PM, Sun. 8:30AM–5PM – concerts (check the website for the schedule).*
Massive pillars support the central tower and early English Gothic **choir** with harmonious proportions dating back to the 13th century, making this the oldest Gothic sanctuary in England. The building houses a sumptuous 1520 altarpiece. The nave was reconstructed between 1890 and 1897 to align with the choir. Notable features include the **Harvard Chapel** *(north side of the choir)*, the funeral monument (1616) of Alderman Humble and his wives *(north of the altarpiece)*, as well as the twelve **vault keys** from the 15th-century wooden frame that collapsed in 1830 *(western end of the north side)*. The cathedral also boasts an archaeological room, an education center, a cafeteria, and a store.

Golden Hinde

G5 *Pickfords Wharf, Clink St. –* ⊖ *London Bridge –* ☎ *020 7403 0123 – www.goldenhinde.co.uk – 10AM–6PM; Nov.–Mar.: 10AM–5PM – £6.*
Docked at St Mary Overie Dock, the *Golden Hinde* is a full-size replica of navigator Francis Drake's galleon (1540–1596). Discover the interior on a guided and costumed tour.

Rose Theatre

G4–5 *56 Park St. –* ⊖ Cannon Street or London Bridge – ☎ *020 7261 9565 – www.roseplayhouse.org.uk – until* restoration works are completed, performances are held on nearby theater stages.

Part of the foundations of Bankside's first theater (1587), discovered in 1989, has been unearthed. You can view the site, also known as **The Rose Playhouse**, during guided tours or performances.

Shakespeare's Globe ★★

G4 *21 New Globe Walk – ⊖ London Bridge or Cannon Street – 🕾 020 7902 1400 – www.shakespearesglobe.com – ♿ – guided tour (50 min) by online reservation – £20/22.*

😊 *The Swan Bar within the theater offers an excellent afternoon tea inspired by Shakespeare's plays (£39.50).*

In this shrine to Shakespeare, a replica of the Globe Theatre, destroyed in 1644, has been erected using historically accurate materials and techniques. The circular theater with an open-air orchestra surrounded by stands is the ideal spot to watch one of Shakespeare's dramas. For authenticity, the plays are performed as in the author's day, in the afternoon and without artificial lighting.

Millennium Bridge ★

G4 ⊖ *Blackfriars.*

Designed by **Norman Foster**, the elegant Millennium Footbridge (2000), with its suspension and curved balustrades, is a true architectural and technical achievement. At night, it looks like a stream of light crossing the Thames.

Tate Modern ★★★

FG4 *Bankside – ⊖ Blackfriars – North entrance via Queen's Walk (Natalie Bell Building, 1st Floor), west entrance*

And in the Midst Flows the Thames

The main river of Great Britain, the Thames (215 miles) winds its path through the heart of London along an east–west axis, dividing the capital between the north and south banks. A major communication route until the end of the 17th century, it transformed the city into a grand port and remains an integral part of London life. Many bridges and footbridges span the river, such as **London Bridge**, considered the oldest in the capital, and the **Millennium Bridge**, built in the year 2000 by architect Norman Foster. As part of the **Illuminated River** project *(www.illuminatedriver.london)*, launched in 2019, nine of these structures are illuminated at night. Eventually, 14 of the city's bridges will have this feature.

To learn more about the history of the Thames and the London canals, visit the **Museum of London Docklands★★** *(☞ p. 104)*, the **London Canal Museum** *(☞ p. 93)*, or, at certain times of the year, the **Thames Barrier** *(www.gov.uk/the-thames-barrier)*, which is intended to protect the city from floods. Enjoy a leisurely trip along the water by boarding a barge in **Little Venice** *(☞ p. 82)* and make use of the **Thames Clippers** *(☞ p. 161)* to travel across the city.

on Holland St. (Turbine Hall, Ground Floor), and south entrance on Sumner St. (Blavatnik Building, 1ˢᵗ Floor) –
📞 020 7887 8888 – www.tate.org.uk –
♿ – 10AM–6PM – free.
😊 River shuttles on the Thames (🧭 p. 161) make it easy to reach Tate Modern, notably from Tate Britain.

The former power station, standing on the riverbank since 1960 and topped with a glass superstructure with large overhanging windows, has become one of the world's temples of modern and contemporary art.

Turbine Hall – The reception hall, the former **turbine room** (509 feet long and 115 feet high), where the overhead crane recalls the building's industrial past, is impressive.

The extensive permanent collections are presented with a thematic approach, relying heavily on the curators' subjectivity: works from different times are shown in parallel, and historical and stylistic associations are highlighted to challenge preconceived notions about contemporary art.

Natalie Bell Building – The most famous names in modern art, and all notable artistic movements, are represented here. Picasso, Dalí, Duchamp and his followers, Picabia and Ernst, Twombly and Bacon, Stella and Manzoni, Fontana, Klimt, Cézanne, Pollock, and many others converse freely in this immense space.

In the basement, **The Tanks**, former oil reservoirs, have been converted into a space dedicated to the performing arts, dance, performances, and installations.

Blavatnik Building – On the south side, a 10-floor pyramid-shaped extension, designed by architects Herzog & de Meuron and named **Tate Modern** or **Switch House**, opened in 2016. Connected to the Natalie Bell wing by a walkway on the 4ᵗʰ floor, it increased the exhibition area by 60%, accommodating works by 250 artists from 50 countries, including Mark Rothko, Ai Weiwei, Louise Bourgeois, and Henri Matisse. You'll also find educational and meeting spaces, a store, bar, restaurant, and terrace offering a superb **panoramic view★★★** of London.

South Bank★★

This district, stretching between Waterloo and Blackfriars bridges, forged a new identity with the developments linked to the millennium festivities. Today, it stands out as a major cultural and tourist hotspot.

▶**Access:** ⊖ Southwark, Waterloo, Westminster, Lambeth North.

Neighborhood map pp. 66–67. Detachable map EF4–5–6.

▶**Tip:** There is always a large crowd around Jubilee Gardens, especially in nice weather: if possible, visit during the week.

☾ *Where to Go pp. 121, 139, and 148.*

Oxo Tower

F4 *Barge House St. –* ⊖ *Southwark or Blackfriars –* www.coinstreet.org/oxotowerwharf.

Dominated by a stunning Art Deco tower, this building was initially designed as a power station in the 1900s before being bought and revamped by Liebig for the production of their famous OXO bouillon cubes. Today, it houses art galleries, artists' studios, fashion and design stores, residences, and a panoramic restaurant. ☾ *Where to Go/Dining p. 121/"Shopping" p. 139.*

Gabriel's Wharf

F4 *56 Upper Ground –* ⊖ *Waterloo.*
The wharf brings together craft shops and cafés around a pleasant square.

National Theatre ★

F4–5 ⊖ *Waterloo –* ☏ *020 7452 3000 –* www.nationaltheatre.org.uk – ♿ – *guided tour in English Mon.–Fri. at 5PM, Sat. at 12PM – £18.*

The **National Theatre** is part of the third phase of the South Bank development downstream from Waterloo Bridge. Inaugurated in 1976, it's a fine example of brutalist style. Its architect, **Sir Denys Lasdun**, merged three theaters (the Olivier, the Dorfman, formerly Cottesloe, and the Lyttelton). With nearly 300 actors and 500 costumes, it boasts a vast repertoire covering Shakespearean classics, musicals, contemporary plays, and operas.

British Film Institute

F5 ⊖ *Waterloo –* ☏ *020 7928 3535/3232 –* www.bfi.org.uk.
Among the world's top cinematheques, it boasts two screening rooms and hosts the London Film Festival.

Waterloo Bridge

E4 ⊖ *Waterloo or Temple.* Architect **Giles Gilbert Scott** designed this 1945 bridge with five arches of Portland stone over concrete; it replaced a structure inaugurated in 1817 to mark the 2nd anniversary of the Battle of Waterloo. Nestled under the bridge is the secondhand **Southbank Book Market**, (10AM–7PM, Sun. 11AM–7PM).

Southbank Centre ★

E5 *Belvedere Rd –* ⊖ *Waterloo –* ✆ *020 3879 9555 – www. southbankcentre.co.uk –* ♿.
For some, this ensemble of stone and gray concrete buildings that looms large

and stark on the Thames' banks is a blemish on the landscape. A symbol of 1970s brutalist architecture, London's most renowned cultural complex nevertheless boasts top-notch programming and perfect acoustics.

It includes three prestigious venues dedicated to classical and contemporary music and dance: the **Queen Elizabeth Hall** and **Purcell Room** (1967), and the **Royal Festival Hall★** (1951), an architectural

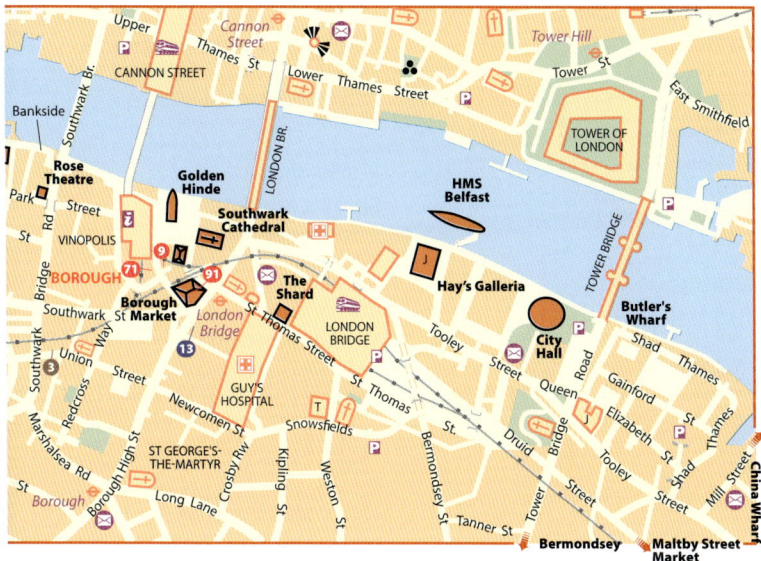

DINING		SHOPPING	
Arabica Bar & Kitchen	9	Oxo Tower Wharf	45
Southbank Centre Food Market	10	GOING OUT	
Oxo Tower Restaurant & Brasserie	42	Flat Iron Square	3
Elliot's	71	Ministry of Sound	6
Borough Market	91	ACCOMMODATION	
GRAB A DRINK		The Mad Hatter	12
The George Inn	13		

SOUTHWARK SOUTH BANK

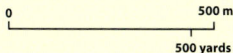

0   500 m
0   500 yards

masterpiece boasting a concert hall with 3,000 seats and marvelous acoustics, a dedicated chamber music room, a ballroom, and a restaurant. The Southbank Centre also hosts contemporary art exhibitions at the **Hayward Gallery** (*Wed.–Fri., Sun. 10AM–6PM, Sat. 10AM–8PM – prices vary with exhibitions*).

> **Picnic Idea**
> Is it nice out? Stock up at the **Southbank Centre Food Market** and have lunch at Jubilee Gardens. *p. 121.*

Jubilee Gardens

E5 Waterloo or Westminster. Jubilee Gardens commemorate the 25 years of Queen Elizabeth II's reign, celebrated in 1977. This green space and the banks facing it are very popular sites.

London Eye ★★★

E5 Waterloo – *087 0990 8883 – www.londoneye.com – ♿ – Mon.–Fri. 11AM–6PM, weekends 10AM–8:30PM – starting at £30 online (£42 on-site); combo tickets available with five other attractions, online discounts.*
This **ferris wheel**, a true technological triumph, towers at 443 feet and weighs 2,100 tons, serving as a spectacular landmark on the Thames since 2000. For 30 minutes, visitors in 32 enclosed capsules enjoy an **exceptional view** for up to 12 miles around.

County Hall

E5 *Belvedere Rd – Waterloo or Westminster.* This classical style building (1912–1922) served as the seat of the Greater London Council until its dissolution in 1986. It hosts various attractions (*combined tickets: see London Eye*).

SEA LIFE London Aquarium★

www.visitsealife.com. This "underwater cathedral" spans two levels below the Thames. You'll discover more than 500 species across 14 themed zones.

Shrek's Adventure

www.shreksadventure.com. For those traveling with children: this attraction invites you to meet Shrek and his friends.

The London Dungeon

www.thedungeons.com. The tour (*90 minutes*) of London's dungeons is for thrill-seekers only (*not recommended for young children*). It offers a grim retrospective of criminal punishments, major epidemics, and more harrowing events through London's history.

Imperial War Museum ★★★

F6 *Lambeth Rd – Lambeth North – 020 7416 5000 – www.iwm.org.uk – ♿ – 10AM–6PM – free.*
This exceptional museum focuses on the armed conflicts involving Great Britain and the Commonwealth since 1914.
The **First World War** is particularly well-documented: models, dioramas, and a reconstructed trench offer an idea of the soldiers' harsh living conditions.

QQ7/Getty Images Plus

London Eye (arch. Julia Barfield and David Marks).

Visitors also learn about a nation mobilized for war efforts and the social changes prompted by the conflict, especially women's roles. The visit ends with a question: is the armistice synonymous with peace? Sadly, we know the answer... The highly educational **Second World War** section raises other big questions: How did the war start? How did it spread across Europe and the world? Through a chronological journey, the major historical events blend with personal stories to make the visit engaging. The **Holocaust** galleries focus on personal stories from some of the six million Jewish people murdered during the Holocaust, providing a deeply human perspective on this tragic period. The exhibition also examines the complex relationship between the Holocaust and the Second World War.

The **Peace and Security: 1945–2014** section addresses the post-war world. The **Lord Ashcroft Gallery** celebrates 250 "extraordinary heroes," all recipients of the Victoria Cross or the George Cross, originated in 1940 for the purpose of acknowledging civilians' acts of courage and bravery.

Belgravia★★ and Knightsbridge★★

Luxury and calm... These neighborhoods, the most affluent in the capital, are a feast for the eyes. If you're a shopaholic, chances are your steps will lead you to the department stores and chic – and costly – boutiques frequented by a wealthy and discerning public.

▶ **Access:** ⊖ Knightsbridge, Sloane Square.
Neighborhood map pp. 72–73. Detachable map BC5–6.
☞ *Where to Go pp. 121, 133, 139, and 148.*

Belgrave Square ★★

C6 The square has preserved its original look with its central garden, rows of houses, and, at the corners, its townhouses. Although the whole gives the appearance of great unity, the colonnades and porticos on each side have a different design, as do the corner pavilions.

Harvey Nichols

C5 *109-125 Knightsbridge.*
Founded in 1813 and set up at the current **Knightsbridge** location in 1880, this temple of luxury has since spread worldwide.

The Squares

B5-6 The triangle formed by Knightsbridge and **Brompton Road** makes up a typically Georgian residential area, centered around three squares: **Trevor Square** (1818), **Brompton Square** (1826), and **Montpelier Square★** (1837). The residences, with stuccoed ground floors and brick upper floors, are adorned with tall windows and doors as well as magnificent balconies. Between these squares is a web of alleys, cottages with faded colors (Rutland Street), and flower-filled gardens.

Though laid out shortly after the squares, **Ennismore Gardens** displays a Victorian style with its stucco houses and rectangular pillar porches.

All Saints, the All Saints Church, built in the Early English style, is now used for Russian Orthodox worship.

Harrods and Harvey Nichols

Just a 4-minute walk apart, these two iconic temples of luxury shopping are a must-visit. ☞ *p. 139.*

The facade of the famous Harrods department store.

Harrods ★★

B5 *87-135 Brompton Rd.*
London's most elegant department store, once frequented by Oscar Wilde, dates back to 1849, though its current building only emerged at the start of the 20th century. Inside, the food halls dazzle with mosaic tiles and colorful stained glass windows – a rare example, alongside the Michelin House (**☞** *p. 76*), of Art Nouveau decor in London.

Beauchamp Place

B6 This street is home to elegant boutiques. At No. 27 you'll find Caroline Charles' store, known for dressing the world's elites, including Princess Diana.

Sloane Street

C5-6 The street, created in 1773 to connect Knightsbridge to Chelsea and the Thames, has been gradually reconstructed.
The **Danish embassy** (1976-1977), at No. 55, was designed by Ove Arup. The western part of Sloane Street (late 18th century) is known as **Hans Town**.

Cadogan Square

BC6 The shaded neighborhood of Cadogan Square and Cadogan Gardens, built at the end of the 19th century, owes its nickname, "Dutch Pont Street," to its high gabled houses, built in red brick with white stone trims.

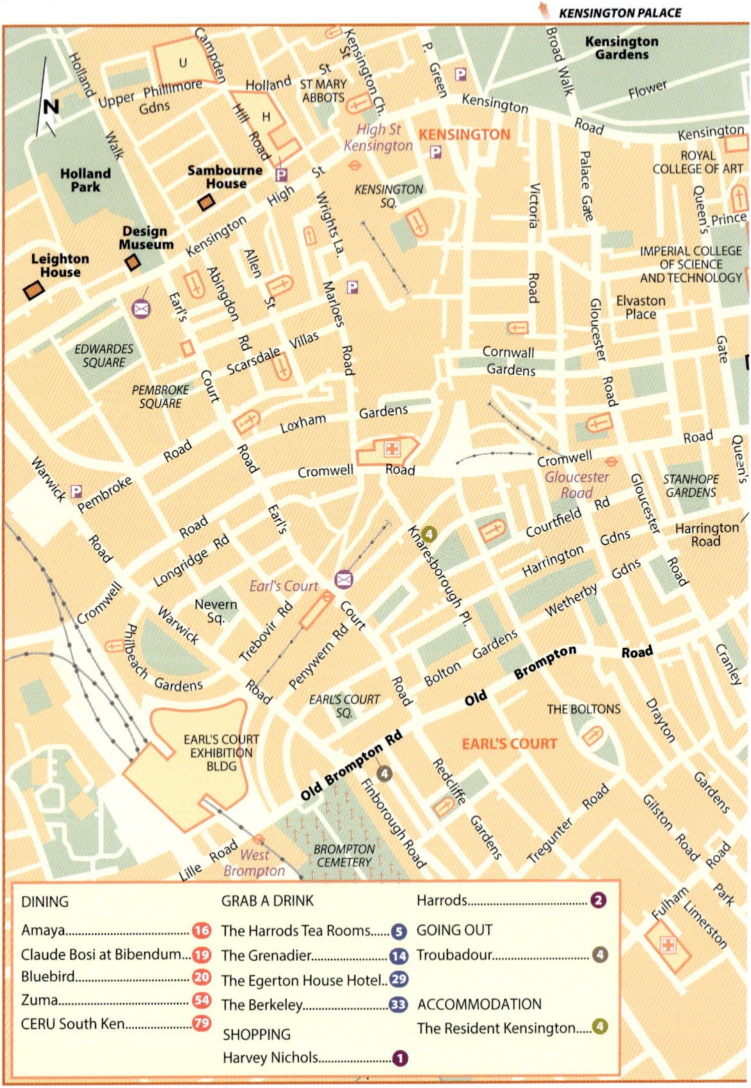
KENSINGTON PALACE
N
Kensington Gardens
Flower
Broad Walk
Kensington Road
Kensington
P. Green
Kensington Ch. St
ST MARY ABBOTS
Holland St
Campden Hill Road
Upper Phillimore Gdns
Holland Walk
Holland Park
Sambourne House
Design Museum
Leighton House
High St Kensington
KENSINGTON
Kensington High St
KENSINGTON SQ.
Wrights La.
Allen St
Abingdon Rd
Earl's Court Road
Marloes Road
Scarsdale Villas
EDWARDES SQUARE
PEMBROKE SQUARE
Loxham Gardens
Pembroke Road
Warwick Road
Cromwell Road
Longridge Rd
Victoria Road
Palace Gate
ROYAL COLLEGE OF ART
Queen's Gate
Prince
IMPERIAL COLLEGE OF SCIENCE AND TECHNOLOGY
Elvaston Place
Gloucester Road
Cornwall Gardens
Gloucester Road
Courtfield Rd
STANHOPE GARDENS
Harrington Road
Harrington Gdns
Wetherby Gdns
Knaresborough Pl.
Earl's Court
Nevern Sq.
Trebovir Rd
Penywern Rd
Philbeach Gardens
EARL'S COURT SQ.
Bolton Gardens
Old Brompton Road
THE BOLTONS
EARL'S COURT
Drayton Gardens
Cranley
Gilston Road
Redcliffe Gardens
Tregunter Road
Finborough Road
Old Brompton Rd
EARL'S COURT EXHIBITION BLDG
BROMPTON CEMETERY
West Brompton
Lille Road
Fulham Road
Limerston
Park Road
DINING
Amaya 16
Claude Bosi at Bibendum 19
Bluebird 20
Zuma (54)
CERU South Ken (79)
GRAB A DRINK
The Harrods Tea Rooms 5
The Grenadier 14
The Egerton House Hotel 29
The Berkeley 33
SHOPPING
Harvey Nichols 1
Harrods 2
GOING OUT
Troubadour 4
ACCOMMODATION
The Resident Kensington 4

SERPENTINE GALLERY

Hyde Park

Walk

Albert Memorial

Royal Albert Hall

Gore

Road

Carriage

Road

Knightsbridge

Hyde Park Corner

LANESBOROUGH HOTEL

Harvey Nichols

Knightsbridge

WILTON CRESCENT

ROYAL GEOGRAPHICAL SOCIETY

Ennismore Gardens

Rutland Gate

Montpelier Square

Trevor Square

Knightsbridge

All Saints

Wilton Pl.

Kemerton Pl.

Grosvnor Cres.

Consort Rd

ROYAL COLLEGE OF MUSIC

Exhibition Road

KNIGHTSBRIDGE

Brompton Square

HYDE PARK CHAPEL

Montpelier St.

Harrods

Knightsbridge

Hans

LOWNDES SQUARE

Lowndes

Belgrave Square

Belgrave Pl.

SCIENCE MUSEUM

Natural History Museum

VICTORIA AND ALBERT MUSEUM

BROMPTON ORATORY

Beauchamp Pl.

Beaufort Gdns

Brompton

Hans Rd

Hans

Crescent

DANISH EMBASSY

Hans Place

Pont Street

Chesham Pl.

Lyall

Eaton

Cromwell Road

THURLOE SQUARE

Brompton Rd

Walton

Street

Pont

Street

Sloane

Cadogan Place

Chesham St.

Eaton Square

Eaton Pl.

King's Rd

INSTITUT FRANÇAIS

Queensberry Pl.

South Kensington

Pelham St

ST COLUMBA

Lennox Gardens

Minner Street

Cadogan Square

Sloane Street

Old Brompton Rd

Onslow Sq.

PELHAM CRESCENT

Michelin House

Sloane

Draycott

Cadogan Gt.

Draycott Pl.

Holy Trinity

Sloane Square

Royal Court Theatre

Sloane Square

Christie's

ONSLOW GDNS

Sidney

Onslow

Road

Ixworth Pl.

Elysian

Chelsea St.

Whiteheads Gr.

Avenue

Avenue

PETER JONES

Lower Sloane St.

Bourne Street

Hobelin Pl.

Pimlico Rd.

ROYAL MARSDEN

ST LUKE

Cale Street

Chelsea Green

Jubilee Place

Markham St.

King's

Road

Royal Avenue

Saatchi Gallery

Chelsea Bridge

Gardens

Fulham

South Parade

CHELSEA SQ.

ROYAL BROMPTON

Dovehouse Street

Burnsall St

Radnor Walk

Wellington Square

Smith Street

St Leonard's Terrace

Franklin's Row

Burton's Court

RANELAGH GARDENS

ELM PARK GARDENS

CARLYLE SQ.

Manresa Road

CHELSEA

Chelsea

Shawfield St.

Tedworth Sq.

Hospital

Royal Hospital

Elm Park

Beaufort

Road

Church Street

Oakley

Glebe Pl.

King's

Road

Manor Street

Flood Street

Christchurch

Royal

NATIONAL ARMY MUSEUM

CARLYLE'S HOUSE

QUEEN'S HOUSE

Chelsea Physic Garden

Chelsea

Embankment

Danvers Street

CHELSEA OLD CHURCH

Lawrence St

Cheyne

Walk

Albert Br.

THAMES

CROSBY HALL

ROPERS GARDEN

BELGRAVIA & KNIGHTSBRIDGE
CHELSEA & SOUTH KENSINGTON
HYDE PARK & NORTH KENSINGTON

0   500 m
500 yards

LINDSEY HOUSE

Chelsea★★ and South Kensington★★

Along the charming streets of Chelsea, you'll find elegant and unique stores, antique dealers, cafés, and restaurants, all creating a lively and bohemian atmosphere. Over in South Kensington, a residential neighborhood with tree-lined streets and beautiful Victorian houses, you'll discover three of London's largest museums.

▶ **Access:** ⊖ Sloane Square, South Kensington, and Gloucester Road.
Neighborhood map pp. 72–73. Detachable map ABC5-6-7-8.
ⓖ *Where to Go pp. 122 and 148.*

Sloane Square

C6 ⊖ *Sloane Square.*
In this bustling square, you'll find the **Royal Court Theatre** (specializing in avant-garde theater since 1870) and the department store **Peter Jones** (1936). Note the plaque honoring the inventor of daylight savings, William Willett.

Holy Trinity

C6 *Sloane St. –* ⊖ *Sloane Square –* 📞 *020 7730 7270 – www. sloanechurch.org –* ♿ *– Mon.–Fri. 10AM–5PM.*
The **Holy Trinity Church** was rebuilt in 1888. It was Edward Burne-Jones of the Pre-Raphaelite movement who designed the 48 choir windows. The decoration and architecture achieve a rare unity here. Also, note the delicate metalwork.

King's Road ★

A8–BC7 ⊖ *Sloane Square and South Kensington.*
Welcome to a shopper's paradise. Originally just a path, King's Road got its name from Charles II, who widened it in hopes of reaching Fulham, where his lover Nell Gwynn lived, quickly. This major shopping street is renowned for its fashion boutiques, antique stores, restaurants, and pubs. The streets to the north are lined with traditional houses built for craftspeople.

Saatchi Gallery

C7 *Duke of York's HQ, King's Rd –* ⊖ *Sloane Square –* 📞 *020 7811 3070 – www.saatchigallery.com –* ♿ *– 10AM–6PM – variable prices depending on the exhibition.*

Victor Korchenko/Getty Images Plus

Cromwell Road with the Natural History Museum on the left.

The 13 spacious rooms of this contemporary art space host 3 to 4 annual exhibitions, showcasing artists who are often still relatively unknown or have never been exhibited in the UK.

Royal Avenue

BC7 🚇 *Sloane Square.*
Planted with trees in the 17th century, this double avenue opens up a view of the central pavilion of the Royal Hospital through a path that cuts across **Burton's Court**, limited to the north by **St Leonard's Terrace** (Georgian facades at Nos. 14–31). Fans of James Bond know that this is where the famous secret agent lives!

Royal Hospital ★★

C7 *Royal Hospital Rd – 🚇 Sloane Square – 📞 020 7881 5200 – www. chelsea-pensioners.co.uk – guided tours Mon.–Fri. at 10AM, Mon.– Wed. and Fri. at 2PM – £15 (online reservations recommended).*
Founded in 1682 by Charles II, inspired by the Hôtel des Invalides built by Louis XIV in Paris, the Royal Hospital was later expanded by James II, and then by William and Mary, who entrusted the work to **Christopher Wren**. Note the main entrance under its octagonal porch, crowned with a lantern. War veterans (Chelsea pensioners) are still its residents, as well as the famous **RHS Chelsea Flower Show** (📍 *p. 165*).

Chelsea Physic Garden ★

B8 *66 Royal Hospital Rd – ⊖ Sloane Square – ☏ 020 7349 6458 – www.chelseaphysicgarden.co.uk – ♿ – daily except Sat. 11AM–4PM – £13.*
Founded in 1673 by the Worshipful Society of Apothecaries, the oldest botanic garden in London carries on its role as research grounds for students.

Cheyne Walk ★

AB8 ⊖ *Sloane Square.*
A pleasant stroll along the Thames when traffic isn't too heavy. Beautiful red-brick houses line the street where artists such as writer George Eliot (No. 4), Pre-Raphaelite poet and painter D. G. Rossetti (No. 16), singer Mick Jagger (No. 48), and painters Whistler (No. 96) and Turner (No. 119) once lived.

Michelin House

B6 *81 Fulham Rd – ⊖ South Kensington.*
Opened in 1910, this building was the first in England to feature a reinforced concrete structure. It was occupied by Michelin until 1985. Admire its **Art Nouveau decoration**, expansive bay windows, and tiled facade★.

🍴 Claude Bosi at Bibendum

Michelin House now hosts a two-Michelin-star restaurant.
𝒞 *p. 122.*

Victoria and Albert Museum ★★★

B6 *Access via Exhibition Rd (main entrance), Cromwell Rd, or through the underground tunnel from ⊖ South Kensington – ☏ 020 7942 2000 – www.vam.ac.uk – ♿ – 10AM–5:45PM (Fri. until 10PM) – free (except for temporary exhibitions). Cafeteria-restaurant, shop.*
The **national museum of decorative arts and design**, the Victoria and Albert Museum was established to house works created for the 1851 Great Exhibition. Its initially disparate collection rapidly expanded with new acquisitions to encompass fine arts and applied arts from around the world, across all styles and periods: 2 million objects spread over 6 miles of galleries! Even those allergic to museums will find joy at the V&A, as Londoners affectionately call it; you can admire the collection of furniture, British sculptures, textiles, ceramics, silverware, and watercolors from 1500 to 1900. Additionally, there are sculptures from the Italian Renaissance, Islamic art carpets, Japanese lacquers, contemporary glasswork, a dazzling collection of jewelry, and a photography gallery from the 19th century to the present, among countless works from all civilizations and eras.
It won't be possible to see everything in a single visit. To navigate this abundance of objects, arm yourself with a map and head toward the galleries that naturally attract you, based on the geographical area or period they cover.

Natural History Museum ★★

AB6 *Cromwell Rd – ⊖ South Kensington – ✆ 020 7942 5000/11 – www.nhm.ac.uk – ♿ – 10AM–5:50PM – closed Dec. 24–26 – free – themed tours (dinosaurs, hidden treasures…).* The grand palace designed by Alfred Waterhouse, inspired by medieval Rhineland architecture, has housed the National Museum of Natural History since 1881. The Irish naturalist and collector **Sir Hans Sloane** (1660–1753) bequeathed over 80,000 specimens of animals, plants, stones, and minerals amassed throughout his lifetime. The botanist **Joseph Banks** (1740–1820) donated the herbarium he cultivated during his around-the-world voyage with Captain James Cook (1768–1771). The museum later enriched its collections with items from the East India Company (1858), the Zoological Society of London (1938), and more recently, the Geological Museum (1985). Today, its collections illustrate all forms of life, from the tiniest bacteria to the largest creatures, including fossils, dinosaurs, minerals, and rocks.

The collections are organized into large color-coded "zones." The **Blue Zone** explores the diversity of life on Earth, from dinosaurs to mammals to the most surprising marine creatures. The **Green Zone** traces the evolution of our planet, featuring minerals, fossils of all kinds, meteorites, and the world of birds and insects. The **Red Zone** continues the exploration of Earth, focusing on natural phenomena (earthquakes, volcanoes) and human evolution. The **Orange Zone** houses

Inside the Victoria and Albert Museum.

the "cocoon" of the Darwin Centre, where visitors can see insects, and provides access to the **Wildlife Garden**, an outdoor space where wildlife and plants change with the seasons. A fascinating visit rich in discoveries for all ages.

Science Museum ★★★

AB6 *Exhibition Rd – ⊖ South Kensington – ✆ 087 0870 4868 – www.sciencemuseum.org.uk – ♿ – 10AM – 6PM – themed evenings for adults ("lates") – activities free, except for flight simulators, IMAX cinema, Wonderlab, and some special exhibitions and activities.* From 19th-century calculating machines to 3D printers, from Stephenson's

Rocket (the first steam locomotive) to the Rolls-Royce Conway jet engine, from new materials to nuclear physics tools... more than 10,000 objects (out of the museum's 300,000!) are on display over 5 floors in this temple of popular science, considered one of the most impressive science museums in the world. The entire Western history of science and technology is on display: knowledge of the Earth, space exploration, secrets of the human body, information technology, the energy sources of yesterday and tomorrow... The permanent galleries, like the remarkable temporary exhibitions, emphasize interactivity wherever possible.

You likely won't be able to see everything in a single day, so check the welcome guide for themes of interest to you. Some of the most popular exhibits include the Space Exploration Gallery, featuring a life-size model of the International Space Station and the Apollo 10 command module; the **Flight Gallery,** dedicated to advancements in air travel; the **Fly Zone**, with its flight simulators (ticketed); and **Wonderlab** (ticketed), an interactive gallery where young visitors can explore hands-on science.

The Wellcome Wing houses the **IMAX cinema** (ticketed), along with a rotating exhibition gallery.

The **Energy Revolution** Gallery focuses on climate change and renewable energy, addressing some of the most pressing issues concerning our planet's future.

Royal Albert Hall ★

A5 *Kensington Gore –* ⊖ *South Kensington or Knightsbridge –* ☎ *020 7589 8212 – www.royalalberthall. com –* ♿ *– guided tour £18.50 (online reservations); ticket + afternoon tea £51.*

The Royal Albert Hall, designed by royal engineer Captain Fowke, is a circular red-brick building topped with a metal dome. It stands in stark contrast to the Albert Memorial nearby (⊙ *p. 80*), differing both in form and decoration: its only adornment is a terracotta frieze depicting the Triumph of Art and Letters.

Dedicated to an extremely diverse range of activities (concerts, dance performances, circus shows, etc.), the venue hosts the famous **BBC Proms**, or promenade concerts, each summer for two months, drawing up to 7,000 spectators at a time (⊙ *p. 166*).

Hyde Park★★, Kensington Gardens★★, and North Kensington★★

The true green lungs of the capital, Hyde Park and Kensington Gardens together form the largest public park in the city. In every season, Londoners come here to bike or rollerblade, run, canoe, or listen to a concert. With its beautiful houses adorned with white stucco and its shopping streets lined with elegant boutiques, the North Kensington neighborhood boasts a high-end clientele. It offers shopping enthusiasts a pleasant alternative to Knightsbridge and Oxford Street.

▶ **Access:** ⊖ Marble Arch, Hyde Park Corner, Lancaster Gate, Queensway, Bayswater, High Street Kensington, Notting Hill Gate.

Detachable map ABC4–5.

☾ *Where to Go pp. 122, 129, 144, and 148.*

Hyde Park ★★

BC4–5 ⊖ *Hyde Park Corner, Marble Arch, or Lancaster Gate – www.royalparks.org.uk – 5AM–12AM.*
East of the Serpentine Bridge and West Carriage Drive, this large park attracts Londoners at the first sign of sunshine. In the summer, they listen to orchestras, canoe under the Serpentine, ride horses, or showcase their golf skills.
At the northeast corner of Hyde Park stands **Marble Arch**, a white marble triumphal arch designed in 1827 by **John Nash** to mark the main entrance to Buckingham Palace. Too narrow for carriages, it was dismantled and rebuilt here, where the gallows of Tyburn once stood.

Not far away, **Speakers' Corner** is a place for public debate established in 1872, a testament to British freedom of expression.
Located in the southwest of the park, the **Princess Diana Memorial Fountain** was established in 2004.

Kensington Gardens ★★

AB4–5 ⊖ *Queensway or Lancaster Gate – www.royalparks.org.uk – 6AM-dusk.*
Kensington Gardens experienced their prime under Queens Mary, Anne, and Caroline (wife of George II) with the royal gardeners Henry Wise and his 1728 successor, Charles Bridgeman.
In the 18th century, the **Round Pond** was excavated, from which avenues radiate

xeipe/Getty Images Plus

Hyde Park.

toward the Serpentine and the Long Water. Another creation from this period is the **Orangery★** of Kensington Palace.

Serpentine South Gallery

℘ 020 7402 6075 – www. serpentinegalleries.org – ♿ – Tue.–Sun. and holidays 10AM–6PM – free.
In the southeast part of the park, this charming pavilion offers quality contemporary art exhibitions.

Serpentine North Gallery

Across the Serpentine, this annex designed by Zaha Hadid also houses a restaurant.

Albert Memorial ★

Inaugurated in 1876 in the south of the park, this monument is distinguished by its neo-Gothic spire designed by George Gilbert Scott. At the center, surrounded by allegorical statues and a frieze of 169 effigies of artists, sits a gilded bronze statue of Queen Victoria's husband, a promoter of the arts and education. Prince Albert (1819–1861) is notably responsible for establishing the great museums of Kensington, a district once nicknamed "Albertopolis."

Kensington Palace ★

A5 *West of Kensington Gardens – ⊖ Queensway or High Street Kensington – ℘ 033 3320 6000 – www.hrp.org.uk – ♿ – Wed.–Sun. 10AM–4PM (last entry 3PM) – reservation required – £24.*
Since its acquisition in 1689 by William III, this early 17th-century house has gone through three phases: under the house of Orange, it was the private residence of the monarch, and **Christopher Wren** was the main architect; under the early Hanoverians, it became a royal palace, decorated by Campbell and Kent; since 1760, it's been a residence reserved for the royal family. Queen Victoria, to whom an entire room is dedicated, lived here, as did Charles, the Prince of Wales, and Princess Diana. Today, it is the official London residence of the heir Prince William and his wife Kate – though the princely couple mostly resides at Adelaide Cottage, not far from Windsor Castle. The palace plays up its Crown credentials for its exhibition program, featuring ceremonial garments, objects, and paintings in its collections.

NORTH KENSINGTON ★★

Sambourne House ★

A5 *18 Stafford Terrace – ⊖ High Street Kensington – 📞 020 7602 3316 – www.rbkc.gov.uk/museums – Wed.– Sun. 10AM–5:30PM – £14 – combined ticket with Leighton House £22.*
The famous illustrator **Linley Sambourne** (1844–1910) moved into this house in 1875 and worked to embellish it in the so-called "aesthetic" style, popular during the Victorian era. The rooms have retained their intimate decor and original furnishings.

Holland Park ★

A5 *Entrance via Kensington High St., Abbotsbury Rd and Holland Park Ave. – ⊖ Holland Park or High Street Kensington – www.rbkc.gov.uk – 7:30AM–sunset.*
This lovely 54-acre park is very popular with London families, who enjoy the tranquility of its shaded paths and Japanese garden, children's playgrounds, and many sports facilities.

Design Museum ★★

A5 *224–238 Kensington High St. – ⊖ High Street Kensington – 📞 020 3862 5900 – www. designmuseum.org – ♿ – Mon.–Thu. 10AM–5PM, Fri.–Sun. 10AM–6PM – closed Dec. 25–26 and Jan. 1 – free.*
This impressive 107,000-square-foot space deserves a visit mainly for its top floor, where one can discover the evolution of contemporary design with the permanent collection "Designer Maker User," which features key objects from each major design domain: home, transportation, computing, automotive, textiles, etc. Sit on the steps in the entrance hall to admire the parabolic **ceiling**. The recent renovation led by John Pawson highlights the very 1960s concrete structure of the former Commonwealth Institute. Temporary exhibitions are shown on the ground floor, next to the café and shop.

Leighton House ★

A5 *12 Holland Park Rd – ⊖ High Street Kensington – 📞 020 7602 3316 – www.rbkc.gov.uk/museums – Wed.– Mon. 10AM–5:30PM – £14 – combined ticket with Sambourne House £22.*
☺ *Cozy café overlooking the garden.*
This house was built in 1866 by Lord Leighton (1830–1896), painter, president of the Royal Academy, and "a fervent advocate of eclectic beauty." Organized around the artist's studio and illuminated by its large skylight, the house wonderfully reflects the **Victorian style** of the era, as well as Leighton's taste for travel: there is a **Moorish living room**★★ decorated with mosaics, Arabic calligraphy, precious blue Damascene tiles, and an indoor fountain. These influences are present in his numerous works (paintings, sculptures and drawings) exhibited in the various rooms of the house.

Notting Hill★★ and Little Venice★

The facades of raspberry pink, canary yellow, seafoam green, and royal blue, along with the peaceful mews (cobbled lanes) in Notting Hill, make for one of London's most picturesque postcards. Along Portobello Road, the neighborhood's main street, you'll find a string of restaurants and cafés, chic designer boutiques, thrift stores, and art galleries. Don't miss the famous flea market, which draws crowds of bargain hunters on weekends. You can also escape the hustle and bustle by taking side streets to the northern part of the neighborhood, which is less touristy.

▶ **Access:** ⊖ Notting Hill Gate, Ladbroke Grove, Warwick Avenue. **Notting Hill off detachable map A3, Little Venice on detachable map A2–3. Notting Hill map opposite.**

▶ **Tip:** Visit on Fridays and Saturdays, the days of the Portobello Road market. *◉ Where to Go pp. 122, 133, 139, 144, and 148.*

Portobello Road ★

A3 toward ⊖ *Notting Hill Gate, Ladbroke Grove.*
This winding street, once a countryside path from the Notting Hill tollgate, comes alive on Fridays and Saturdays, when the **flea market** is in full swing *(9AM–7PM).* At the end of August, Portobello Road becomes the hub of the **Notting Hill Carnival** *(◉ p. 166).*
From Chepstow Villas to the junction with Lonsdale Road, there's a series of vintage stores, antique dealers, and Nepalese or Indian stores alternating with a few upscale restaurants. The atmosphere is more relaxed as you head north, especially near **Golborne Road**, where charming cafés sit next to grocery stores and Moroccan and Portuguese bakeries.

🍴 Iconic Cuisine
Don't miss the renowned Anglo-Israeli chef Yotam Ottolenghi's spot! *◉ p. 122.*

Kensington Park Road

A3 toward ⊖ *Ladbroke Grove.*
Kensington Park Road rivals Portobello Road in terms of liveliness. Bars and restaurants stay open late into the evening.

Little Venice ★

A2–3 *On Bloomfield Rd, west of Edgware Rd –* ⊖ *Warwick Avenue.*
Little Venice is a charming triangular basin bordered by weeping willows. It's the starting point for canal walks to Camden via Regent's Park Zoo.

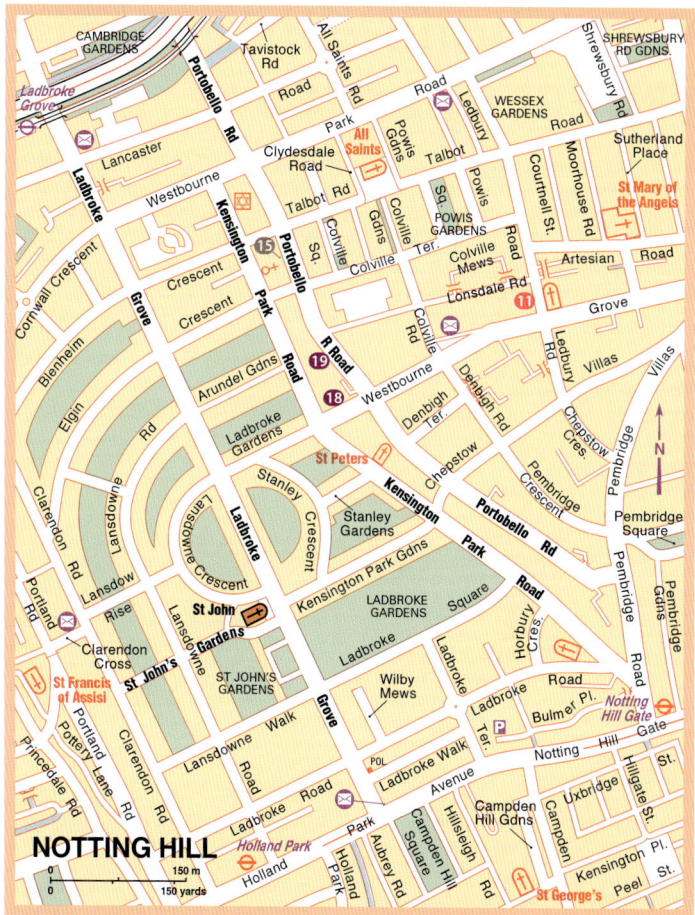

DINING		GOING OUT	
Ottolenghi	17	Electric Cinema	15
		Portobello Road	19
SHOPPING			
Paul Smith	18		

Marylebone★ and Regent's Park★★★

You don't need to be Sherlock Holmes to figure out that Oxford Street – Europe's longest shopping street – and the surrounding areas are a magnet for window shoppers. But the upscale neighborhood of Marylebone also offers pleasant surprises for those exploring its quiet alleys and squares, where stunning 18th-century homes can be found, one of which houses the treasures of the Wallace Collection. To completely escape the urban environment, head north to the green expanses of the beautiful Regent's Park.

▶ **Access:** ⊖ Regent's Park, Great Portland Square, Baker Street, Marble Arch, Bond Street.

Neighborhood map p. 87. Detachable map BCD1-2-3-4.

▶ **Tip:** If you want to visit Madame Tussauds, buy your ticket in advance to avoid the long lines.

⦿ *Where to Go pp. 123, 135, 140 and 148.*

MARYLEBONE ★

Oxford Street ★

CD3–4 ⊖ *Bond Street.*
This busy road extends west as far as Marble Arch (⦿ *p. 79*) and Hyde Park. At No. 400 stands the famous **Selfridges** store, a shrine to luxury built in 1908 by Gordon Selfridge, identifiable by its grand Ionic columns reaching three levels to a balustraded attic. Its various restaurants and food counters make it an endlessly exciting destination.

Other department stores alternate with international fast-fashion brands and empty storefronts, highlighting Oxford Street's struggle to regain its pre-Covid-19 success.

At Nos. 334–348, the large Debenhams store, among many others, awaits a revival project after falling into bankruptcy during the pandemic, and may possibly transform into a mix of stores, offices, and leisure spaces. To be continued...

The 2022 opening of the **Twist Museum** (*248 Oxford Street – www.twistmuseum.com – Mon.–Thu. 11AM–7:30PM, Fri.–Sat. 10AM–9PM, Sun. 10AM–6:30PM – £26*) in the heart of this shopping mecca suggests a shift in entertainment preferences. An immersive and colorful experience, Twist combines science, art, and fun to engage visitors in optical illusion games.

Opened across from Tottenham Court Road subway station, the **Outernet** (*corner of Oxford St. and Charing*

R. Leaver/Loop Images/age fotostock

Oxford Circus.

Cross Rd) delights passersby with ultra-HD photo and video projections on giant floor-to-ceiling screens. To the east, the street connects with Bloomsbury (⚲ p. 46).

The Squares ★

BC3 ⊖ *Bond Street, Baker Street.*
St Christopher's Place is a charming pedestrian area known for its terrace cafés and small stores.
Gloucester Place beckons visitors with its small alleyways and wrought-iron balconies.
At the northeast corner of **Portman Square** are two beautiful houses (Nos. 20 and 21). The first, built by **Robert Adam** from 1772 to 1777, was intended for Elizabeth, Countess of Hume.

Montagu Square, dating from the early 19th century, features residences with ground floors illuminated by small bow windows. The writer **Anthony Trollope** lived at No. 39 (1873–1880).
Bryanston Square, from the same period, is adorned with stucco terraces.

Wallace Collection ★★★

C3 *Hertford House, Manchester Sq. –* ⊖ *Bond Street –* ☏ *020 7563 9500 – www.wallacecollection. org –* ♿ *– 10AM–5PM – free.*
In the heart of Marylebone, on a Georgian square, **Hertford House** has a superb collection of French art gathered by the 4th Marquess of Hertford (1800–1870), who mostly resided in Paris, at the Bagatelle

castle in the Bois de Boulogne. To the family collection of Italian masters and 17th-century Dutch paintings, he added 18th-century French furniture, Sèvres porcelains, and paintings by Watteau, Boucher, and Fragonard. His son, **Richard Wallace** (1818–1890), further expanded the collection, brought it to England, and his widow donated it to the British nation in 1900.

On the ground floor is a gallery dedicated to the **Renaissance**, featuring Italian, French, and Flemish sculptures and paintings. Following this are vast rooms displaying ancient European and Eastern arms.

On the 1st floor, the **Great Gallery★★**, beautifully restored in 2022, gathers the greatest paintings from the 17th and 18th centuries: among others, *Perseus and Andromeda* by Titian, *The Lady with a Fan* by Velázquez, two striking full-length portraits of Philippe Le Roy by Van Dyck, the superb *Laughing Cavalier* by Frans Hals (not actually a cavalier and only hinting at a vague enigmatic smile), *The Rainbow Landscape* by Rubens, whose counterpart is at the National Gallery; several religious paintings including *The Adoration of the Shepherds* by Murillo, and a touching portrait by Rembrandt depicting his son Titus. There are also works by Nicolas Poussin, Philippe de Champaigne, and English portraitists Thomas Gainsborough and Thomas Lawrence. Lavishly decorated lounges showcase rich and colorful 18th-century French canvases: Greuze, Boucher, Fragonard, and more.

Madame Tussauds ★

C2 *Marylebone Rd – ⊖ Baker Street – ☏ 020 7487 0351 – www.madametussauds.com – ♿ – 9/10AM–4/5PM – from £42 (£37 online); combined tickets with South Bank attractions (☉ p. 68), online discounts.*

This famous wax museum features, alongside the French royal family (Louis XVI and Marie Antoinette) crafted by Mme Tussaud herself, effigies of distinguished figures from all countries and eras, including statesmen, athletes, artists, and English murderers, depicted in sometimes very realistic settings.

Sherlock Holmes Museum

C2 *221B Baker St. – ⊖ Baker Street – ☏ 020 7224 3688 – www.sherlock-holmes.co.uk – 9:30AM–6PM – £16.*

The choice to dedicate a museum to someone who never existed may be surprising. But it's delightful to step into the Victorian apartment where Sherlock Holmes and Dr. Watson "lived" from 1881 to 1904, set up according to descriptions found in Sir Arthur Conan Doyle's novels. Fans will recognize the iconic cap-pipe-magnifying glass set, as well as clues, evidence, and crime weapons drawn from the detective's celebrated adventures.

MARYLEBONE AND REGENT'S PARK

0 500 m
500 yards

Circle
London Zoo

REGENT'S PARK

Outer

Circle

Albert   Road   Parkway   Delancey St   Camden High St   Crowndale St

Circle

Park Village East   Mornington Crescent   Eversholt St

ST JOHN'S WOOD

REGENT'S PARK

Euston

Hampstead   Euston Square

OPEN AIR THEATRE   **Inner**

Boating Lake   Queen Mary's Gardens

Regent's University

Chester Rd   Robert St

Albany   Street

POL

Terraces

Terraces

Terraces

Prince   Outer

Regent's   Park Road

MARYLEBONE

Lisson   Rossmore Rd

Clenworth St

Sherlock Holmes Museum

Ulster   Terrace   Road

Regent's Park

FITZROY SQ.

Euston   Road

Great Portland Street   **Warren Street**

Broadley St   Grove

Marylebone

Baker Street

Madame Tussauds   3

Devonshire Street

Portland   Great Portland St   Cleveland Street

BRITISH TELECOM TOWER

Edgware Road   Marylebone

Gloucester   Crawford St

Baker   Paddington St   3   Devonshire Street

10

5

Wimpole   Harley   Cavendish

New

Mortimer Street   Wells St   Newman Street

Edgware Road

Bryanston Sq.   60   1

WALLACE COLLECTION   55

ALL SOULS CHURCH

40   Great Castle St.

7

Montagu Sq.   George St   66

MANCHESTER SQ.

—Marylebone La.

CAVENDISH SQ.

Portman Sq.   Wigmore

James St

St Christopher's Place   **Twist Museum**

Regent Street   **Street**

Oxford Circus

Seymour St   Orchard   Duke St   **Oxford**   New Bond St

Marble Arch   **Selfridges**   *Bond Street*

HANNOVER SQ.   LIBERTY

Brook   Street

Conduit St   Regent   Beak Street

Upper Brook St   *GROSVENOR SQ.*   Heddon St

Hyde

South Audley Street

BERKELEY SQ.

Savile Row   Old Bond St   Vigo St   ROYAL ACADEMY OF ART

Mount   Street   Albermarle St   Dover St

MAYFAIR

Park   Lane   Curzon   Street   Piccadilly   *Green Park*

Jermyn St

N

DINING

Fischer's	3
31 Below	5
ROVI	7
The Golden Hind	55
Chiltern Firehouse	60
Pachamama	66
Honey & Co	68

GRAB A DRINK

Artesian	40

SHOPPING

The Conran Shop	3
Contemporary Applied Arts	10

ACCOMMODATION

Gunmakers	1

REGENT'S PARK ★★★

BC1-2 ⊖ *Regent's Park – www. royalparks.org.uk – 5AM–7PM (pedestrian access)/midnight (vehicle access).*

In the early 19th century, vast lands previously granted by Oliver Cromwell to various operators were returned to the Crown, which decided to develop them. At the time, large-scale real estate operations were in vogue, and it was **John Nash** who devised the plan for a new neighborhood. Only part of it was realized between 1817 and 1825: the villas, the pantheon, and its halo of buildings never saw the light of day. The interior circular road, **Inner Circle**, surrounds a former botanical garden, now transformed into **Queen Mary's Gardens**, a floral garden that includes an open-air theater. The Holme, which sits outside the Inner Circle, is one of the few villas planned by Nash, while **Regent's University** occupies another villa rebuilt and expanded in the 20th century. The **Outer Circle**, a road built around the periphery of the park, is in line with the original plan. Three of its outer edges are lined with splendid **palaces★★**.

The Terraces to the West of the Outer Circle ★★

BC2 *Follow the walk clockwise.*
Park Crescent (1821) is a graceful classical-style semicircle designed by Nash to connect Portland Place to Regent's Park. The buildings (1823–1824) forming the east and west wings of **Park Square** are adorned with a simple Ionic colonnade.
Ulster Terrace (1824) is distinguished by its pair of bays attached to each end of the building.
Stretching nearly 1,083 feet – half the width of the park! – **York Terrace** (1821) consists of two symmetrical blocks centered around York Gate and ancillary houses. Villas adorned with imposing Corinthian columns flank the central body; the York Gate houses are Ionic in style.
Cornwall Terrace (1822) is a long building (558 feet) with Corinthian colonnades designed to evoke a receding perspective.
The central body and corners of **Clarence Terrace** (1823) feature heavy Corinthian pediments atop an Ionic arcade.
Sussex Place (1822) presents a curved structure, housing the London

asmithers/Getty Images Plus

Bridge in Regent's Park.

Business School, and surprises viewers with its domed helmet-shaped towers connected by a row of Corinthian columns.

The pale blue pediments of **Hanover Terrace** (1823) serve as the backdrop to a plaster frieze and plinth for statues silhouetted against the sky.

Behind a small octagonal pavilion at Hanover Gate stands the **mosque** (1977), with its white minaret topped by a golden dome and a slender crescent. Its light gray facade is punctured by high windows.

Hanover Lodge consists of a row of modern villas (1989) harmonizing with an 18th-century villa.

The Terraces to the East of the Outer Circle ★★

C1–2 At the same time as neighboring buildings, **Cambridge Terrace** (1825) underwent restoration, while **Cambridge Gate** (1875), on the site of the former Coliseum where exhibitions and dioramas were held, remains a fully Victorian structure with pavilion roofs.

Chester Terrace (1825) boasts the longest uninterrupted facade (940 feet) with imposing Corinthian columns. At each end, triumphal arches open onto the interior access road.

Cumberland Terrace (1826) features a monumental facade (794 feet) with Ionic columns.

Gloucester Gate (1827) is flanked by stuccoed porticos, contrasting with the red of the tympanums and the statues standing against the sky.

Pass through the gate and make a detour to Albany Street to see **Park**

Village West. More modest terraces, smaller houses, and cottages give a provincial feel to this charming horseshoe-shaped street.

London Zoo ★

C1 *Regent's Park, Outer Circle – ⊖ Camden Town – access possible by boat via Regent's Canal – ☏ 034 4225 1826 – www.londonzoo.org – ♿ – Nov. to mid-Feb.: 10AM–4PM; mid-Feb.–Mar. and Sep.–Oct.: 10AM–5PM; Apr.–Aug.: 10AM–6PM – £27/33 – reduced rates and fast-track tickets online.*

In 1828, the Zoological Society of London opened the zoo on a site of 5 acres. It now covers 35 acres. More than 20,000 animals from 260 species are on display. The Zoological Society continues to play a key role in the protection of endangered species, particularly by studying their breeding conditions.

Camden Town and King's Cross-St Pancras

Camden Town and its markets are still riding the mod revival wave of the 1970s to attract visitors, who flock there in droves on weekends. Not far from there, the opening of the British Library in 1998, right in the middle of a railroad junction – three of the capital's stations are within less than a half-mile radius! – marked the start of the transformation of a long-neglected area. Today, the district is dotted with new construction and renovated buildings dedicated to business, culture, and nature. It has turned into a popular weekend spot for strolling, made even more pleasant by Regent's Canal, which runs through it.

▶ **Access:** ⊖ Camden Town, Euston Square, King's Cross-St Pancras.

Camden Town map opposite. Detachable map DE1-2.

▶ **Tips:** For cultural events and updates on the area's transformation, inquire at the King's Cross Visitor Centre *(11 Stable St. – www.kingscross.co.uk).*
☾ *Where to Go pp. 124, 125, 133, 140, 145, and 149.*

CAMDEN TOWN

D1 ⊖ *Camden Town.*
Camden Town, iconic for housing London's counterculture, was the hub of British rock and pop in the 1990s. The area boasts residential spots with large, elegant homes favored by artists, writers, and actors. Nowadays, people mostly visit for the **flea markets**, the vibrant atmosphere, and immersion in the cutting-edge culture that still dominates the area. The eclectic storefronts and signage add to this hub of street art with bold, quirky, and sometimes provocative touches.

At the corner of Camden High Street and Buck Street, **BoxPark** (fomerly Buck Street Market) comprises around sixty recycled containers, bringing together bars, restaurants, and stores.
Camden Lock Market★★ is the first and most renowned of Camden's markets. Situated along the banks of Regent's Canal, it's also the most picturesque, featuring stalls of crafts and world cuisines.
From there, continue to the **Stables Market**, where art stores, vintage clothing stores, and a few antique dealers occupy old stables. A **statue**

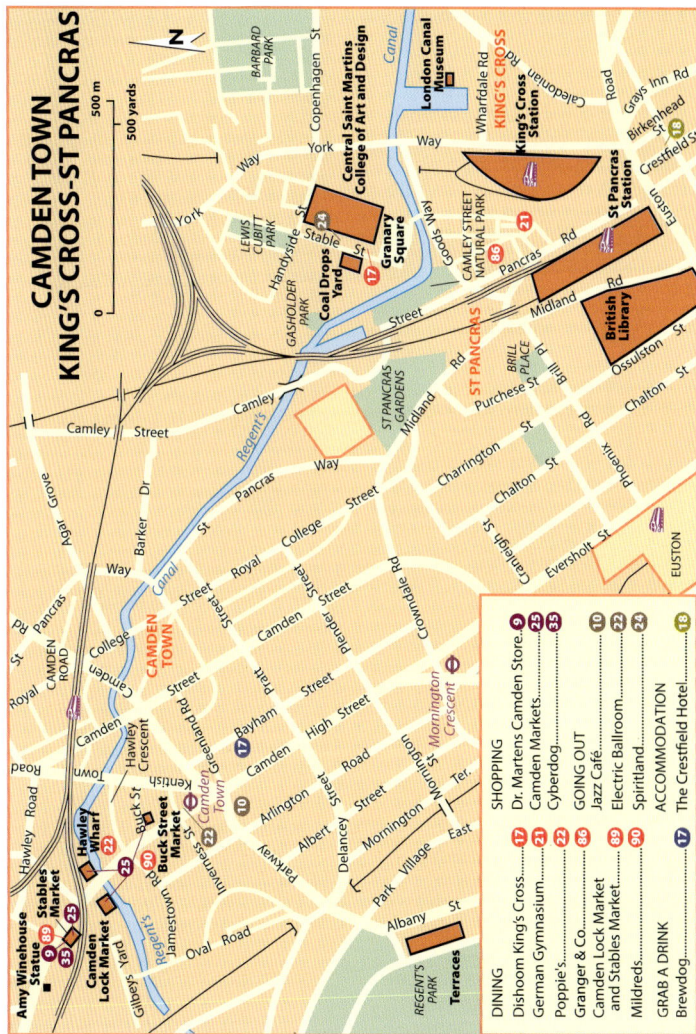

CAMDEN TOWN
KING'S CROSS-ST PANCRAS

N

500 m
500 yards

0

BARBARD PARK

Copenhagen St

Canal

London Canal Museum

Wharfdale Rd

KING'S CROSS

King's Cross Station

Caledonian Rd

Grays Inn Rd

Birkenhead St

Crestfield St

Central Saint Martins College of Art and Design

York Way

LEWIS CUBITT PARK

Handyside St

Stable St

Granary Square

Coal Drops Yard

Goods Way

CAMLEY STREET NATURAL PARK

St Pancras Station

Pancras Rd

Euston Rd

Midland Rd

ST PANCRAS

British Library

Ossulston St

York Way

GASHOLDER PARK

Street

ST PANCRAS GARDENS

Midland Rd

BRILL PLACE

Purchese St

Brill St

Chalton St

Regent's Canal

Camley Street

Camley Street

Barker Dr

Agar Grove

Pancras Way

Way

Charrington St

Chalton St

Crestfield St

Phoenix Rd

Eversholt St

EUSTON

College Street

Royal College St

Camden St

Pratt St

Bayham St

Camden High Street

Pancras Rd

Pancras Rd

St Pancras Way

Royal College St

Greenland Rd

Camden St

Camden Rd

CAMDEN TOWN

CAMDEN ROAD

Camden Rd

Kentish Town Rd

Hawley Crescent

Camden St

Arlington Road

Albert Street

Mornington Crescent

Mornington St

Mornington Ter.

Mornington Crescent

Mornington Cres

Delancey Street

Parkway

Crowndale Rd

Park Village East

Albany St

REGENT'S PARK

Terraces

Hawley Road

Hawley Road

Amy Winehouse Statue

Stables Market

Hawley Wharf

Camden Lock Market

Buck Street Market

Inverness St

Jamestown Rd

Regent's Canal

Gilbey's Yard

Gloucester Ave

Oval Road

Royal College St

Pancras Rd

College St

Camden Town

DINING
Dishoom King's Cross 17
German Gymnasium 21
Poppie's 22
Granger & Co. 86
Camden Lock Market and Stables Market 89
Mildreds 90

GRAB A DRINK
Brewdog 18

SHOPPING
Dr. Martens Camden Store 9
Camden Markets 25 35
Cyberdog 35

GOING OUT
Jazz Café 10
Electric Ballroom 22 21
Spiritland 21

ACCOMMODATION
The Crestfield Hotel 17

91

of **Amy Winehouse** was erected there in memory of the British singer who lived in the area and passed away in 2011 at age 27.

Further east, along Regent's Canal and the old railroad arches, the **Hawley Wharf** warehouses have been completely renovated to host a vast complex of stores, bars, restaurants, rooftops, housing, and leisure facilities (cinema, boxing gym, etc.).

Wellcome Collection

D2 *183 Euston Rd – ⊖ Euston Square – ☏ 020 7611 2222 – www. wellcomecollection.org – ♿ – Tue.– Sun. 10AM–6PM – free.*
Housed in a bright building, the unique collections amassed by pharmacist and businessman **Henry Wellcome** (1853–1936) offer a fascinating journey through the world's medical history.

KING'S CROSS-ST PANCRAS

British Library ★★

E1–2 *96 Euston Rd – ⊖ Euston Square or King's Cross-St Pancras – ☏ 019 3754 6060 – www.bl.uk – ♿ – 9:30AM–8PM (6PM on Fri., 5PM on Sat.), Sun. 11AM–5PM – free.*
The John Riblat Gallery's three exhibition rooms house the **Treasures of the British Library**: three millennia of writings from all over the world. Some have been digitized, providing a unique opportunity to peruse these rare manuscripts. Among the historically

Reading Room of the British Library.

significant documents are ancient maps, copies of the **Magna Carta** extracted in 1215 from King John by a group of nobles, and Shakespeare's signature (1623).

St Pancras Station ★

E1 ⊖ *King's Cross-St Pancras.*
Under the neo-Gothic spires of the impressive St Pancras Station (1864), a masterpiece of Victorian architecture, the scenes of **Harry Potter** departing for Hogwarts were filmed, even though the series references King's Cross Station.

🍴 **Between Two Trains**

Grab lunch at the **German Gymnasium**, located in a beautifully restored industrial building. 📷 *p. 124.*

King's Cross Station

E1 🚇 *King's Cross-St Pancras.*
Although the clock of King's Cross Station (1852) continues to impress, today the semi-circular metal structure of the **departure hall**, designed in 2012 by John McAslan + Partners, captures all the attention. *Harry Potter* fans can have their pictures taken in front of the famous **Platform 9¾** before popping into the adjacent souvenir shop.

London Canal Museum

E1 *12–13 New Wharf Rd –* 🚇 *King's Cross-St Pancras –* 📞 *020 7713 0836 – www.canalmuseum.org.uk –* ♿ *– Tue.– Sun. 10AM–4:30PM – £7.*
The museum occupies a former ice warehouse on the edge of Regent's Canal, where blocks of natural ice from Norway were once stored. The warehouse notably supplied Carlo Gatti, the most famous ice cream manufacturer of the Victorian era, among other clients. The exhibition traces the fascinating history of England's canal construction, the life of the canal workers, the industry's decline in the 20th century, and the rise of leisure boats.

Around Granary Square

E1 🚇 *King's Cross-St Pancras.*
The symbolic heart of the "new King's Cross," this vast pedestrian square extends behind the station along Regent's Canal. Popular day and night for its **fountain** with a thousand water jets, it is overshadowed by a former grain silo, repurposed to host the renowned **Central Saint Martins College of Art and Design**, part of the University of the Arts London (UAL). Several cafés, restaurants, and cultural venues are gradually taking over the surrounding former industrial wastelands.

Not far from here, in a large hall, the **Canopy Market** *(West Handyside Canopy – Fri. 12PM–8PM, weekend 11AM–6PM)* takes place each weekend, with a friendly ambiance uniting "taste artisans" – bakers, cheesemakers, chocolatiers, roasters, and more – and independent designers. You can eat and listen to music there.

Nearby, the **Coal Drops Yard** *(Stable St. – www.kingscross.co.uk)* shopping gallery occupies restored former coal warehouses (19th century), while the King's Road **Gasholders** have been converted into luxury apartments. This is the starting point for walks along the canals to Camden and Little Venice (📷 *pp. 82, 90 and 162).*

Clerkenwell

F2 🚇 *King's Cross-St Pancras.*
In this neighborhood extending southeast of the train stations, the **Quentin Blake Centre for Illustration** *(www.qbcentre.org.uk)* is set to open in 2025, serving as a new home and new name for the House of Illustration, which closed its doors at Granary Square in 2020.

Hampstead★★ and Highgate★

From atop its hill, the chic and charming neighborhood of Hampstead looks down on the rest of London. It's hard to resist the allure of its maze of alleys and passageways dotted with trendy stores, bars, restaurants, and historic pubs. It's always been a favorite spot for affluent artists, drawn by its peaceful atmosphere and proximity to a stunning wild heath. Across the park, the village of Highgate boasts plenty of character, with its houses, cemetery, and traditional pubs.

▶ **Access:** ⊖ Hampstead, Highgate, Archway, Hampstead Heath (Overground).
Neighborhoods map Cover flap.
▶ **Tip:** Visit Hampstead in the morning, then cross the heath *(approx. 2 miles)* to Highgate.
☉ *Where to Go pp. 125 and 134.*

HAMPSTEAD ★★

⊖ *Hampstead.*
The village has always attracted a large community of artists, including the painter John Constable and writers Robert Louis Stevenson, D.H. Lawrence, and **John Keats**, whose house you can visit *(10 Keats Grove – 𝄞 020 7332 3868 – www.cityoflondon. gov.uk, "Things to do" section – Wed.– Fri. and Sun. 11AM–1PM, 2PM–5PM – £9).* Even today, you're likely to run into some stars in this upscale neighborhood.
As soon as you exit the subway, you'll fall in love with the charming stores on **Flask Walk**, a pedestrian street almost too picturesque to be real. Not far from there begins the beautiful line of brick houses on **Church Row** (1720).

Freud Museum

20 Maresfield Gardens – ⊖ Finchley Road – 𝄞 020 7435 2002 – www.freud.org.uk – Wed.–Sun. 10:30AM–5PM – £15.
After leaving Vienna to escape Nazi persecution, **Sigmund Freud** (1856–1939) spent the last year of his life in Hampstead. His preserved house contains, among other curiosities, his famous **couch**, as well as an incredible collection of books, paintings, and antiques.

Fenton House ★★

Hampstead Grove – ⊖ Hampstead – 𝄞 020 7435 3471 – www.nationaltrust. org.uk – ♿ – Fri., Sun. and public holidays 11AM–4PM – closed Nov.–Mar. – £12.
A gate designed by **Tijou** (1707) opens onto a red brick house (1693), the oldest and largest in Hampstead.

Highlights include the magnificent Benton-Fletcher collection of **18 keyboard instruments**, made between 1540 and 1805, as well as a beautiful **garden**.

Hampstead Heath ★★

⊖ *Belsize Park, Hampstead or Hampstead Heath (Overground).*
This is one of the few examples of heathland in an urban setting. The site (790 acres) is a popular place for walking and entertainment *(large fairs on Easter Monday and during spring and summer holidays)*. Three ponds and a swimming pool are open for bathing.
From **Parliament Hill★**, there is a stunning view of the London skyline.

Kenwood House ★★

Hampstead Lane – ⊖ *Archway, Golders Green then bus 210 –* ℘ *020 8348 1286 – www.english-heritage.org.uk –* ♿ *– 10AM–5PM (4PM in winter); park: 8AM–7PM (4PM in winter) – free.*
The white stucco mansion presides over a harmonious landscape. Its elegant architecture, inspired by Antiquity, reflects the Adam style *(see pp. 36 and 175)*.
Note the **Adam Library★★**, designed as a reception room, and the beautiful collection of **paintings★★**. In the dining room: *Self-Portrait at the Age of 63* by Rembrandt, *Man with a Cane* by Frans Hals, *The Guitar Player* by Vermeer; in the small lounge: seascapes by Van

de Velde and a Turner. On the landing and in the breakfast room: paintings by Gainsborough. On the 1st floor, there is a fine series of portraits from the **Suffolk collection**.

HIGHGATE ★

⊖ *Archway, Highgate.*
Though it was just a green hill in the 16th century, Highgate attracted wealthy merchants, who built summer residences there in the 17th century and beyond. Apart from select modern buildings, the village, centered on Pond Square and High Street, has preserved a rural atmosphere.

Highgate Cemetery ★★

Swain's Lane – ⊖ *Archway –* ℘ *020 8340 1834 – www.highgatecemetery. org – 10AM–5PM (Nov.–Feb. 4PM) – closed Dec. 25–26 – £10.*
Shrouded in mystery, this cemetery, in operation since 1839, contains about 53,000 graves of both unknown and known individuals, such as the writer **George Eliot** (1819–1880) and **Karl Marx** (1818–1883). The western section features some remarkable funerary monuments, as well as the graves of **Michael Faraday** (1791–1867) and painter **Dante Gabriel Rossetti** (1828–1882). It's also here, in an area closed to visitors, that singer **George Michael** was laid to rest after he died in 2016.

East End

More than Notting Hill or Camden, the East End is where you'll discover a cosmopolitan and authentic London. When, in the early 1990s, cash-strapped artists sensed the potential of London's East and its spacious and affordable accommodations, they didn't foresee that the buzz of a new Eldorado would spread like wildfire. Since then, a multitude of galleries, bars, restaurants, and trendy clubs have sprung up. Despite this, the East End retains its cultural diversity.

▶ **Access:** ⊖ Liverpool Street, Aldgate East, Shoreditch High Street (Overground), Old Street, Bethnal Green.

Neighborhood map p. 98. Detachable map H1–2–3.

▶ **Tips:** Visit the area on a Sunday to enjoy the markets (☞ *"Shopping" p. 142)*. Start at Columbia Road Flower Market, Ideally early in the morning to avoid the crowds, head down to Brick Lane Market, continue to the Sunday Upmarket, and finish at Old Spitalfields Market.

☞ *Where to Go pp. 126, 131, 134, 142, 146, and 149.*

The Cockney

The "Cockney" moniker refers to a Londoner born within such a radius of the St Mary-le-Bow church in Cheapside that he or she can hear the sound of the Bow Bells when they chime. In practice, the area includes residents of the East Side, notably the City, but especially the neighborhoods of Spitalfields, Bethnal Green, Shoreditch, and Whitechapel. The Cockney often present themselves with enormous friendliness, humor, and camaraderie, and the story of working-class Cockney folks – complete with the colorful banter they're known for – has been widely popularized by the television series *East Enders*, which has been airing nonstop on the BBC since 1985.

SPITALFIELDS

H3 ⊖ *Liverpool Street.*

Once a historic textile industry district, Spitalfields marks the border between the City and the East End, with its large covered market. Vibrant and diverse, it is full of galleries, stores, underground clubs, and street art. Walk down **Artillery Lane**, one of the narrowest and oldest streets in the area. A typical house can be found at No. 9 Artillery Passage.

Old Spitalfields Market ★

www.spitalfields.co.uk – 10AM–8PM, Thu. 8AM–6PM, Sat. 10AM–6PM, Sun. 10AM–5PM.

Founded in 1862, the largest goods depot in London was moved to Leyton in 1991 and Spitalfields Market was transformed into a vibrant place of pop-up stores, food trucks, and restaurants of all kinds. The site has retained its Victorian arch (1892) on the east side, which runs along Commercial Street. On the west side, toward the City, much of the market was torn down to make way for a **Norman Foster** project combining office buildings and a shopping gallery.

Dennis Severs' House

18 Folgate St. – 🚇 Liverpool Street or Shoreditch High Street (Overground) – 📞 020 7247 4013 – www. dennissevershouse.co.uk – Thu.–Sun. 12PM–4PM – £8, "silent" visit £16, night visit £25 – book online.
Restored, or rather staged, the Georgian house of **Dennis Severs**, an American artist who died in 1999, tells a story spanning the 18th and early 20th centuries. Smells and soundscapes contribute to the complete immersion, further enhanced during a candlelit visit.

BRICK LANE ★

H2–3 🚇 *Shoreditch High Street, Aldgate East, Liverpool St.*
Brick Lane, though now manifestly gentrified, is still home to a significant Bangladeshi community. It is a lively thoroughfare on Sundays, worth exploring: on one side are fabric stores (reminders of the strong textile tradition), hardware stores, and barbers; on the other, Bangladeshi restaurants.
Connecting with Commercial Street, **Fournier Street** boasts beautiful Georgian houses (1718–1728), once inhabited by silk weavers.
The history of the **mosque** *(corner*

R. Harding/hemis.fr

Brushfield Street.

of Brick Lane/Fournier St.), which was initially a chapel and later a synagogue, reflects the area's various waves of immigration. Standing 98 feet high, its stainless steel minaret (2010) now serves as a neighborhood landmark and lights up in the evening.
On Sundays *(9:30AM–1PM),* a **flea market** takes over the area around Bethnal Green Road, Sclater Street, and Cheshire Street.

Old Truman's Brewery

This 18th-century former brewery is recognizable by its tall brick chimney marked with the Truman name. Its buildings stretch across both sides of Brick Lane and now house bars, stores,

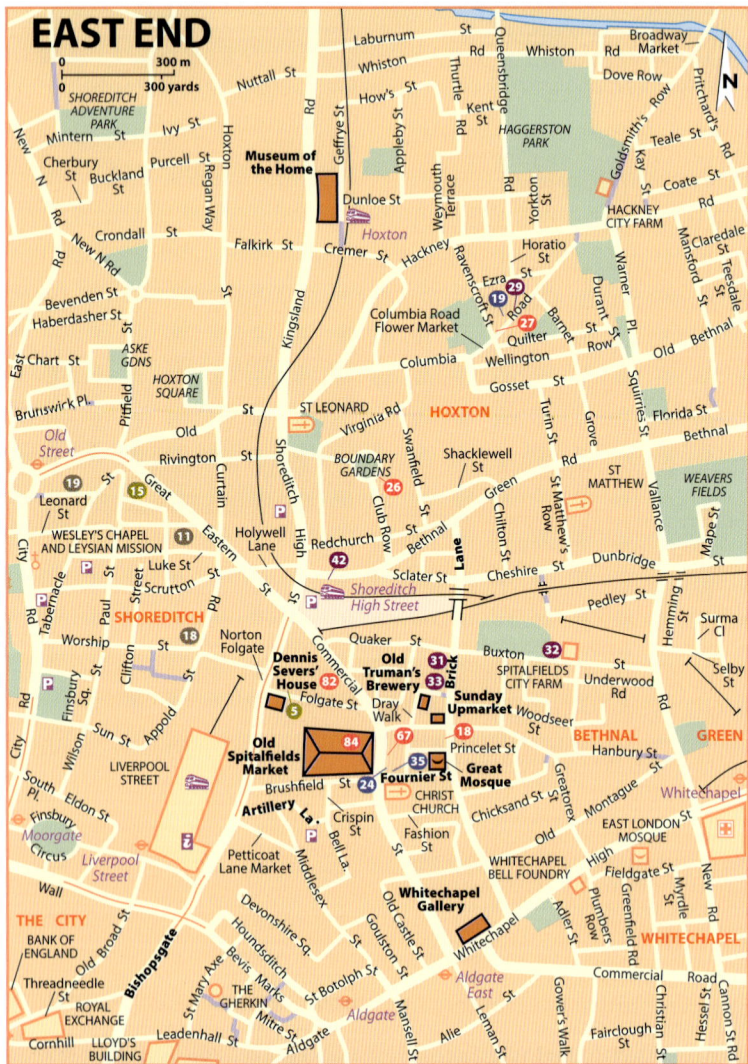

EAST END

0 — 300 m
0 — 300 yards

SHOREDITCH ADVENTURE PARK

Laburnum St
Whiston
How's St
Nuttall St
Mintern St
Ivy St
Cherbury St
Buckland St
Purcell St
Regan Way
Geffrye St
Appleby St
Whiston Rd
Queensbridge Rd
Thurtle Rd
Kent St
Dove Row
Broadway Market
Pritchard's Rd
Goldsmith's Row
Teale St
Kay St
Coate St
HACKNEY CITY FARM
Claredale Rd
Teesdale St
Mansford St

Museum of the Home
Dunloe St
Hoxton
Falkirk St
Cremer St
Hackney Rd
Weymouth Terrace
Yorkton St
Warner Pl

HAGGERSTON PARK

Crondall St
New N Rd
Bevenden St
Haberdasher St
Chart St
ASKE GDNS
HOXTON SQUARE
Brunswick Pl
Pitfield St
Kingsland Rd
Columbia Road Flower Market
Columbia Rd
Ezra St
Horatio St
Quilter St
Barnet Gr
Durant St
Row St
Old Bethnal
Wellington Row
Gosset St
HOXTON
Squirries St
Florida St
Bethnal

Old Street
Leonard St
Great Eastern St
Curtain Rd
Shoreditch High St
ST LEONARD
Virginia Rd
BOUNDARY GARDENS
Swanfield St
Shacklewell St
Green St
Chilton St
Turin St
Grove
ST MATTHEW
Vallance Rd
WEAVERS FIELDS
Mape St

WESLEY'S CHAPEL AND LEYSIAN MISSION
Tabernacle St
Paul St
Luke St
Scrutton St
Holywell Lane
Redchurch St
Club Row
Bethnal
Sclater St
Brick Lane
Cheshire St
Pedley St
Dunbridge St
Hemming St
Surma Cl

SHOREDITCH
Worship St
Clifton St
Finsbury Sq
Appold St
Norton Folgate
Commercial St
Shoreditch High Street
Quaker St
Buxton St
Selby St
Underwood Rd
SPITALFIELDS CITY FARM
BETHNAL GREEN

Dennis Severs' House
Old Truman's Brewery
Dray Walk
Sunday Upmarket
Woodseer St
Folgate St
Hanbury St
Greatorex St
Montague St
Whitechapel
EAST LONDON MOSQUE

LIVERPOOL STREET
Old Spitalfields Market
Brushfield St
Artillery La
Crispin St
Fournier St
Great Mosque
Princelet St
CHRIST CHURCH
Fashion St
Chicksand St
Old Montague St
Hanbury St
Fieldgate St
WHITECHAPEL

South Pl
Eldon St
Finsbury
Moorgate
Liverpool Street
Circus
Wall
Wilson St
Sun St
Petticoat Lane Market
Bell La
Middlesex St
WHITECHAPEL BELL FOUNDRY
Whitechapel Gallery
High St
Myrdle St
Greenfield Rd
New Rd

THE CITY
BANK OF ENGLAND
Threadneedle St
ROYAL EXCHANGE
Cornhill
LLOYD'S BUILDING
Bishopsgate
St Mary Axe
Bevis Marks
THE GHERKIN
Houndsditch
Devonshire Sq
Mitre St
Leadenhall St
St Botolph St
Aldgate
Aldgate East
Goulston St
Old Castle St
Whitechapel
Aldgate
Mansell St
Alie St
Leman St
Gower's Walk
Plumbers Row
Adler St
Commercial Rd
Fairclough St
Christian St
Back Church La
Cannon St Rd

offices, and the **Sunday Upmarket** (🕐 p. 142).

WHITECHAPEL

H3 🚇 *Aldgate East, Whitechapel.* The southern edge of the East End – where Jack the Ripper struck in 1888 – is still a very popular neighborhood. Visitors come for the colorful markets and specialty African and East Asian stores.

Whitechapel Gallery ★

H3 *77–82 Whitechapel High St. – 🚇 Aldgate East – 𝄞 020 7522 7888 – www.whitechapelgallery. org – ♿ – Tue.–Sun. 11AM–6PM (9PM Thu.) – free.*
😊 *A particularly well-stocked bookstore.*
Opened in 1901 to exhibit works in the Arts & Crafts style, this gallery has hosted future masters of modern art like Picasso – who exhibited *Guernica* here for the first time in 1938 – Pollock, Rothko, and Frida Kahlo, as well as contemporary artists **David Hockney** and Gilbert & George, who were unknown at the time.

SHOREDITCH, HOXTON, AND BETHNAL GREEN

GH1-2 🚇 *Old Street, Shoreditch High Street or Hoxton (Overground).*
Already popular before being taken over by artists and night owls, Shoreditch and, to a lesser extent, Hoxton, are gradually gentrifying. Rivington Street, Redchurch Street, and Chance Street are adorned with stencils, graffiti, and stickers that reveal both entrenched and emerging local attitudes (🕐 box p. 100).

Victoria Miro Gallery

G1 *16 Wharf Rd – 🚇 Old Street – 𝄞 020 7336 8109 – www.victoria-miro. com – Tue.–Sat. 10AM–6PM – gardens: Apr.–end Oct.*
Hidden in a former furniture factory, this contemporary art gallery showcases nearly 11,000 square feet of paintings and installations by major international artists as well as some top new talents.

Museum of the Home ★

H1 *136 Kingsland Rd – ⊖ Old Street or Hoxton (Overground) – ☎ 020 7739 9893 – www.museumofthehome.org.uk – ♿ – Tue.–Sun. 10AM–5PM – free.* This museum illustrates the everyday life of the British middle class from the 16th to 20th centuries, through reconstructions of interiors and themed rooms. In addition to the herb garden, other plots have been laid out in styles from different periods.

Young V&A ★

H2, toward *Cambridge Heath Rd – ⊖ Bethnal Green – www.vam.ac.uk/young – ♿ – 10AM–5:45PM – free.* In 2023, the Victoria and Albert Museum opened this museum dedicated to children, enhanced by its vast collections of games and toys from around the world. A remarkable presentation and real educational effort make it appealing for all ages – including adults! It offers three permanent galleries – "Imagine," "Play" (with play areas for the little ones and a video game room for teenagers), and "Design." Fun workshops are led by museum staff to explore art and creativity. Excellent temporary exhibitions.

V&A East Storehouse and Museum

H2, toward *Queen Elizabeth Olympic Park – Stratford – ⊖ Hackney Wick – www.vam.ac.uk/east.* As part of the redevelopment of the Stratford Olympic Park, this Kensington-based Victoria and Albert Museum annex is positioned as a new cultural landmark. The "Storehouse" section makes more than 250,000 objects from the V&A's extraordinary collection visible to the public in a state-of-the-art storage space. The "Museum" section explores themes of making and creativity, illuminating our capacity to change the world.

Shoreditch, the Hotspot of London Street Art

The streets and alleys of Shoreditch are favorite playgrounds for street artists, who showcase their inspiration and creativity side by side with other luminaries. Protest pieces, satire, humor, poetry, graffiti, murals, collages, mosaics, and sculptures cover the brick walls of the neighborhood. Besides well-known names like the prolific **Banksy**, whose provocative stencils have animated the nooks and crannies of the capital since the 1990s, artists both British and international have claimed East London as their open-air studio. By nature ephemeral, urban art is constantly renewing itself, and it may be wise to follow a **guided tour**.

☛ Shoreditch Street Art Tour *(www.shoreditchstreetarttours.co.uk)*, Street Art London Tour *(www.streetartlondon.co.uk)*, Strawberry Tours *(www.strawberrytours.com)*.

The Southern Districts

In the wake of a revitalization of the south bank of the Thames, the once working-class neighborhoods of Brixton and Peckham have become go-to spots for fashionable young Londoners in just a few years. Naturally, coffee shops are springing up, trendy restaurants are opening, and there's a new surge of culture and nightlife. More upscale, the Battersea district, across from Chelsea, is undergoing a major transformation. Visit soon as the entire new urban area, Nine Elms, literally rises from the ground.

▶ **Access:** Refer to each district.

Detachable map BD8 (Battersea and Nine Elms) and cover flap.

▶ **Tips:** Visit Peckham on the weekend for a livelier atmosphere. Brixton is a 15-minute subway ride (Victoria line) from St Pancras. Convenient for a last visit before catching the Eurostar. In warmer seasons, consider taking the river shuttle to Battersea.

◉ *Where to Go pp. 127, 134, 135, and 146.*

PECKHAM

⊖ *Peckham Rye (Overground).*
Located in the borough of Southwark, this neighborhood is popular with young Londoners, earning it the nickname "new Shoreditch." Climbing prices are threatening to displace the African and Asian communities who have made Peckham their home for generations.

Close to the overground station, **Rye Lane** was considered the "Oxford Street" of South London in the early 19th century. Today, it's a bustling popular shopping street with African markets, rare fruits, and music that gives it a permanent festive atmosphere! At No. 133, the former warehouses of **Copeland Park** and **Bussey Building** (*www.copelandpark.com*) form the cultural heart of Peckham, hosting a theater, artist workshops and galleries, cafés, a record store, and even a rooftop bar and cinema during pleasant weather (*schedules on www.rooftopfilmclub.com*).

Parallel to Rye Lane, **Bellenden Road**, with its bohemian-chic feel, offers a wide range of stores and cafés where the latte is king, all in a charming village atmosphere.

South London Gallery

65–67 Peckham Rd – www.southlondongallery.org – 11AM–6PM, Wed. 11AM–9PM – closed Mon. – free.

This art museum was founded in 1868 by philanthropist William Rossiter on Blackfriars Road before moving to its present location at the end of the 19th century. It features stunning gardens created by Mexican artist Gabriel Orozco (*weekends 11AM–6PM*) and has highlighted young British artists since the 1950s. An annex of the museum has opened in the former fire station on Peckham Road.

BRIXTON

⊖ *Brixton.*

In the wake of World War II, Brixton (☞ *p. 178*) became home to a thriving community of Caribbean migrants. Following a period of social unrest in the 1980s, Brixton has continued to develop and now even has its own currency, the Brixton Pound, created in 2009 to encourage local commerce.

Brixton Village and Market Row

www.brixtonvillage.com – 8AM-midnight (until 6PM on Mondays). **Electric Avenue**, one of London's first electrified streets, leads to the largest Afro-Caribbean market in Europe. A must-visit to feel the pulse of the neighborhood. Under the large glass roofs of these two covered passages, the stalls overflow with African fabrics, artisanal jewelry, home decor, and more. Numerous restaurants offer cosmopolitan cuisine at a reasonable price.

Not far away, on Windrush Square, a **memorial** dedicated to Afro-Caribbeans who fought during both World Wars, as well as the **Black Cultural Archives** (*1 Windrush Sq. – www.blackculturalarchives.org*), show that Brixton doesn't forget its past.

Brockwell Park

www.lambeth.gov.uk/parks/ brockwell-park – 7:30AM-sunset. The 123 acres of lawn in this park offer a breathtaking view of the City.

Brixton Windmill

Blenheim Gardens (about 0.6 miles south of the subway station) – www. brixtonwindmill.org – Mar. to Oct.: guided tours on the 2nd weekend of the month – £5. On the left of Brixton Hill, you can visit the last **windmill** in the capital, which operated from 1816 to the 1930s.

Brixton and Music: The Perfect Match

Most Londoners see Brixton, a bastion of reggae, as a music capital. The neighborhood is known for housing one of the capital's legendary venues, the **Brixton O2 Academy** (*www.academymusicgroup.com/o2academybrixton*), and for having given us **David Bowie**, whose colorful memorial is worth seeing (*464 Brixton Rd, at the corner of Tunstall Rd*). This magnificent mural, created by Australian artist Jimmy C., is located not far from the artist's former home.

BATTERSEA AND NINE ELMS

BD8 ⊖ *Battersea Power Station or Battersea Park (Overground or Southern train from Victoria Station or Clapham Junction).*
The borough of Wandsworth is now home to the second largest urban renovation project in Europe (after La Courneuve in the Paris region): the new neighborhood of Nine Elms, around the former Battersea power station, set to become a mixed-use district (residential, commercial and business) by 2030. This area, once dedicated to asparagus farming and industrial activities, is writing one of the great chapters of London's future. In comparison, the charming Battersea seems quite calm and traditional, with its old churches and large park.

Battersea Power Station ★

⊖ *Battersea Power Station or Thames Clippers river shuttles (⊙ p. 161) – www.batterseapowerstation.co.uk – Mon.–Sat. 10AM–9PM, Sun. 12PM–6PM.*
In operation from 1939 to 1983, this was the country's first large coal-fired power station. It has since undergone an incredible transformation, becoming the center of a brand-new neighborhood. It took nearly 10 years to rehabilitate, from 2013 to 2022, with architects from around the world, including **Foster + Partners** and **Gehry Partners**. Once long abandoned, the red brick structure, recognizable by its four tall chimneys and immortalized on the cover of **Pink Floyd**'s *Animals* album, now houses an impressive complex of stores (over 150),

restaurants, bars, cafés, a cinema, and residential units.
An elevator, **Lift 109** *(www.lift109. co.uk – 10AM–6PM, 8PM Fri., Sat., and public holidays – closed Dec. 25 – £17/24 – variable rates depending on the time and demand)*, ascends to the top of the northwest chimney, reaching a heigh of 358 feet: the 360° view of London showcases the extent of the renovations. All around, many buildings have already emerged, bringing a new neighborhood to life, particularly on the **Circus West Village** side, which boasts around twenty trendy bars and restaurants.

Battersea Park ★

⊖ *Battersea Park – www.wandsworth. gov.uk/batterseapark – 8AM–sunset.*
Created in the mid-19th century on marshy land, this beautiful park covering 205 acres along the River Thames serves as the green lung of the neighborhood. It features a lake for boating, playgrounds, sports facilities, two cafés, a riverside pagoda, and a small zoo. Numerous activities (concerts, exhibitions) are organized here.
⊙ *For more information about the Nine Elms projects, see p. 178 and www. nineelmslondon.com.*

103

Docklands★

Where the Thames meanders to Greenwich, between Tower Pier and the Thames Barrier, the landscape undergoes a radical transformation. The most striking element is Canary Wharf, which overshadows other points of interest. It's recommended to arrive on the Docklands Light Railway: the impression of entering a futuristic city highlights the extent of the Docklands' regeneration, a sign of London's ongoing expansion eastward.

▶ **Access:** ⊖ Tower Hill, Canary Wharf, Canary Wharf (DLR), West Shadwell (DLR), West India Quay (DLR).

Neighborhood map pp. 106–107. Off the detachable map.

▶ **Tip:** Visit the Docklands during the week: the area tends to be less busy on weekends.
𝐂 *Where to Go pp. 134, 135, and 149.*

St Katharine's Docks ★

⊖ *Tower Hill.*

Situated just a stone's throw from the Tower of London (𝐂 *p. 58*), this pleasant **marina** lined with offices, stores, restaurants, and luxury apartments replaced the docks that had occupied the site since 1828, 140 years later, in 1968. Nothing remains of the St Katharine-by-the-Tower hospice (1148) that welcomed refugees from Europe and would eventually give the docks their name. The land was purchased in 1825 by the St Katharine Dock Company, which built warehouses and two docks. Several terraces allow visitors to enjoy the picturesque setting, particularly delightful on sunny days.

Museum of London Docklands ★★

West India Quay – ⊖ *West India Quay (DLR) –* 𝄞 *020 7001 9844 –* *www.museumoflondon.org.uk –* ♿ *– 10AM–5PM – free.*

A visit to this fascinating museum, housed in warehouse No. 1, reveals the importance of the Thames in London's development and the history of the Docklands. Across two floors, the docks' complex functioning during the heyday of maritime trade is explained, as well as how port activity affected the city's social and economic life from Roman times to the present day. Exhibits depict the dance of ships entering the port, directed to specific docks depending on their origin. The exhibition also examines the diverse array of goods arriving from all over the globe.

The Docklands were also home to a hardworking population of laborers, dockers, and families living under harsh conditions, whose demands sparked numerous social conflicts and strikes. A reconstruction of a set of dark alleys, with taverns, stores, and poor housing, helps visitors grasp this reality.

Isle of Dogs ★

⊖ *West India Quay (DLR) or Canary Wharf (DLR).*
This strip of land nestled in a bend of the Thames was named in reference to kennels set up in the 16th century by King Henry VIII. At that time, the land was covered in marshy grasslands where cattle would graze.
In the early 19th century, the introduction of the **West India Docks** quickly transformed the area. A populous neighborhood developed around the three docks erected in 1802 and 1806 and the main quay, Canary Wharf. Following the closure of the docks in the 1980s, the Isle of Dogs became the focus of a redevelopment project aimed at creating an "annex" of the City in East London. With the renovation of Canary Wharf, the project was successful.

Canary Wharf ★

⊖ *Canary Wharf (DLR).*
The resurgence of Canary Wharf, which became a leading business district in under two decades, began in 1988 with the construction of new skyscrapers around Cabot Square, including **One Canada Square** (774 feet high). Erected in 1991 by Argentinian architect César Pelli, this 50-floor steel-clad obelisk reflects light like a beacon. Entirely funded by private investment, Canary Wharf has attracted prestigious firms, banks, and media groups since its inception. More recently, to counter the rise of remote work, Canary Wharf has sought to establish itself as a shopping hub with the establishment of large **shopping centers** such as Cabot Place, Jubilee Place, Canada Place, and Churchill Place, comprising hundreds of stores. Today, the area continues to evolve, with many residential towers being built, including the **Landmark Pinnacle**, completed in 2020; with its 75 floors (764 feet), it is one of the tallest residential towers in Europe.

The O2

Peninsula Square – ⊖ North Greenwich, Royal Victoria (DLR), then IFS Cloud Cable Car (https://tfl.gov.uk/modes/london-cable-car/£6 AS). Thames Clippers ferries: stop at North Greenwich (🕐 p. 161) – ☎ 020 8463 2000 – www.theo2.co.uk – ♿ – free, except for activities.
Located on the Greenwich Peninsula, on the south bank of the Thames loop, the former Millennium Dome designed by **Richard Rogers** (2000) is a vast fiberglass fabric structure 1,200 feet in diameter and 164 feet high, supported by 12 steel masts, with a volume equal to ten times that of St Paul's Cathedral. It has been converted into a leisure complex including stores, restaurants, bars, nightclubs, a cinema, bowling, and several concert halls, including one with 20,000 seats (O2 Arena).

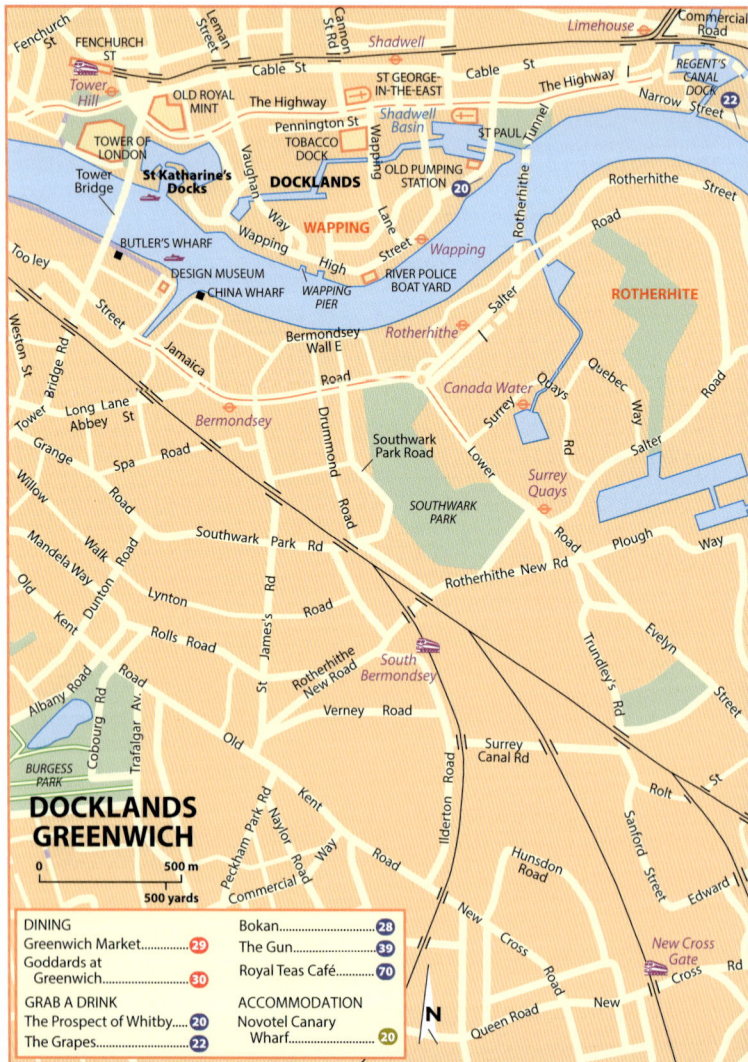

DOCKLANDS GREENWICH

0 — 500 m
500 yards

BURGESS PARK

N

DINING		Bokan	28
Greenwich Market	29	The Gun	39
Goddards at Greenwich	30	Royal Teas Café	70
GRAB A DRINK		**ACCOMMODATION**	
The Prospect of Whitby	20	Novotel Canary Wharf	20
The Grapes	22		

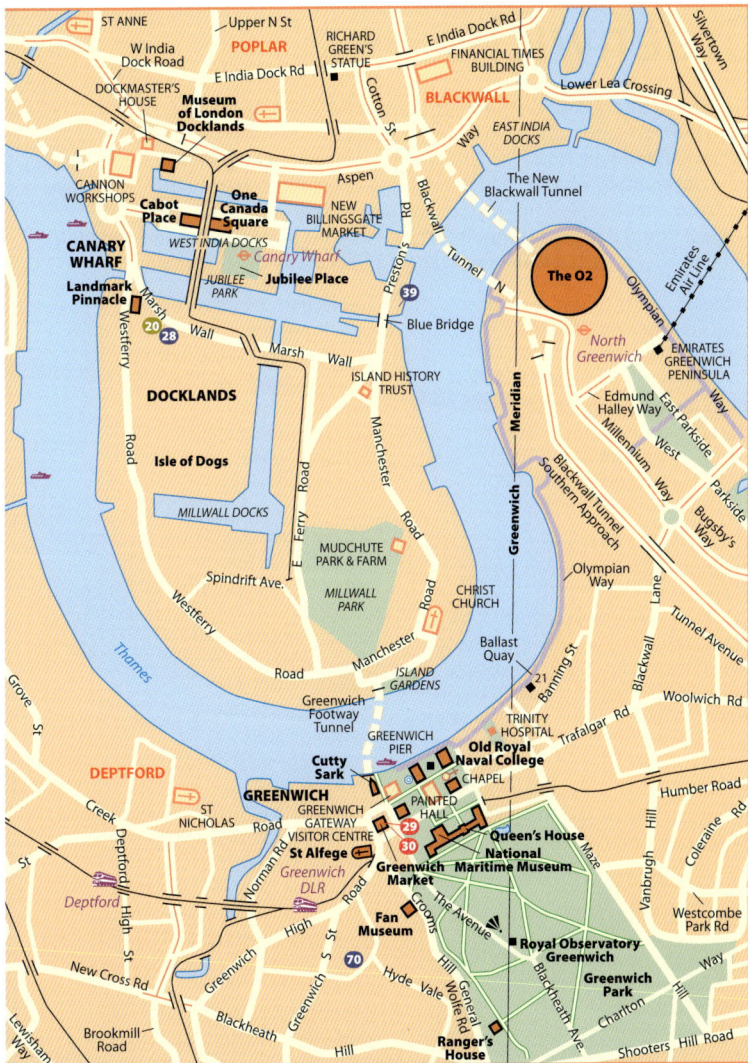

ST ANNE
Upper N St
RICHARD GREEN'S STATUE
E India Dock Rd
Silvertown Way

W India Dock Road
POPLAR
E India Dock Rd
FINANCIAL TIMES BUILDING
Lower Lea Crossing

DOCKMASTER'S HOUSE
Museum of London Docklands
Cotton St
Way
BLACKWALL
EAST INDIA DOCKS

CANNON WORKSHOPS
Aspen
Blackwall
The New Blackwall Tunnel

Cabot Place
One Canada Square
NEW BILLINGSGATE MARKET
Preston's Rd
Tunnel N
Emirates Air Line

CANARY WHARF
WEST INDIA DOCKS
Canary Wharf
The O2
Olympian

Landmark Pinnacle
JUBILEE PARK
Jubilee Place
39
North Greenwich
EMIRATES GREENWICH PENINSULA

Westferry
Marsh Wall
Blue Bridge
East Parkside
Way

20 28
Marsh Wall
ISLAND HISTORY TRUST
Meridian
Edmund Halley Way
West
Parkside
Bugsby's Way

DOCKLANDS
Manchester
Millennium Way

Isle of Dogs
Road
Blackwall Tunnel Southern Approach

Road
E Ferry Road
MILLWALL DOCKS
Greenwich

Spindrift Ave.
MUDCHUTE PARK & FARM
Olympian Way

Westferry
MILLWALL PARK
Manchester Road
CHRIST CHURCH
Tunnel Avenue
Lane
Blackwall

Thames
Road
ISLAND GARDENS
Ballast Quay
Banning St
21
Woolwich Rd

Grove St
Greenwich Footway Tunnel
TRINITY HOSPITAL
Trafalgar Rd
Humber Road

GREENWICH PIER
GREENWICH PIER
Old Royal Naval College
CHAPEL

DEPTFORD
Cutty Sark
Maze Hill
Coleraine Rd

ST NICHOLAS
GREENWICH
GREENWICH GATEWAY VISITOR CENTRE
PAINTED HALL
Queen's House
Vanbrugh Hill

Deptford Creek
Road
Norman Rd
29
30
National Maritime Museum
Westcombe Park Rd

St George's St
St Alfege
Greenwich DLR
Greenwich Market
The Avenue

Deptford
High St
Crooms Hill
■ **Royal Observatory Greenwich**
Way

Fan Museum
General Wolfe Rd
Blackheath Ave
Greenwich Park
Charlton

New Cross Rd
70
Hyde Vale

Lewisham Way
Brookmill Road
Blackheath
Greenwich
South St
Hill
Ranger's House
Shooters Hill Road

Greenwich★★★

The name of this district on the south bank of the Thames, facing the Docklands, is known worldwide due to the Prime Greenwich Meridian. However, Greenwich is not limited to this imaginary line, nor to the observatory where the first longitude calculations were made. This former royal residence boasts a rich history and remarkable architecture, granting it UNESCO World Heritage status. Its Royal Park – the largest in London – and the riverside offer pleasant walks to escape the heat of the city in summer.

▶**Access:** ⊖ Cutty Sark, Greenwich (DLR). Greenwich is located on the south bank of the Thames, opposite the Isle of Dogs. A pedestrian tunnel under the Thames (Greenwich Footway Tunnel) connects the two areas. Access by boat with the Thames Clippers river shuttles (☉ p. 161).

Neighborhood map pp. 106–107. Off the detachable map.

▶**Tip:** Avoid weekends, as it gets crowded around the market, the Royal Park, and at certain museums like the Cutty Sark and the Maritime Museum.
☉ *Where to Go pp. 128 and 131.*

Greenwich Market

www.greenwichmarket.london – 10AM–5:30PM.
Just steps from the DLR Cutty Sark station, this charming covered market adds to the village-like atmosphere of Greenwich. Established in 1700, it gathers delightful stores and a few cafés, and has craft, food, and antique stalls.

St Alfege

Greenwich Church St. – ☎ 020 8853 0687 – www.st-alfege.org.uk – Tue.– Sun. 11AM–4PM – concerts.

> 🍴 **Lunch at Greenwich**
> For a pleasant stroll or a quick bite, **Greenwich Market** is the perfect spot. ☉ p. 128.

This primitive church was built on the site of the martyrdom of Alphege, Archbishop of Canterbury, killed by the Danes in 1012, and it hosted the baptism of **Henry VIII**.

Cutty Sark ★★

King William Walk – ☎ 020 8858 4422 – www.rmg.co.uk – ♿ – 10AM–5PM – £20; combined ticket with the Royal Observatory £30.
Launched in 1869 from the Dumbarton shipyards in Scotland, this majestic three-masted ship was intended for importing tea from China. It quickly became famous due to its speed: its best one-day run, with its 107,640 square feet of fully deployed sails, was 360 miles. After the opening of the Suez Canal, the *Cutty Sark* competed with steamships carrying

M. Brand/imageBROKER/age fotostock

Old Royal Naval College.

wool from Australia. The trip, including the dangerous rounding of Cape Horn, took 70 days going and 80 days returning with a full load of 5,000 bales of wool. Sold to a Portuguese company in 1895, the ship returned to England in 1922 and was converted into a training ship before being transferred to Greenwich in 1954, set in dry dock and transformed into a maritime museum. A very enjoyable interactive visit, popular with families.

Old Royal Naval College ★★

King William Walk – ✆ 020 8269 4747 – www.ornc.org – ♿ – 8AM–11PM; Painted Hall, Visitor Centre, and chapel: 10AM–5PM – £16.50.

This college houses the University of Greenwich campus. King Charles's pavilion is occupied by the Trinity College of Music, and the buildings facing the Thames house a naval school.

National Maritime Museum ★★

Romney Rd – ✆ 020 8312 6565 – www. rmg.co.uk – ♿ – 10AM–5PM – free, except for guided tours and exhibits. The collections of the National Maritime Museum illustrate the naval history of Great Britain. Particular emphasis is placed on commercial development, with a focus on the triangle trade and the East India Company, as well as the figure of Admiral Nelson and the impact of modern progress on marine life. Numerous activities are aimed at children.

Queen's House ★★

☎ 020 8858 4422 – www.rmg.co.uk – 10AM–5PM – free – closed Jan.–Feb.
This elegant villa, which hosts temporary exhibitions, stands out for its beautiful horseshoe staircase, which descends from the terrace on the northern facade, and its loggia on the south side, facing the park.

Fan Museum ★

12 Crooms Hill – ☎ 020 8305 1441 – www.thefanmuseum.org.uk – ♿ – Tue.–Sat. 11AM–5PM – closed mid-Dec.

View of the Old Royal Naval College and London from Greenwich Park.

Circle Creative Studio/Getty Images Plus

to end Jan. – £5 – fan-making workshop by reservation.
This magnificent museum displays around 2,000 **fans** organized by their production methods, materials, and origins. There are temporary exhibits based on decorational themes.

Greenwich Park

www.royalparks.org.uk – 6AM–sunset.
Enclosed by a fence in 1433 and walled under the Stuarts, this park is the oldest enclosed royal estate. Covering almost 222 acres, its chestnut tree avenues and vast lawns rise to a hill peaking at 171 feet above the Thames, crowned by the old Royal Observatory and the Wolfe Monument. The hill provides a beautiful **view** of London.

Royal Observatory Greenwich ★★

Blackheath Ave. – ☎ 020 8858 4422 – www.rmg.co.uk – ♿ – 10AM–5PM – £20 for observatory; £12 for planetarium; combined ticket with the Cutty Sark £30, reduced prices online.
In 1675, Charles II asked **Christopher Wren** to build a small observatory in Greenwich Park. His goal was to perfect navigational methods through intensive studies of the stars and planets. Wren, a former astronomer, built a red brick house topped with a balustrade and several small roofed domes to serve as an astronomer's residence "and add a certain pomp." At exactly 1PM each day, a red ball, which was placed atop one of the domes in 1833, slides down a mast, allowing navigators on the Thames to set their watches.

In the courtyard, the **Greenwich Meridian**, which sits at zero longitude, is marked by a copper rail. Close by, you can discover **Flamsteed House**, the house of the royal astronomer John Flamsteed. The **Octagon Room**, high-ceilinged and nicely proportioned, has been restored and refurbished to its original state. A multimedia presentation traces the history of calculating latitude and longitude. **Peter Harrison Planetarium** – *reserve at www.rmg.co.uk/whats-on/planetarium-shows.* Built in the shape of a cone, it consists of 250 welded and polished bronze panels. The north side of the cone is aligned with the perpendicular line to the horizon perceived from Greenwich (the zenith). The south side points to the North Star. The slope angle (51° 28' 44") equals the latitude of the Royal Observatory. Lastly, the planetarium is aligned on the Greenwich Meridian. The upper part is covered with reflective glass to give viewers a glimpse of changes in the sky. Inside, presentations take visitors into space to view Earth from above, complete with to-the-minute images sent by satellites.

Ranger's House ★

Chesterfield Walk, Greenwich Park – ☎ 020 8853 0035 – www.english-heritage.org.uk/visit/places/rangers-house-the-wernher-collection – ♿ – Wed.–Sun. 10AM–5PM – £12.70. This mansion was originally a small brick villa. Rounded wings were added by Philip Stanhope, 4th Earl of Chesterfield (1694–1773) and a politician, diplomat, and wit. The south gallery was then created. Measuring 82 feet in length, it features a coffered ceiling and is illuminated by three bow windows, of which the owner, quite pleased, remarked: "All three different, and the best views in the world." The gardens have retained all their beauty. The paneled rooms on the ground and 1st floors house the magnificent **Wernher Collection** of European art, reflecting the eclectic taste of **Sir Julius Wernher** (1850–1912), a philanthropist and mining industry magnate. This collection brings together rare religious paintings by Filippo Lippi and Dutch masters' canvases (Van Ostade, de Hooch), as well as Renaissance jewelry and bronzes.

Getaways nearby★★

Here are some ideas for day trips, easily accessible from central London and great for a green escape in good weather. If it rains, you might want to visit the Harry Potter film studios. So, aspiring wizards, head to Platform 9¾!

Kew Gardens ★★★

⊖ *Kew Gardens. Southwest of London.*
▶ *By boat: with Thames River Boats (www.thamesriverboats.co.uk – Apr.–Oct.).*
℘ *020 8332 5655 – www.kew.org 10AM–7PM (5PM or even 4PM in winter, last entry 1 hour before closing) – Feb.–Oct.: weekdays/weekends £22/24; Nov.–Jan. £14/16 – discounts online.*

The Thames makes a long loop around Kew, a residential area with a village-like atmosphere. In good weather, it's lovely to wander through the royal botanical gardens, bordered to the north by the river, to discover rare species, large greenhouses, and beautiful features. An elevated walkway (Treetop Walkway) 59 feet above ground (118 steps) lets you stroll among the treetops.
☺ *Don't miss: Kew Palace; the Palm House; the bamboo garden; the view from the pagoda.*

Richmond ★★

⊖ *Richmond. Southwest of London.*
▶ *By boat: with Thames River Boats (www.thamesriverboats.co.uk – Apr.–Oct.).*

Located on the banks of the Thames, Richmond enjoys a country atmosphere thanks to its lush parks and golf courses. The small town is popular for its historic pubs, restaurants, antique stores, and chic boutiques. **Richmond Palace**, one of the Tudors' favorite residences, and other beautiful homes remind visitors of a noble past.
☺ *Don't miss: Richmond Park with its view and free-roaming deer; a walk along the Thames.*

Hampton Court ★★★

14 miles southwest of London.
▶ *By train: 30 minutes from Waterloo Station.*
▶ *By boat: from Westminster or Richmond (Apr.–Sep.) with Thames River Boats (www.thamesriverboats. co.uk) or Turks (www.turks.co.uk).*
℘ *033 3320 6000 – www.hrp.org.uk – varied hours – £30.*

Set in a romantic location on the Thames, King Henry VIII's favorite **royal palace** was an ideal retreat for many monarchs. These splendid buildings and gardens showcasing a variety of styles bear witness to royal power and wealth.
☺ *Don't miss: the kitchens; the apartments; the tennis court; the maze.*

Windsor Castle ★★★

22 miles west of London.
▶ *By train: 50 minutes from Waterloo Station (stop Windsor & Eton Riverside), then a 15-minute walk.*
▶ *By bus: 1h10 from Victoria Station, bus no. 702 of London Line (www.reading-buses.co.uk).*
☎ *030 3123 7334 – www.rct.uk – open Tue.–Wed. 10AM–5:15PM (Nov.–Feb.: 4:15PM) – from £30, advance purchase, audioguide included.*

Perched on a steep cliff in a beautiful park, the turrets of **Windsor Castle** overlook a charming town nestled in the Thames Valley. Windsor illustrates the transformation of a medieval castle into a sumptuous royal residence. Its monarchical character adds a lot of charm to the town.

Across the bridge stand the buildings of **Eton College** (*www.etoncollege.com*), also worth seeing.

😊 *Don't miss: St George's Chapel; the state apartments.*

Warner Bros. Studios

Behind the Scenes of Harry Potter ★★

Leavesden, 20 miles northwest of London.
▶ *By train: 20 minutes from Euston Station (stop Watford Junction), then a 15-minute bus ride.*
▶ *By bus: shuttles (1h15) leaving from Victoria Station or Baker Street.*
☎ *084 5084 0900 – www.wbstudiotour.co.uk – from £53.50 – reservations essential well in advance.*

In the old Rolls-Royce factory hangars on the Leavesden aerodrome, Warner Bros. Studios welcome Harry Potter fans in a 150,700-square-foot space. This is where Daniel Radcliffe (Harry), Rupert Grint (Ron), and Emma Watson (Hermione) filmed the eight movie adaptations of the book series over 10 years.

😊 *Don't miss: the Hogwarts model in the Model Room.*

113

The Final Resting Place of Elizabeth II

Queen Elizabeth II, who passed away on September 8, 2022, at her Balmoral estate in Scotland, now rests in the King George VI Memorial Chapel within St. George's Chapel at Windsor Castle. She is buried alongside her father, George VI (who died in 1952), her mother, Elizabeth Bowes-Lyon (2002), her sister, Princess Margaret (2002), and her husband, Prince Philip (2021).

WHERE TO GO

Portobello Road shop.
G.Masci/age Fotostock

🍴 Dining

At lunchtime, **cafés, pubs** (☞ *"Grab a Drink" p. 129*) and quality chain restaurants (Pret A Manger, Wasabi Sushi & Bento, Wagamama, Yo! Sushi, Itsu, Tortilla, Pizza Express, Benugo, etc.) offer decent meals at reasonable prices. Don't forget to explore the food stands and food trucks at markets, as well as the fresh sections in supermarkets (Marks & Spencer, Waitrose, Sainsbury's or Tesco), stocked with sandwiches and salads. Plus, cafés and restaurants in museums often offer very good, or even excellent, food in impressive settings, like the cafeteria at the Victoria and Albert Museum or the charming and refined restaurant at the Wallace Collection. For **dinner**, take the chance to explore cuisines from around the world.

Vegetarians will easily find menus to their liking. Most restaurants clearly display allergens for those with intolerances.

😊 *The price ranges indicated below correspond to a meal of an appetizer and a main course or a main course and a dessert, excluding drinks. A service tax of 10 to 15% is typically added to menu prices, and in establishments where no tax is noted, you may choose – or not – to leave a tip instead.*

☞ *"Dining" p. 157 and "London Dining" p. 185.*

☞ **Locate the addresses on our maps using numbered markers (e.g. 🔴 1). The coordinates in red (e.g. C2) refer to the detachable map.**

Westminster – Victoria

Map p. 17

Less than £25

🔴 76 **Market Hall Victoria** – **D6** – *191 Victoria St. – ⊖ Victoria.* Perfect for grabbing a quick bite without breaking the bank: world cuisine stalls are set up under the market's glass roof, across from the station. Heated rooftop terrace.

🔴 78 **Regency Café** – **D6** – *17–19 Regency St. – SW1P 4BY – ⊖ St James's Park or Pimlico – ☎ 020 7821 6596 – www.regencycafe. has.restaurant – 🚭 – Mon.–Fri. 7AM–2:30PM, 4PM–7:15PM, Sat.*

7AM–12PM – under £20. An institution since 1946, serving simple and hearty dishes at unbeatable prices! The perfect place to dive into a proper English breakfast with beans, sausages, and eggs, served on formica tables in a bustling yet friendly canteen atmosphere. Expect a bit of a wait.

❤️ 13 **Cellarium Café & Terrace** – **E6** – *20 Dean's Yard – Westminster Abbey (entrance through the cloisters) – SW1P 3PA – ⊖ St James's Park or Westminster – ☎ 020 7222 0516 – www.benugo.com – Mon.–Fri. 8AM–3:30PM, Sat. 9AM–3PM – £20–25.* With its vaulted rooms – the abbey's former pantry – and beautiful terrace, this café is perfect for a full English breakfast or a light lunch: sandwiches, salads, soups, quiches. Also afternoon tea.

73 Kazan – **D6** – *93–94 Wilton Rd – SW1V 1DW –* ⊖ *Victoria –* ℘ *020 7233 7100 – www.kazan-restaurant.com – 12PM–10PM except Sun. – £20/£25, lunch menu £17.* Head to Istanbul with menu selections of cold or hot mezze. A lovely range of flavors to enjoy in a trendy setting. There's a pleasant lounge for tea.

From £25 to £50

23 The Cinnamon Club – **E6** – *30–32 Great Smith Street – SW1P 3BU –* ⊖ *St James's Park or Westminster –* ℘ *020 7222 2555 – www.cinnamonclub.com – 12PM–3PM, 6:30PM–11PM – closed Sun. – £35/£50.* Modern and refined Indian cuisine in the unique setting of the former Westminster library, a superb Victorian building. Shelves filled with books in old bindings surround diners, mostly business people and politicians.

Trafalgar Square

Map p. 17

From £25 to £50

87 Bancone – **E4** – *39 William IV St. – WC2N 4DD –* ⊖ *Charing Cross –* ℘ *020 7240 8786 – www.bancone.co.uk – daily, continuous service – £25/£30.* A gourmet address worth praising. Here, fresh pasta is the star. The specialty: "silk handkerchiefs" with walnut butter. Start with shared focaccia or a plate of Sardinian prosciutto. The name means "counter," which is where

everyone wants to sit, but tables are also available.

8 The Portrait – **E4** – *National Portrait Gallery – St Martin's Place – WC2H 0HE –* ⊖ *Charing Cross –* ℘ *020 3872 7610 – www. theportraitrestaurant.com – Wed.– Sat. 12PM–10:30PM, Sun.–Tues. 12PM–5:30PM – £45/£60, menus £34/£39 on Sat.* Chef Richard Corrigan offers refined and original contemporary cuisine (duck heart with grapes and sage, braised rabbit with chanterelles...) served in a glass-walled room on the 4th floor of the National Portrait Gallery, with views of Trafalgar Square. Efficient and friendly service in this elegant establishment.

St James's

Map p. 24

Less than £25

1 St James's Café – **D5** – *Horse Guards Rd – St James's Park – SW1A 2BJ –* ⊖ *Charing Cross or Westminster –* ℘ *020 7839 1149 – www. benugo.com – 8AM–6PM – £15/£25.* Right in the heart of St James's Park, this is an ideal spot for breakfast just before going to watch the changing of the guard at Buckingham Palace or Horse Guards Parade. Full English breakfast, sweet or savory toasts, followed at noon by quality dishes prepared with seasonal ingredients. Rooftop terrace in good weather.

From £25 to £50

63 Gymkhana – **D4** – *42 Albemarle St. – W1S 4JH –* ⊖ *Green Park –* ℘ *020 3011 5900 – www. gymkhanalondon.com – 12PM–2:45PM,*

5:30PM–10:45PM – £30/£40, lunch menu £48. From the copper percolator to the fans, the woodwork to the intricately designed cutlery, every detail at Gymkhana exudes a quiet, elegant atmosphere. Indian cuisine infused with European influences and featuring local products, especially game. Two Michelin stars in the 2024 Guide.

Mayfair – Piccadilly

Map pp. 28–29

From £25 to £50

70 **L'Autre** – **C5** – *5B Shepherd St. – W1J 7HP –* ⊖ *Greenpark –* ☎ *020 7499 4680 – www.lautrerestaurant. co.uk – Mon.–Sat. 5PM–11PM – dishes £28/£40.* Torn between goulash and guacamole? This little restaurant is made for you: it might be the only one in the world offering both Polish and Mexican specialties on the same menu! Very good food. Be sure to reserve.

57 **Scott's** – **C4** – *20 Mount St. – W1K 2HE –* ⊖ *Bond Street –* ☎ *020 7495 7309 – www.scotts-mayfair.com – daily, continuous service – dishes £38/£50.* For seafood lovers. The decor, food, and service are all sophisticated and flawless. Good wine list.

Soho

Map pp. 28–29

Less than £25

64 **Koya Bar** – **D4** – *50 Frith St. – W1D 4SQ –* ⊖ *Leicester Square or Tottenham Court Road – www.koya. co.uk – daily, continuous service – under £20.* This bar in the busy heart

The traditional fish and chips.

of Soho has a zen atmosphere and specializes in udon. Sit at the counter to enjoy thick noodles served in broth, hot or cold, with about twenty side dishes. Perfect for a quick and healthy lunch.

❤ **62** **Golden Union** – **D3** – *38 Poland St. – W1F 7LY –* ⊖ *Oxford Circus –* ☎ *020 7458 4411 – www.goldenunion. co.uk – daily, continuous service – approx. £20.* A reliable fish and chip shop, available for dine-in or takeout. Generous portions, fresh fish, crispy but not greasy fries and a good atmosphere.

2 **BAO** – **D4** – *53 Lexington St. – W1F 9AS –* ⊖ *Oxford Circus or Piccadilly Circus – www.baolondon.com – daily, lunch and dinner – under £25.*

Diana Miller/Getty Images Plus

118

Steamed bao buns filled with braised pork, coriander, and peanut powder, also available with chicken or other fillings, are the specialty here. Served in small portions, accompanied by a variety of mini dishes and reimagined classic drinks such as roasted peanut milk. This place is popular and has several locations in the city.

From £25 to £50

❤ **88** **The Palomar** – **D4** – *34 Rupert St. – W1D 6DN –* ⊖ *Piccadilly Circus –* ✆ *020 7439 8777 – www.thepalomar. co.uk – 12PM–2:30PM, 5PM–10:30PM – lunch menu £24/£28, £30/£40.* The zinc counter in this wood-paneled dining room sets the tone for a fresh and lively atmosphere. A modern take on Middle Eastern cuisine right in the heart of London's cinema district.

14 **10 Greek Street** – **D4** – *10 Greek St. – W1D 4 DH –* ⊖ *Tottenham Court Road – ✆ 020 7734 4677 – www.10greekstreet.com – Tue.–Sat. 12PM–10:30PM – approx. £40.* This neighborhood bistro hasn't just charmed the locals: its excellent value draws visitors from far and wide. The menu changes daily, offering a well-crafted selection of dishes.

❤ **53** **Yauatcha Soho** – **D4** – *15–17 Broadwick St. – W1F 0DL –* ⊖ *Piccadilly Circus – ✆ 020 7494 8888 – www.yauatcha.com/soho – daily, continuous service – £40/£55.* A trendy Chinese restaurant in a theatrical setting (illuminated aquarium, stone walls) designed by Christian Liaigre. Specializes in dim sum and other flavorful small dishes. Desserts to die for.

Covent Garden

Map p. 34

From £25 to £50

48 **Rules** – **E4** – *35 Maiden Lane – WC2E 7LB –* ⊖ *Covent Garden – ✆ 020 7836 5314 – www.rules. co.uk – closed Mon. – £45/£60.* Pork cheeks, teal, sole meunière, game, and rabbit are on the menu at one of London's oldest and best-loved restaurants. A place rich in history. Reservations recommended!

The Strand

Map p. 34

Less than £25

65 **Flat Iron** – **E4** – *17–18 Henrietta St. – WC2E 8QH –* ⊖ *Leicester Square – ✆ 020 3019 4212 – www.flatironsteak. co.uk – daily, continuous service – £25/ £30.* The facade overflowing with greenery is this small restaurant franchise's signature. The limited menu is by design, focusing on their specialty: extremely tender grilled beef. The side dishes are simple but tasty, and the cocktails well-crafted. Free ice cream after the check. Several other locations in London.

41 **MOC Kitchen** – **E4** – *Villiers St. (Unit 2 The Arches) – WC2N 6NG –* ⊖ *Charing Cross or Embankment – ✆ 020 7930 8789 – www.mockitchen. co.uk – daily except Sun., continuous service – approx. £25 – menus £22.50/ £25.50.* An authentic and delicious small Vietnamese eatery, a refreshing change from the numerous Japanese restaurants and chain establishments in the area. On the menu: bò bún, beef lôc lac and phó.

Bloomsbury

From £25 to £50

49 **Lamb's Conduit Street** (**E3**),
A charming, partly pedestrianized street with two historic pubs (The Lamb and The Perseverance) and several other quality spots, including the wine bar **Noble Rot** (✆ 020 7242 8963 – www.noblerot.co.uk) and **La Fromagerie** (✆ 020 7242 1044 – www.lafromagerie.co.uk), serving boards of local cheeses and charcuterie. Everything you need to start the evening off right.

45 **Lima Fitzrovia** – **D3** – *31 Rathbone Pl. – W1T 1JH –* ⊖ *Tottenham Court Road –* ✆ *020 3002 2640 – www. limalondon.com/fitzrovia – daily except Sun., continuous service – lunch menu £28/£36 – approx. £50.* Chef Virgilio Martinez crafts high-quality and original Peruvian cuisine with well-executed flavors. Reservations advised.

The City

Map pp. 50–51

Less than £25

6 **City Càphê** – **G3** – *17 Ironmonger Lane – EC2V 8EY –* ⊖ *Bank – www. citycaphe.com – 11:30AM–3PM – closed weekends – under £15.* A small Vietnamese place that's popular with City workers, as evidenced by the line snaking across the sidewalk every afternoon (fewer people after 1:30PM). Menu includes banh mi, pho, spring rolls, salads.

69 **Caravan City** – **G4** – *22 Bloomberg Arcade – EC4N 8AR –* ⊖ *Cannon Street –* ✆ *020 3957 5555 – www.*

caravanandco.com – daily, continuous service – £20/£25. This spot charms visitors with its large covered terrace, beautiful dining room, and food suitable for any time of the day. Mediterranean-inspired menu with many vegetarian options. Several other locations in the City.

£25 to £50

❤ **35** **Sweetings** – **G4** – *39 Queen Victoria St. – EC4N 4SA –* ⊖ *Mansion House –* ✆ *020 7248 3062 – Mon.– Fri. 11:30AM–3PM – £30/£40.* This institution has been serving excellent fish and seafood to City executives since 1889, who take a seat at the counter when the dining room is full.

Southwark

Map pp. 66–67

Less than £25

To eat quickly, well, and cheaply in this neighborhood, consider the markets that also house street food stalls and restaurants: **91** **Borough Market** (**G5** – ⊙ *p. 62*) is beautiful and well-stocked. **77** **Maltby Street Market** (**H6** – ⊙ *p. 60*) is less touristy than Borough Market and just as vibrant *(weekends only).*

£25 to £50

9 **Arabica Bar & Kitchen** – **G5** – *Borough Market, 3 Rochester Walk – SE1 9AF –* ⊖ *London Bridge –* ✆ *020 3011 5151 – www.arabicalondon.com – daily, continuous service – £25/£30.* Situated under the arches of Borough Market, this is a large modern Lebanese restaurant that's packed every day at lunchtime. No wonder! The dishes are fresh and tasty: mezzes, grilled meats, man'ousheh (Levantine pizza), and more. To finish, order a cardamom coffee, prepared to perfection.

71 Elliot's – **G5** – *Borough Market – 12 Stoney St. – SE1 9AD –* ⊖ *London Bridge –* ℰ *020 7403 7436 – www. elliots.london – daily, continuous service – £28/£40.* Highly popular and unpretentious, this café sources most of its ingredients from Borough Market, crafting simple and hearty local cuisine. Try the sharing plates, such as the 25-day aged Shorthorn beef or lamb shoulder.

South Bank

Map pp. 66–67

To Go

10 Southbank Centre Food Market – **E5** – *Belvedere Rd – SE1 8XX –* ⊖ *Waterloo –* ℰ *020 3879 9555 – www.southbankcentre.co.uk –* ♿ *– Fri. 12PM–8PM, Sat. 11AM–8PM, Sun. and holidays 12PM–6PM – price varies by food stall.* On weekends, food trucks and food stalls with cuisine from around the world set up behind the South Bank Centre. Choose dishes to enjoy in the Jubilee Gardens along the Thames.

£50 to £75

42 Oxo Tower Restaurant & Brasserie – **F4** – *Oxo Tower Wharf – Barge House St. – SE1 9PH –* ⊖ *Southwark or Blackfriars –* ℰ *020 7803 3888 – www. oxotowerrestaurant.com – daily, continuous service – £38/£60.* This restaurant on the top floor of the Oxo Tower offers an extraordinary view. Very professional service. More moderate prices at the Oxo Brasserie Tower, which hosts concerts on its summer terrace.

Belgravia – Knightsbridge

Map pp. 72–73

£50 to £75

16 Amaya – **C6** – *Halkin Arcade (entrance via Lowndes St.) – SW1X 8JT –* ⊖ *Knightsbridge –* ℰ *020 7823 1166 – www.amaya. biz – daily, lunchtime and evening – £35/£50.* This stylish spot offers Indian cuisine highly praised by critics, and rightfully so! A Michelin star in the 2024 Guide.

54 Zuma – **B5** – *5 Raphael St. – SW7 1DL –* ⊖ *Knightsbridge –* ℰ *020 7584 1010 – www. zumarestaurant.com – daily, lunch and dinner – £45/£65.* This attractive Japanese izakaya with a sleek and contemporary look draws a chic and close-knit crowd, especially around the counter. Sushi, maki, yakitori, and tempura are crafted in a fusion style with original flavors. Good cocktails and a wide selection of sake available.

Chelsea – South Kensington

Map pp. 72–73

Less than £25

79 CERU South Ken – **A6** – *7–9 Bute St. – SW7 3EY –* ⊖ *South Kensington –* ℰ *020 3195 3001 – www. cerurestaurants.com – Mon.–Fri. 12PM–10PM, weekend 11AM–10PM – £15/£25.* An excellent lunch option in this "museum district" where restaurants are rare. Mezze plates to share, subtly spiced assortments, seasonal salads, kebabs, etc., for highly flavored Levantine cuisine. Vegan and/or gluten-free options available. Another location at Queensway.

£25 to £50

❤️ **20** **Bluebird** – **A7** – *350 King's Rd – SW3 5UU – ⊖ South Kensington – ☎ 020 7559 1000 – www.bluebird-restaurant.co.uk – daily, continuous service – £35/£45.* The "gastrodrome" floor envisaged by Terence Conran includes a brasserie and a designer restaurant. Modern British cuisine. Weekend brunch.

More than £75

19 **Claude Bosi at Bibendum** – **B6** – *Michelin House – 81 Fulham Rd – SW3 6RD – ⊖ South Kensington – ☎ 020 7581 5817 – www.claudebosi. com – Thu.–Sat. lunch and dinner – menus £75/£145/£165.* Claude Bosi has breathed new life into Bibendum, located on the 1st floor of Michelin's former London headquarters. With its sleek style and iconic stained glass, the interior is impressive. High-end traditional French cuisine, balanced and skillfully executed, enhanced with creative touches and showcasing bold and vivid flavors. Two Michelin stars in the 2024 Guide. Oyster bar on the ground floor: *daily, lunch and dinner.*

North Kensington

Map pp. 72–73

From £25 to £50

Ffiona's – **Off the map** – *51 Kensington Church St. – W8 4BA – ⊖ High Street Kensington – ☎ 020 7937 4152 – www. ffionas.com – Tue.–Fri. 5:30–11:00PM, weekends 9:00AM–3:00PM, 5:30–11:00PM – £25/£30.* Warm decor with candlelit wooden tables decorated with flower pots in this family-run restaurant. Home-style British cuisine, featuring excellent fish and chips and a tasty roast lamb with mint sauce. Weekend brunch.

15 **Cocoro** – **A4** – *45 Moscow Rd – W2 4AH – ⊖ Bayswater – ☎ 020 7221 9790 – www.cocorobayswater. co.uk – Wed.–Sat. 12:00–3:00PM, 6:00–10:00PM, Sun. 12:00–4:00PM, 5:30–10:00PM – £28/£45.* An authentic Japanese restaurant where you can taste coveted delicacies served ln traditional ceramic dishes: depending on the season, sea urchin, sea bream, seaweed salad, Wagyu beef. Selection of vegetarian dishes and original desserts like matcha chocolate fondant and cherry blossom ice cream (a delight!). Good for sake and umeshu (plum wine) enthusiasts. Other locations and menus: 31 Marylebone Lane, ⊖ Bond Street; 25 Coptic St., ⊖ Tottenham Court Road.

Notting Hill

Map p. 83

To Go

❤️ **11** **Ottolenghi** – **Off the detachable map** – *63 Ledbury Rd – W11 2AD – ⊖ Westbourne Park, Notting Hill Gate – ☎ 020 7727 1121 – www.ottolenghi. co.uk – 8:00AM–7:00PM (Sun. 6:00PM) – approx. £20/£25.* The first London establishment opened by the renowned Anglo-Israeli chef

Terrace on Portobello Road.

Yotam Ottolenghi is now dedicated to take-out, starting from breakfast. The daily salads, made with fresh ingredients and presented in large bowls, pair perfectly with the hot dishes (chicken with red onions, eggplant quiche with goat cheese). The brand has several other locations with different styles, always excellent, including a delicatessen in Chelsea (*261 Pavillion Rd, ⊖ Sloane Square*) and the more sophisticated ROVI in Fitzrovia (*⦿ p. 124*).

Less than £25

On Fridays and Saturdays, flea market days, you'll find numerous stalls with food from around the world along **Portobello Road**. Don't hesitate to also visit **Golborne Road**, a pleasant street lined with cafés and Moroccan food stalls.

Marylebone – Regent's Park

Map p. 87

To Go

68 **Honey & Co** – **D2** – *25A Warren St. – W1T 5LZ – ⊖ Warren Street – ✆ 020 7388 6175 – www.honeyandco. co.uk – 9AM–7PM except Sun.* The couple running this lovely little café used to head the kitchens at **Ottolenghi**; so expect colorful and fresh lunch boxes inspired by Israeli and Middle Eastern flavors.

Less than £25

5 **31 Below** – **C3** – *31 Marylebone High St. – W1U 4PP – ⊖ Baker Street – ✆ 020 3912 2007 – www.31below. co.uk – Mon.–Wed. 9AM–10PM, Thu.– Sat. 9AM–11PM, Sun. 10AM–8PM – £18– 25.* This place fits multiple categories. Enjoy breakfast, a tasty salad, or a sandwich for lunch. Have afternoon tea or sip excellent cocktails in the basement bar while sharing small tapas-style plates for dinner.

From £25 to £50

55 **The Golden Hind** – **C3** – *71a–73 Marylebone Lane – W1U 2PN – ⊖ Bond Street – ✆ 020 7486 3644 – www.goldenhindrestaurant. com – daily except Sun. Lunch and dinner – £25/£35.* An institution for fish and chips since 1914, delighting Londoners with squid, cod, haddock, plaice, and other seafood treats. Perfect for a lunch break.

3 **Fischer's** – **C3** – *50 Marylebone High St. – W1U 5HN – ⊖ Baker*

123

Street – ☏ 020 7466 5501 – www.fischers.co.uk – daily, continuous service – £30/£40. A guaranteed escape at this authentic Viennese brasserie, worthy of the Austrian capital! Serving Central European specialties from breakfast to dinner (brunch on weekends): herring, charcuterie, Wiener Schnitzel, strudel, and Sachertorte.

⬤66 Pachamama – **C3** – 18 Thayer St. – W1U 3JY – ⊖ Bond Street – ☏ 020 7935 9393 – www.pachamamalondon. com – daily, lunch and dinner – £38/£55. Modern Peruvian cuisine with fusion touches. Excellent seafood and generous waffles (sweet or savory) for brunch. Tastefully decorated dining room and very pleasant service.

❤ ⬤7 ROVI – **D3** – 59 Wells St. – W1A 3AE – ⊖ Oxford Circus – ☏ 020 3963 8270 – www.ottolenghi. co.uk – lunch and dinner – closed Sun. evening – approx. £50. ROVI, one of nine locations in the **Ottolenghi** empire, does not disappoint: sophisticated modern decor, original cocktails, and predominantly vegetarian cuisine (but not exclusively). The menu changes seasonally, and dishes are served as small plates, perfect for sampling. Outdoor seating in the summer.

From £50 to £75

❤ ⬤60 Chiltern Firehouse – **C3** – 1 Chiltern St. – W1U 7PA – ⊖ Bond Street or Baker Street – ☏ 020 7073 7676 – www.chilternfirehouse. com – daily, continuous service – daily special £28 – £45/£60. This magnificent Victorian-style firehouse was transformed into a luxury hotel by André Balazs. The restaurant offers a chic and cozy setting beloved by the in crowd. In the vast open kitchen, contemporary British cuisine is crafted, slightly minimalist yet refined. Reservations recommended.

King's Cross – St Pancras

Map p. 91

From £25 to £50

⬤86 Granger & Co – **E1** – 1 Stanley Building, 7 Pancras Sq. – N1C 4AG – ⊖ King's Cross-St Pancras – ☏ 020 3058 2567 – www.grangerandco. com – daily, continuous service – £25/£30. A somewhat trendy spot with fresh dishes and unique flavors. The King's Cross location also offers a beautiful glass facade that lets in plenty of light. Very pleasant, especially for breakfast: try the ricotta hotcakes, a specialty. Several other locations in town.

❤ ⬤17 Dishoom King's Cross – **E1** – 5 Stable St. – N1C 4AB – ⊖ King's Cross-St Pancras – ☏ 020 7420 9321 – www.dishoom.com – daily, continuous service – £25/£35. Before boarding the Eurostar or while exploring the King's Cross area, stop by to try the specialties of this superb Indian restaurant. Its decor, inspired by the Irani cafés of Bombay, showcases the exemplary redevelopment of the old industrial district. Everything is delicious and ultra-fresh, including cocktails and fruit lassis. It's a popular spot: try visiting midday during the week to ensure you find a seat. Several other locations in London.

❤ ⬤21 German Gymnasium – **E1** – 1 King's Bd – N1C 4BU – ⊖ King's Cross-St Pancras – ☏ 020 7287 8000 – www.germangymnasium.com – daily, *continuous service – menus £30/£35 – £35/£48.* This is undoubtedly one of the biggest successes in the redevelopment of the King's Cross neighborhood. Dressed in bricks, this former gymnasium, built in 1865 as a training facility for the German gymnastic society, now encompasses a café, two bars, and a chic restaurant serving German and Central European specialties with impressive portions. Cheaper brasserie options available at the café.

Camden Town

Map p. 91

Less than £25

89 Camden Lock Market and **Stables Market** – **Off the detachable map** – ⊖ *Camden Town.* Throughout the week, food stalls fill the courtyards of these two markets, located 3 minutes apart on foot. African mafé, Indian curry, Japanese sushi, Chinese noodles, or chili con carne: enjoy a feast for a low price.

90 Mildreds – **Off the detachable map** – *9 Jamestown Rd – NW1 7BW –* ⊖ *Camden Town –* ℰ *020 7482 4200 – www.mildreds.co.uk – daily, continuous service – less than £25.* Just a step away from Camden High Street, settle into a bright, spacious room to indulge in fresh and tasty vegetarian cuisine, featuring flavors from the UK and abroad (Indian, Japanese, South American, and more). Ideal for a momentary escape from the neighborhood's hustle and bustle.

22 Poppie's – **Off the detachable map** – *30 Hawley Crescent – NW1 8NP –* ⊖ *Camden Town –* ℰ *020 7267 0440 – www.poppiesfishandchips.co.uk – daily, continuous service – £25/£30.* A well-regarded fish and chip shop offering fresh fish and generous portions, all just steps away from the lively Camden scene... What more could you ask for?

Hampstead

Less than £25

Ginger and White – **Off the map** – *4a–5a Perrins Court – NW3 1QS –* ⊖ *Hampstead –* ℰ *020 7431 9098 – www.gingerandwhite.com – daily, continuous service – under £20.* Situated in one of Hampstead's charming alleys, this cozy café is a favorite with locals for its fresh, original breakfasts, sandwiches, soup of the day, and pastries. Perfect for a treat before or after a walk on the heath.

From £25 to £50

❤ **The Wells** – **Off the map** – *30 Well Walk – NW3 1BX –* ⊖ *Hampstead –* ℰ *020 7794 3785 – www.thewellshampstead.co.uk – daily, continuous service – £28/£40.* Newly renovated, one of Hampstead's oldest pubs attracts young crowds to its ground-floor bar. Its charming restaurant, perched at roof height, overlooks the tree-lined street. Enjoy English cuisine with a gastropub twist. Terrace in fair weather.

Delicatessen – **Off the map** – *46 Rosslyn Hill – NW3 1NH –* ℰ *020 7700 5511 – www.delicatessen.company – closed Fri. and Sat. – £30/£45.* A lovely kosher restaurant where diners share

125

reworked Middle Eastern specialties: roasted cauliflower, crunchy salad with pomegranate, lamb hummus… Attentive service and well-presented plates.

East End

Map p. 98

Less than £25

84 Old Spitalfields Market – **H3** – (⊙ p. 96). For an affordable lunch in a youthful, convivial atmosphere, take a seat around the long tables at the food court of this former market, where you'll discover cuisines from around the world.

18 Bengal Village – **H3** – *75 Brick Lane – E1 6QL – ⊖ Shoreditch High Street (Overground) or Liverpool Street – ☎ 020 7366 4868 – www.bengalvillagebricklane.co.uk – daily, continuous service – £20/£25.* A great spot on Brick Lane, home to many affordable curry houses. Fresh and relaxing contemporary decor. Extensive menu with many Bangladeshi specialties and vegetarian dishes, made by a Bangladeshi chef.

From £25 to £50

67 St John Bread and Wine – **H3** – *94–96 Commercial St. – E1 6LZ – ⊖ Liverpool Street – ☎ 020 7251 0848 – www.stjohnrestaurant.com – daily, lunch and dinner – £30/£37.* In this unadorned space opposite Old Spitalfields Market, focus is on highly flavorful meat dishes. Vegetarian options are also good. Traditional dessert choices and a good selection of wines. The menu changes daily.

Restaurant Delamina EAST

Delamina EAST.

82 Delamina EAST – **H3** – *151–153 Commercial St. – E1 6BJ – ⊖ Liverpool Street or Shoreditch High Street (Overground) – ☎ 020 7078 0770 – www.delaminakitchen.co.uk – daily, continuous service – £32/£40.* An aroma of the eastern Mediterranean fills the room and plates, with original dishes full of surprising flavors. Beautifully presented plates in artisan dishware. Courteous and friendly service.

♥ **26 Rochelle Canteen** – **H2** – *16 Playground Gardens – Rochelle School, Arnold Circus – E2 7FA – ⊖ Old Street or Shoreditch High Street (Overground) – ☎ 020 3928 8328 – www.rochellecanteen.com – ♿ – Wed.–Sat. 12PM–3PM, 5:30PM–10PM,*

*Mon., Tue. and Sun. 12PM–3PM –
£28/£40.* You'll need to open the door
of an old school to find this place. The
restaurant is set in the former bike
shed, which features a vine-covered
pergola protected by a glass roof. Here,
you can enjoy authentic and delicious
cuisine made from high-quality
ingredients: braised oxtail, grilled brill,
rabbit pie, etc. The menu changes daily.
Save room for the very British desserts.
Reservations recommended.

④ Caravel – G1 – *172 Shepherdess
Walk – N1 7JL –* ⊖ *Old Street –
✆ 020 7251 1155 – www.
caravelrestaurant.com – Tue.–Sat.
12PM–4PM, 5:30PM–11PM, Sun.
12PM–4PM – £30/£45.* The *Poppy*, a
restored barge moored on Regent's
Canal, serves simple and tasty bistro-
style cuisine. British culinary classics
(excellent braised lamb) sit alongside
modern European dishes. Slow but
attentive service.

㉗ Brawn – H2 – *49 Columbia Rd –
E2 7RG –* ⊖ *Hoxton (Overground) –
✆ 020 7729 5692 – www.brawn.co
– closed Sun. and Mon. lunch –
£30/£45.* In the open kitchen of this
charming gastronomic spot, seasonal
and local ingredients take center stage.
Everything is fresh and excellent.
Reservations recommended.

Southern neighborhoods

To go

**㊄ The Battersea General Store –
C8** – *9–10 Circus Rd West – SW11 8EZ –*
⊖ *Battersea Power Station or
Battersea Park (Overground) –* ✆ *020
3196 1300 – www.thegeneral.store –
daily, continuous service – under £20.*

A beautiful gourmet grocery with an
appetizing deli section. You'll find
everything you need for a delicious
picnic along the Thames, opposite
Battersea Power Station.

Less than £25

Franco Manca – Off the map –
4 Market Row – SW9 8LD –
⊖ *Brixton – ✆ 020 7738 3021 – www.
francomanca.co.uk – daily, continuous
service – pizzas approx. £10/£15.* It
was in Brixton, under the roof of the
covered market, that the first Franco
Manca pizzeria was born. The delicious
wood-fired Neapolitan pizzas quickly
became a staple in the neighborhood.
Here, everything is organic, even
the wine. Excellent value for money.
Numerous other locations in the city.

**㉛ Megan's Battersea Power
Station – C8** – *27 Circus West Village –
SW11 8NN –* ⊖ *Battersea Power
Station – ✆ 020 3468 0218 – www.
megans.co.uk – daily, continuous
service – £20/£25.* Featuring
Mediterranean-inspired decor and a
spacious terrace on the Thames, this is
one of the latest additions to the small
chain of Turkish specialty restaurants
(kebab, mezze). A pleasant stop at any
time. Very good coffee.

From £25 to £50

㊴ Wright Brothers – C8 –
26 Circus West Village – SW8 4NN –
⊖ *Battersea Power Station – ✆ 020
7324 7734 – www.thewrightbrothers.
co.uk – daily, continuous service –
£30/£45.* Known for their seafood
specialties, this establishment offers a
large terrace overlooking the Thames,
right by Battersea Power Station.

Greenwich

Map pp. 106–107

To go

❤ **㉙ Greenwich Market – Off the detachable map** – *5B Greenwich Market – SE10 9HZ –* ⊖ *Cutty Sark –* ☎ *020 8269 5096 – www. greenwichmarket.london – 10AM–5:30PM – prices vary by food stall.* To eat on a budget, visit the international food stalls set up in Greenwich Market alongside artisans and creators. Enjoy your food along the Thames under the masts of the *Cutty Sark*.

Under 25 £

㉚ Goddards at Greenwich – Off the detachable map – *22 King William Walk – SE10 9HU –* ⊖ *Cutty Sark –* ☎ *020 8305 9612 – www. goddardsatgreenwich.co.uk – daily, continuous service – under £15.* This unpretentious spot has been serving a classic British dish since 1890: pie and mash, a savory pie with mashed potatoes. Hearty and affordable and offered with meat, vegetables, or eel, it's considered one the best in London.

Grab a drink

Many of the cafés, pubs, and tea rooms we list here are also great spots for a quick and light lunch, more affordable than dining at a restaurant.

⊙ **Locate the addresses on our maps using the numbered markers (e.g. ❶).** The **red coordinates** (e.g. **C2**) refer to the detachable map.

CAFÉS, TEA ROOMS

Trafalgar Square

Map p. 17

34 Muriel's Kitchen – **E4** – *National Gallery – Trafalgar Sq. – WC2N 5DN – ⊖ Charing Cross – no* 🕿 *– www.murielskitchen.co.uk – 11AM–5:45PM (8:45PM on Fri.).* Full of fresh food, a self-service café with a relaxed atmosphere for a sweet or savory break during your National Gallery visit. Open to all, museum visitors or not.

St James's

Map p. 24

12 Ole and Steen – **D4** – *56 Haymarket – SW1Y 4RP – ⊖ Piccadilly Circus – 🕿 020 3828 8242 – www.oleandsteen.co.uk – 7AM–8PM, weekend 8AM–8PM.* You'll take a number and wait for your turn in this elegant pastry shop where French-inspired cakes sit alongside well-stuffed Danish *smørrebrød.*

38 Maison Assouline – **D4** – *196A Piccadilly – W1J 9EY – ⊖ Piccadilly Circus – 🕿 020 3034 1197 – www.maisonassouline.com – 10:30AM–7PM, Thu.–Sat. 10:30AM–9PM – closed Sun.* The elegant bookstore of this art book publisher serves as a cozy bar-tea room: a strong contrast with the hustle and bustle of Piccadilly.

Covent Garden

Map p. 34

❤ **31 Brigit's Bakery** – **E4** – *6–7 Chandos Pl. – WC2N 4HU – ⊖ Leicester Square or Covent Garden – 🕿 020 3026 1188 – www.b-bakery.com – 10AM–7PM.* Whatever your tastes and dietary restrictions (gluten-free, halal, vegan), there's a tea time made for you here (*£40–£55*), served in adorable flowery crockery. You can also simply enjoy a drink and a pastry or sandwich. You can hop on a double-decker bus to explore London while having tea!

North Kensington

❤ **Candella Tea Room** – **Off the map** – *34 Kensington Church St. – W8 4HA – ⊖ Notting Hill Gate – 🕿 020 7937 4161 – www.candellatearoom.com – 11AM–6PM, weekend 10AM–6PM.* Hidden behind Kensington Palace, this charming little tea room has vintage British flair and offers a good afternoon tea at an affordable price (*£25/person*). Nice selection of tea (available for sale). Be sure to book ahead as it's tiny.

129

Traditional Afternoon Tea

Take advantage of your stay in London to indulge in the ritual of afternoon tea
(⌖ p. 185). It is advisable to make a reservation, sometimes several weeks in advance,
and proper attire is required. Among the popular spots (though there are others!):

1 **The Ritz London** – **D5** – *150 Piccadilly – W1J 9BR – ⊖ Green Park – ℘ 020 7300
2345 – www.theritzlondon.com – afternoon tea at 11:30AM, 1:30PM, 3:30PM, 5:30PM, and
7:30PM – starting from £75/person (children £53).* The greats of the world have graced
the Ritz with their presence for a classic English tea ritual in the Palm Court! Reservations
need to be made nearly 6 weeks in advance, but the experience is unforgettable.

2 **Fortnum & Mason's Restaurants** – **D4** – *181 Piccadilly – W1A 1ER – ⊖ Piccadilly
Circus – ℘ 020 7734 8040 – www.fortnumandmason.com – The Diamond Jubilee:
11:30AM–8PM (6PM Sun.); The Parlour: 10AM–8PM, Sun. 11:30AM–6PM – starting from
£80/person.* The famous gourmet store has several restaurants, including The Parlour
(1st floor) and the chic Diamond Jubilee (4th floor), both with a pianist.

3 **The Savoy** – **E4** – *The Strand – WC2 R 0EZ – ⊖ Charing Cross or Covent Garden –
℘ 020 7836 4343 – www.thesavoylondon.com – 12:30PM–7PM (last seating 5:15PM) –
starting from £92/person.* A unique experience in an exceptional hotel.

4 **Claridge's** – **C4** – *Brook St. – W1K 4HR – ⊖ Bond Street – ℘ 020 7107 8860 – www.
claridges.co.uk – 2:45PM–5:30PM – starting from £90/person.* The most chic address to
introduce you to the afternoon tea ritual: complete with Art Deco decor!

5 **The Harrods Tea Rooms** – **B5** – *87–135 Brompton Rd – SW1X 7XL –
⊖ Knightsbridge – ℘ 020 7225 6800 – www.harrods.com – 12PM–7PM, Sat.
11:30AM–8PM, Sun. 12PM–6PM – starting from £73/person.* Mahogany woodwork,
crystal chandeliers, and damask linen tablecloths for an exceptional tea in this iconic
department store.

15 **Sketch** – **D4** – *9 Conduit St. – W1S 2XG – ⊖ Oxford Circus – ℘ 020 7659 4500 –
www.sketch.london – 11AM–4:30PM – starting from £80/person.* A quirky place that's
worth a look: a room decorated in pink with velvet sofas and sketches on the walls.

29 **The Egerton House Hotel** – **B6** – *17–19 Egerton Terrace – SW3 2BX –
⊖ Knightsbridge – ℘ 020 7589 2412 – www.egertonhousehotel.com – afternoon tea
at 2PM and 4PM – starting from £75/person.* A wide selection of high-end teas. Vegan,
vegetarian, and gluten-free options available. Even dogs have their own tea time for £30!

33 **The Berkeley** – **C5** – *Wilton Place – SW1X 7RL – ⊖ Knightsbridge – ℘ 020 7107
8866 – www.the-berkeley.co.uk – 1PM–5:30PM – starting from £85/person.* For
fashionistas, "Prêt-à-Portea" is inspired by the latest fashion collections.

36 **One Aldwych** – **E4** – *1 Aldwych – WC2B 4BZ – ⊖ Charing Cross – ℘ 020 7300
0300 – www.onealdwych.com – Wed.–Fri. 12PM–3PM (till 4:30PM on weekends) –
starting from £70/person.* For fans of Willy Wonka and his famous chocolate factory.

37 **Rosewood Hotel** – **E3** – *252 High Holborn – WC1V 7EN – ⊖ Holborn – ℘ 020 3747
8620 – www.rosewoodhotels.com – 12PM–5:45PM – starting from £78/person.* A daring
afternoon tea blending traditional flavors and iconic artworks.

⌖ *www.afternoontea.co.uk: list of establishments, reservations, discounts.*

East End

Map p. 98

19 **The Lily Vanilli Bakery** –
H2 – *6 The Courtyard, Ezra St. –
E2 7RH – Old Street or Hoxton
(Overground) – 020 3186 4356 –
www.lilyvanilli.com – Wed. 5PM–9PM,
Thu.–Fri. 11AM–5PM, Sat. 10AM–5PM,
Sun. 9AM–4:30PM.* If you're a fan of
deliciously "Instagrammable" cakes,
this is the place for you! Tucked away in
a charming courtyard, it's very popular
on Sundays, the day of the Columbia
Road flower market. People come here
for the cupcakes, pies, and brownies.
Prefer something savory? Try one of
the massive sausage rolls straight out
of the oven.

35 **Townhouse** – **H3** – *5 Fournier
St. – E1 6QE – Liverpool Street or
Shoreditch High Street (Overground) –
020 7247 4745 – www.
townhousespitalfields.com – Tue.–Sat.
11AM–6PM, Sun. 11:30AM–5:30PM.* In the
basement of this antique and pottery
gallery-shop, the old kitchens of an
18th-century townhouse house a cozy
café, known for its homemade cakes.

Greenwich

Map pp. 106–107

70 **Royal Teas Café** – *76 Royal Hill –
SE10 8RT – Greenwich – 020
8691 7240 – www.royalteascafe.co.uk –
Mon.–Wed. and Fri. 9AM–4PM, Sat.
9AM–5PM, Sun. 10:30AM–5PM.* Nestled
on a quiet street, this discreet café is a
lovely spot to indulge in a homemade
treat accompanied by good coffee,
tea, or hot chocolate. Light vegetarian
lunch options (soups, salads, pies).

Eva-Katalin/Getty Images Plus

131

Tea time.

TRADITIONAL PUBS

Pubs (short for public houses) are the
proud descendants of medieval inns
and taverns. Many have been around
for centuries, retaining their original
decor. They play an important role in
social life, hosting groups of friends,
business discussions, or darts players
over beer, served on tap (draught)
or in bottles. They also serve good
food. You place orders and pay at the
counter in most places.

Westminster

Map p. 17

7 **St Stephen's Tavern** – **E5** – *10 Bridge
St. – SW1A 2JR – Westminster –
020 7925 2286 – www.*

ststephenstavern.co.uk – 10AM–10:30PM. Located across from Big Ben, this pretty Victorian pub with a cozy atmosphere makes for a pleasant stop during your visit to Westminster.

St James's

Map p. 24

❤️ **8** **Golden Lion** – **D5** – *25 King St. – SW1Y 6QY –* ⊖ *Green Park –* ☎ *020 7925 0007 – www.greeneking-pubs.co.uk – 12PM–11PM, Fri., Sat. 11:30AM–11PM, Sun. 12PM–10:30PM.* Though the neighboring theater has long since vanished, this pub from 1762 remains an institution.

St Stephen's Tavern

The traditional St Stephen's Tavern pub.

Soho

Map pp. 28–29

9 **Argyll Arms** – **D3** – *18 Argyll St. – W1F 7TP –* ⊖ *Oxford Circus –* ☎ *020 7734 6117 – www.nicholsonspubs. co.uk – 11AM–11PM, Fri.–Sat. 11AM–12AM, Sun. 11AM–10:30PM.* This historic pub (1716) has preserved its stunning 18th-century decor: large mirrors, wood paneling, and sculpted ceilings, with a mahogany wood counter. Its location in the bustling Oxford Circus area explains why it's packed at all hours.

Covent Garden

Map p. 34

❤️ **10** **Lamb & Flag** – **E4** – *33 Rose St. – WC2E 9EB –* ⊖ *Covent Garden –* ☎ *020 7497 9504 – www. lambandflagcoventgarden.co.uk – 12PM–11PM, Sat. 11AM–11PM, Sun. 12PM–10:30PM.* Nestled in a narrow alleyway, the oldest tavern in the area (1623) continues to draw a crowd of regulars and tourists thanks to its cozy and friendly atmosphere and a good selection of beers.

Holborn

21 **Princess Louise** – **E3** – *208 High Holborn – WC1V 7EP –* ⊖ *Holborn –* ☎ *020 7405 8816 – 12PM–11PM, Sun. 3PM–10PM.* This late 19th-century pub, named in honor of Queen Victoria's fourth daughter, is worth a visit for its magnificent Victorian decor.

Chancery Lane

Map p. 41

27 **Craft Beer Co** – **F3** – *82 Leather Lane – EC1N 7TR –* ⊖ *Chancery*

Lane – ☎ 020 7671 0906 – *www.thecraftbeerco.com* – *12PM–11PM except Sun.* Affiliated with the best craft breweries in the country, this pub boasts no less than thirty hand pumps for casks, the small barrels used for the natural carbonation of real ale, unpasteurized and unfiltered. A delight for beer enthusiasts!

The City

Map pp. 50–51

26 **The Blackfriar** – **F4** – *174 Queen Victoria St. – EC4V 4EG –* ⊖ *Blackfriars –* ☎ *020 7236 5474 – www.nicholsonspubs.co.uk – 11:30AM–11PM, Sun. 12PM–6PM.* This historic pub located in a peculiar triangular building occupies the site of a former Dominican monastery. It features facade engravings and admirable Arts & Crafts interior decor (1905). Good choice of real ales.

Southwark

Map pp. 66–67

13 **The George Inn** – **G5** – *75–77 Borough High St. – SE1 1NH –* ⊖ *London Bridge –* ☎ *020 7407 2056 – www.greeneking-pubs.co.uk – 11AM–11PM, Fri.–Sat. 11AM–12AM, Sun. 12PM–11PM.* This establishment, tucked away in a narrow alley, is worth a visit for its unique architecture and warren of time-worn rooms.

Knightsbridge

Map pp. 72–73

14 **The Grenadier** – **C5** – *18 Wilton Row – SW1X 7NR –* ⊖ *Knightsbridge or Hyde Park Corner –* ☎ *020 3205*

2905 – *www.grenadierbelgravia.com –* *12PM–11PM, Sun. 12PM–10:30PM.* This historic pub, adorned in red, white, and blue, was once frequented by the Duke of Wellington and his grenadiers. A good selection of beers and traditional cuisine.

Notting Hill

The Cow – **Off the map** – *89 Westbourne Park Rd – W2 5QH –* ⊖ *Royal Oak –* ☎ *020 7221 0021 – www.thecowlondon.com – 11AM–11PM, Sun. 12PM–10:30PM.* One of the most pleasant pubs in Notting Hill. The regular clientele, quite fashionable, knows it well. People come here to enjoy some oysters with a pint of Guinness or to savor quality Irish-influenced cuisine. Beautiful terrace.

Camden Town

Map p. 91

17 **Brewdog** – **Off the detachable map** – *113 Bayham St. – NW1 0AG –* ⊖ *Camden Town –* ☎ *020 7284 4626 – www.brewdog.com – Tue. 4PM–11PM, Wed.–Thu. 12PM–11PM, Fri.–Sat. 12PM–12AM, Sun. 12PM–10PM.* A Scottish brewery with lots of house beers, and more! They'll help you choose if you're unsure, and you can even join a tasting workshop to educate your palate *(book online).* They also serve great food: diverse and unique burgers with plenty of vegetarian options.

Hampstead

The Spaniards Inn – **Off the map** – *Spaniards Rd – NW3 7JJ –* ⊖ *Hampstead or East Finchley and 15*

min walk – 📞 020 8731 8406 – www.
thespaniardshampstead.co.uk –
10AM–11PM, Sun. 12PM–10:30PM. This
1585 tavern, found at the bend in the
road, maintains a jovial atmosphere
despite its dark and mysterious interior.
Outdoor barbecue on summer Sundays.

❤️ **The Flask** – **Off the map** –
14 Flask Walk – NW3 1HE – ⊖
Hampstead – 📞 *020 7435 4580 –*
www.theflaskhampstead.co.uk –
11AM–11PM, Sun. 12PM–10:30PM. In
winter, a beautiful fireplace warms
this traditional pub, which was once
frequented by Karl Marx.

East End

Map p. 98

❤️ 24 **The Ten Bells** – **H3** –
84 Commercial St. – E1 6LY –
⊖ *Liverpool Street –* 📞 *020 7247
7532 – www.tenbells.com –*
12PM–12AM, Fri.–Sun. 12PM–1AM. This
historic pub in Spitalfields, located
opposite the market, is known for
having been Jack the Ripper's hangout.
The restored ceramics and woodwork
that decorate the space attract the
City's yuppies.

South Districts

Pop Brixton – **Off the map** – *49 Brixton
Station Rd – SW9 8PQ –* ⊖ *Brixton –*
📞 *020 3879 8410 – www.popbrixton.
org – Tue.–Wed. and Sun. 12PM–11PM,
Thu.–Fri. 12PM–12AM, Sat. 11AM–12AM.*
Built on a former parking lot, this
complex of recycled and modular
containers is a trendsetter, an ideal
spot to sample world cuisines, have a
beer, and listen to live music. Festive
and relaxed atmosphere.

30 **Battersea Brewery** – **C8** – *12–14
Arches Lane – SW11 8AB –* ⊖ *Battersea
Power Station or Battersea Park
(Overground) –* 📞 *020 8161 2366 –
www.batterseabrew.co.uk –
12PM–11PM, Fri.–Sat. 12PM–12AM, Sun.
12PM–10:30PM.* This microbrewery is
tucked under the arches of a railroad,
just steps away from Battersea
Power Station. You can savor the
beers brewed on-site, which can be
paired with some snacks and toasties.
Red brick and post-industrial decor,
outdoor terrace, great atmosphere.

Docklands

Map pp. 106–107

22 **The Grapes** – **Off the detachable
map** – *76 Narrow St., Limehouse – E14
8BP –* ⊖ *Westferry (DLR) –* 📞 *020
7987 4396 – www.thegrapes.co.uk –
12PM–11PM.* This charming historic pub,
once visited by Dickens, has two tiny
terraces overlooking the river. Dining
room upstairs.

❤️ 20 **The Prospect of Whitby** – **Off
the detachable map** – *57 Wapping
Wall – E1W 3SH –* ⊖ *Wapping –*
📞 *020 7481 1095 – www.greeneking-
pubs.co.uk – 11:30AM–11PM, Fri.–Sat.
11AM–1PM, Sun. 12PM–10PM.* This
spacious, delightfully old-fashioned pub
is one of the most touristy spots along
the Thames. Built in 1553, it welcomed
the likes of Samuel Pepys and Charles
Dickens. Its large terrace offers a lovely
view of the river.

39 **The Gun** – **Off the detachable
map** – *27 Coldharbour – E14 9NS –*
⊖ *Canary Wharf –* 📞 *020 7519 0075 –
www.thegundocklands.com –* 🅿 –
11:30AM–11PM, Wed.–Sat.

11:30AM–12AM, Sun. 11:30AM–10:30PM. Situated by the Thames, this historic pub stands firm amid the skyscraper invasion. Offers refined cuisine and decor.

COCKTAIL BARS

Mayfair

Map pp. 28–29

❤️ ⑥ **The Connaught Bar** – **C4** – *Carlos Pl. – W1K 2AL –* ⊖ *Bond Street –* ☎ *020 7499 7070 – www.the-connaught.co.uk – 4PM–1AM except Sun.* With its pearlescent light and light wood paneling, this hotel bar offers a beautiful setting in which to sip the head mixologist's cocktails, including the famous flavored martinis, here preferred "stirred, never shaken."

The City

Map pp. 50–51

⑱ **SushiSamba** – **H3** – *Heron Tower – 110 Bishopsgate – EC2N 4AY –* ⊖ *Liverpool Street –* ☎ *020 3640 7330 – www.sushisamba. com – 12PM–1:30AM.* An elevator takes you to the 38th and 39th floors of this tower, where the bar reveals a magical 360° view over the City, particularly breathtaking from the terrace. Cocktails and a good selection of sakes. There is another bar in Covent Garden.

Marylebone

Map p. 87

⑳ **Artesian** – **D3** – *The Langham Hotel, 1C Portland Pl. – W1B 1JA –* ⊖ *Oxford Circus –* ☎ *020 7636 1000 – www.artesian-bar.*

co.uk – 🅿 *– 4PM–12AM, Thu.–Sat. 4PM–1AM.* In this elegant lounge, the head bartender crafts experimental and sophisticated cocktails. The menu also features wines, Bluebird beers, and spirits from around the world.

The Southern Districts

Frank's Café – **Off the detachable map** – *95A Rye Lane – SE15 4ST –* ⊖ *Peckham Rye (Overground) –* ☎ *075 2860 0924 – www.boldtendencies. com – mid-May to mid-Sep.* Located on the 10th floor of a parking garage, this vast rooftop is the perfect spot to admire the sunset with a cocktail in hand. Dining options during the week and brunch on weekends. Very popular, so expect to wait, as reservations are not possible.

Docklands

Map pp. 106–107

㉘ **Bokan** – **Off the detachable map** – *40 Marsh Wall, Isle of Dogs – E14 9TP –* ⊖ *Canary Wharf (DLR) –* ☎ *020 3530 0550 – www.bokanlondon. co.uk – Mon.–Wed. 4PM–11PM, Thu. 4PM–12AM, Fri. 1PM–1AM, Sat. 12PM–1AM, Sun. 12PM–11PM.* Positioned on the 38th floor of the Novotel in Canary Wharf, this bar offers stunning vistas of the city. Original and delicious cocktails, live music in the evening, and a beautiful rooftop with a 360° view.

🛍 Shopping

Whatever your style and budget, you will find something to delight: big stores on Oxford Street and Knightsbridge, luxury leather goods, art dealers, and high fashion designers on Bond Street, chic boutiques in Marylebone and King's Road, vintage stores in the East End, Notting Hill, and Camden, the Seven Dials shopping area, northeast of Covent Garden... Not to mention museum shops filled with unique, high-quality items.

⟳ **Find the addresses on our maps using the numbered dots (e.g. ❶). The red coordinates (e.g. C2) refer to the detachable map.**

St James's

Map p. 24

Hatter

❽ Lock & Co. Hatters – D5 – *6 St James's St. – SW1A 1EF – ⊖ Green Park – 📞 020 7930 8874 – www.lockhatters.co.uk – closed Sun.* Open since 1759, this historic hatter on St James's Street has adorned the heads of world-renowned figures from Admiral Lord Nelson to Jacqueline Kennedy, as well as Charlie Chaplin, Winston Churchill, and Oscar Wilde, who even left with a debt of £3.30. Enjoy browsing , or equip yourself with a bowler hat, top hat, or wool cap.

Department Stores

❤ **❹ Fortnum & Mason – D4** – *181 Piccadilly – W1A 1ER – ⊖ Green Park or Piccadilly Circus – 📞 020 7734 8040 – www.fortnumandmason.com – daily.* One of the must-visit department stores. An incredible selection of teas, biscuits, sweets, spirits, and more. All beautifully presented. A homemade honey is produced in hives on the roof.

Tailoring

❤ **㉔ Hilditch & Key – D4** – *73 Jermyn St. – SW1Y 6NP – ⊖ Green Park – 📞 020 7930 2329 – www.hilditchandkey.co.uk – daily.* On the legendary Jermyn Street, you'll find the domain of the city's oldest shirtmaker. Choose between bespoke or ready-to-wear. Mostly men's articles and accessories.

Mayfair and Piccadilly

Map pp. 28–29

Chocolates

❤ **⑪ Charbonnel et Walker – D4** – *Royal Arcade, 28 Old Bond St.– W1A 1ER – ⊖ Green Park or Piccadilly Circus – 📞 020 7318 2075 – www.charbonnelchocolates.com – closed Sun.* Established in 1875, this royal purveyor is one of the oldest chocolatiers in the country, favored by Wallis Simpson, Princess Diana, and Sir Alec Guinness. The boutique is charming and the chocolates (truffles being the specialty) are irresistible. Other locations in London include in

The Portobello Road market in Notting Hill.

giorgiogiolano/Getty Images Plus

Selfridges and Harrods department stores.

Fashion

5 Vivienne Westwood – **C4** – *6 Davies St.* – *W1K 3DN* – ⊖ *Bond Street* – ✆ *020 7629 3757* – *www.viviennewestwood.com* – *closed Sun.* The temple of "Queen Viv" (1941–2022), who brought punk to the people.

6 Stella McCartney – **D4** – *23 Old Bond St.* – *W1S 4PZ* – ⊖ *Green Park* – ✆ *020 7518 3100* – *www.stellamccartney.com* – *daily.* The creations of the talented Stella may not be within everyone's budget, but the store is worth a visit.

Soho

Map pp. 28–29

Fashion

47 Beyond Retro – **D3** – *19–21 Argyll St.* – *W1F 7TR* – ⊖ *Oxford Circus* – ✆ *020 7729 9001* – *www.beyondretro.com* – *daily.* One of the temples of London vintage. This gigantic space gathers clothing and accessories for men and women from the 1920s to the 1990s.

Perfumes

❤ **20 Penhaligon's** – **D4** – *125 Regent St.* – *W1B 4HT* – ⊖ *Piccadilly Circus* – ✆ *020 7434 2608* – *www.penhaligons.com* – *daily.* Another venerable British house supplying the Royal

Family, this perfume store founded in 1870 is the originator of the famous Blenheim Bouquet, a favorite of Winston Churchill—and the innovation continues!

Toys

38 **Hamleys** – **D4** – *188–196 Regent St. – W1B 5BT –* ⊖ *Piccadilly or Oxford Circus – ☏ 037 1704 1977 – www.hamleys.com – daily.* Spread over seven floors, this is one of the largest toy stores in the world, bursting with fun and magic. It's a must-see, just for the joy of feeling like a kid again!

Music

12 **Berwick Street** – **D4** – *Berwick St. – W1F 0PH –* ⊖ *Piccadilly Circus.* This street is known for its market and its many specialized record stores (new and second-hand). At number 30 is the famous Reckless Records. At number 75, Sister Ray, specializing in indie rock, is well stocked with vinyls.

7 **The Rolling Stones Store** – **D4** – *9 Carnaby St. – W1F 9PE –* ⊖ *Piccadilly Circus or Oxford Circus – www.therollingstonesshop.co.uk – daily.* The Stones have naturally chosen Carnaby Street to open their first store. The iconic red tongue, the band's logo since the 1970s, sets the tone and is available on every imaginable item. A must for fans.

Covent Garden

Map p. 34

Jewelry, Accessories

40 **Tatty Devine** – **E4** – *36 Neal St. – WC2H 9PS –* ⊖ *Covent Garden – ☏ 020 8617 8688 – www.tattydevine.com – 10AM–6PM, Sun. 11AM–5PM.* Founded by two British designers famous for their eccentric jewelry and custom-made necklaces adorned with charms, crafted within the hour. Colorful, fun, and quirky at affordable prices.

Cosmetics

15 **Neal's Yard Remedies** – **E3** – *15 Neal's Yard – WC2H 9DP –* ⊖ *Covent Garden – ☏ 020 7379 7222 – www.nealsyardremedies.com – daily – Therapy Rooms: 10AM–7PM, Sun. 11AM–6PM.* This is the flagship store of this pioneer in organic cosmetics, which has now spread throughout the UK. Featuring therapy rooms at 2 Neal's Yard for a pampering experience.

Cheese

♥ **14** **Neal's Yard Dairy** – **E4** – *17 Shorts Gardens – WC2H 9AT –* ⊖ *Covent Garden – ☏ 020 7500 7520 – www.nealsyarddairy.co.uk – daily.* Explore this cheese shop with over 50 varieties of excellent products from the British Isles, such as cheddar and stilton. Other locations in London, including near Borough Market.

Books

13 **Magma** – **E3** – *29 Shorts Gardens – WC2H 9AP –* ⊖ *Covent Garden – ☏ 020 7240 7970 – www.magma-shop.com – daily.* A vast selection of books on design, typography, illustration, and art. A must-visit.

Bloomsbury

Accessories

23 **James Smith & Sons** – **E3** – *53 New Oxford St. – WC1A 1BL –* ⊖ *Tottenham*

Court Road – ☎ 020 7836 4731 – www. james-smith.co.uk – closed Sun. Since 1830, this establishment has been selling the essential accessory for any visit to London: the umbrella! The store, still full of Victorian charm, offers a wide range of canes, custom-made accessories, etc.

Temple

Map p. 41

Tea

🔟 **Twinings** – **F4** – *216 The Strand – WC2 R 1AP – ⊖ Temple or Charing Cross – ☎ 020 7353 3511 – www. twinings.co.uk – daily.* Two Chinese tea merchants flanking a lion mark the entrance to this store, where the famous brand has been since 1706. A vast selection of teas is offered for tasting before you make your selection. Master classes are also available to introduce you to the world of tea.

South Bank

Map pp. 66–67

Fashion, Home Decor

45 **Oxo Tower Wharf** – **F4** – *Barge House St. – SE1 9PH – ⊖ Southwark or Blackfriars – ☎ 020 7021 1600 – www.oxotower.co.uk – hours vary by store.* Ceramics, jewelry, textiles, lighting, design, gadgets… About thirty designers and artisans have set up shop over three floors of the former OXO stock cube factory.

Belgravia – Knightsbridge

Map pp. 72–73

Department Stores

1 **Harvey Nichols** – **C5** – *109–125 Knightsbridge – SW1X 7 RJ – ⊖ Knightsbridge – ☎ 020 7235 5000 – www.harveynichols.com – daily.* In this historic department store, you'll find the top fashion brands, beauty products, and home items. The delicatessen section offers unique products from England and beyond.

2 **Harrods** – **B5** – *87–135 Brompton Rd – SW1X 7XL – ⊖ Knightsbridge – ☎ 020 7730 1234 – www.harrods. com – daily.* Harrods boasts that it can provide anything! The food halls are impressively decorated. There's also a hair salon, beauty spa, travel agency, and shipping service. Visit it as you would a museum.

139

Notting Hill

Map p. 83

Fashion

😊 Practically every other store at the beginning of Portobello Road is a **vintage shop**. In some, clothes are well organized and may date back to the 1930s. In others, you have to rummage, and choices are mostly from the 1970s–1980s, or even more recent. In any case, prices are quite high.

❤️ 18 **Paul Smith** – **Off the detachable map** – *122 Kensington Park Rd – W11 2EP – ⊖ Notting Hill Gate – ☎ 020 7727 3553 – www.paulsmith. com – daily.* Halfway between a showroom and a store, Westbourne House showcases the creations of the famous designer. In this typical townhouse setting, visit the rooms adorned with items collected by Sir Paul Smith. The collections, however, are for sale.

Flea Market

19 Portobello Road – **Off the detachable map** – *Portobello Rd – W11 1LU –* ⊖ *Notting Hill Gate –* ☏ *020 7361 3001 – www.portobelloroad.co.uk.* From Notting Hill Gate to the north of Portobello Road, you'll find antique dealers and second-hand stores, vintage clothes, Indian jewelry, crafts, and a food market. Alongside affordable British souvenirs, boutiques and labyrinthine passages sometimes hide treasures, though at exorbitant prices (old toys, jewelry, pottery, etc.). **Portobello Market** runs on Fridays and Saturdays *(8AM–7PM)*. **Portobello Green Market** *(Fri.–Sun. 9AM–5PM)* gathers vintage clothes and fashion.

Marylebone – Regent's Park

Map p. 87

Decor

3 The Conran Shop – **C2** – *55 Marylebone High St. – W1U 5HS –* ⊖ *Regent's Park –* ☏ *020 7723 2223 – www.conranshop.co.uk – daily.* Furniture and decor store by the famous designer Terence Conran (founder of Habitat). Modern and trendy design, with numerous accessories and utensils that are easy to fit in your suitcase. Another, more classic location is at 16 Sloane Square, Chelsea.

10 Contemporary Applied Arts – **C3** – *6 Paddington St. – W1U 5QG –* ⊖ *Baker Street –* ☏ *020 7620 0086 – www.caa.org.uk – closed Sun.–Mon.* Exhibition and sale of decorative and applied arts (pottery, ceramics, glasswork, metals, jewelry, fabrics, and furniture), crafted by modern British designers.

Camden Town

Map p. 91

Fashion

35 Cyberdog – **Off the detachable map** – *Stables Market – Chalk Farm Rd – NW1 8AH –* ⊖ *Camden Town –* ☏ *020 7482 2842 – www.cyberdog.net – daily.* Immersed in darkness and pulsating with deafening music, this store offers punk-futuristic clothing, fluorescent t-shirts, silver dresses, bright cosmetics, and other eccentric gadgets. Salespeople are totally in sync with the vibe.

9 Dr. Martens Camden – **Off the detachable map** – *26–27 Stables Market – Chalk Farm Rd – NW1 8AH –* ⊖ *Camden Town –* ☏ *020 3006 8080 – www.drmartens.com – daily.* From boots to sandals, the iconic air-cushioned soles of Dr. Martens' shoes have always been a hit in London across all generations. Bags and satchels are also available.

Flea Markets

25 Camden Markets – **Off the detachable map** – *Camden Lock Pl. – Chalk Farm Rd – NW1 8AF –* ⊖ *Camden Town – www.camdenmarket.com – daily.* While most stores are open during the week, the

Namaste Store on Camden High Street.

real fun happens on weekends. This is one of London's major attractions, even if the markets aren't quite what they used to be. Be sure to check out the Stables Market, set in old stables.

East End

Map p. 98

Markets

For vintage or artisanal shopping, don't miss **Old Spitalfields Market** (☞ *p. 96*).

♥ **29** **Columbia Road Flower Market** – **H2** – *Columbia Rd – E2 7 RG – Hoxton (Overground) – ✆ 020 7613 0876 – www.columbiaroadmarket. co.uk – Sun. 8AM–2PM.* This flower market is experiencing a remarkable revival since East London has become one of the city's trendiest areas. It's complemented by artisan shops based in the low houses of Columbia Road. There's a plethora of compelling decor concepts, galleries, cafés, and restaurants, some of which are also open during the week. Come early to avoid the crowds.

32 **Spitalfields City Farm** – **Off the detachable map** – *Buxton St. – E1 5AR – Whitechapel or Shoreditch High Street (Overground) – ✆ 020 7247 8762 – www.spitalfieldscityfarm. org – closed Mon.* Just steps away from Brick Lane, this is one of the most centrally located urban farms. Built on the site of a former railroad goods

yard, it hosts colorful residents – goats, donkeys, rabbits, and pigs. The farm offers various activities, including cooking classes, vegetable picking, and a junior farmers' club.

42 **Boxpark Shoreditch** – **H2** – *2–10 Bethnal Green Rd – E1 6GY – Shoreditch High Street (Overground) – ✆ 020 7186 8800 – www.boxpark.co.uk – daily.* About sixty containers house pop-up stores from over fifty well-known brands and young designers, as well as restaurants, some of which are on rooftops.

Fashion

31 **Sunday Upmarket** – **H3** – *Old Truman's Brewery – 91 Brick Lane – E1 6QL – Shoreditch (Overground) – ✆ 020 7770 6028 – www.sundayupmarket.co.uk – Sat. 11AM–6PM, Sun. 10AM–6PM.* This large warehouse in the courtyard of the old Truman Brewery hosts young designers, vintage sellers, and a range of food stalls.

Music

33 **Rough Trade East** – **H3** – *Old Truman Brewery, 91 Brick Lane – E1 6QL – Shoreditch High Street (Overground) or Aldgate East – ✆ 020 7392 7788 – www.roughtrade. com – daily.* A must-visit independent record store if you're heading to Brick Lane. Great advice from the staff.

Going out

London never sleeps, but each hour of the night has its own special places. The **pubs** (⊙ *p. 131*) are must-visits at the start of the evening. The **bars** of Soho, Clerkenwell, Islington, and the East End come alive later, drawing a younger crowd. Musical ambiance is often provided by bands or DJs, and it's not uncommon to dance until 2AM. Bars also offer a cheaper alternative to the **clubs**, known to be quite pricey, where the vibe rarely picks up before midnight.

Alternatively, consider booking a ticket for a **musical** or a play (⊙ *p. 144)*, and enjoy the many **concerts** held in churches, like the famous St Martin-in-the-Fields (⊙ *p. 22),* or at the prestigious Royal Opera House (⊙ *p. 35)*.

⊙ Find addresses on our maps using the numbered markers (e.g. ❶). The **red coordinates** (e.g. **C2**) refer to the detachable map.

Soho

Map pp. 28–29

❷ Bar Rumba – **D4** – *36 Shaftesbury Ave. – W1D 7EP –* ⊖ *Piccadilly Circus –* ☏ *020 7287 6933 – www. barrumbadisco.co.uk – 7:30PM–3AM.* Bar Rumba is one of London's best clubs despite its modest dance floor. The atmosphere is always friendly, with a variety of music: jazz, house, funk, reggaeton... Comedy club on Tuesdays, Thursdays, Fridays, and Saturdays, early in the evening.

㉑ Cirque le Soir – **D4** – *15–21 Ganton St. – W1F 9BN –* ⊖ *Oxford Circus –* ☏ *020 7287 8001 – www.cirquelesoir. com – 11PM–3AM – closed Tue., Thu., and Sun.* Wild, even decadent vibe in this extravagant club centered on burlesque cabaret and circus acts. Jugglers, fire eaters, and dancers perform to the latest house and hip-hop hits.

The City

Map pp. 50–51

❼ Fabric – **F3** – *77a Charterhouse St. – EC1M 6HJ –* ⊖ *Farringdon –* ☏ *020 7336 8898 – www.fabriclondon. com – Fri.–Sun. from 11PM and as scheduled – minimum age 19 years.* A huge venue (three rooms) with exceptional acoustics, hosting the top techno, house, and drum and bass DJs and attracting a crowd aged 20–30. "Bodysonic" dancefloor to feel the bass.

❶ Barbican Centre – **G3** – *Silk St. – EC2Y 8DS – The City –* ⊖ *Barbican –* ☏ *020 7638 8891 – www.barbican.org. uk –* ♿. Europe's largest arts center offers a remarkable cultural program in cinema, theater, dance, and opera. The country's most prestigious classical, contemporary, and experimental music groups regularly perform here, including the London Symphony Orchestra, the BBC Symphony Orchestra, and the Academy of Ancient Music.

Southwark

Map pp. 66–67

⑥ Ministry of Sound – G6 – 103 Gaunt St. – SE1 6DP – ⊖ Elephant and Castle – ☏ 020 7740 8600 – www.ministryofsound.com. This club attracts a crowd aged 20–35 every weekend. Outstanding sound and a dizzying experience, but expect long lines at the entrance. House, garage, and techno music.

③ Flat Iron Square – G5 – 64 Union St. – SE1 1TD – ⊖ London Bridge – ☏ 020 3179 9800 – www.flatironsquarc.co.uk – Noon–11PM, Sun. 12PM–8PM, closed Mon. This unique spot tucked under a railroad arch is home to several bars and street food stalls. Gather around large wooden tables for a snack before heading to the club and its underground tequila bar to party.

North Kensington

Map pp. 72–73

④ Troubadour – Off the detachable map – 263–267 Old Brompton Rd – SW5 9JA – ⊖ Earl's Court or West Brompton – ☏ 020 7341 6333 – www.troubadourlondon.com – Noon–12AM, Thu. 12PM–2AM, Fri.–Sat. 10AM–2AM. A haven for artists and intellectuals in the 1960s, this bar hosted great music legends like Bob Dylan and Jimi Hendrix. Expect eclectic programming in the basement venue: poetry readings, movie nights, and concerts from emerging talents.

Notting Hill

Map p. 83

❤ ⑮ Electric Cinema – Off the detachable map – 191 Portobello Rd – W11 2ED – ⊖ Ladbroke Grove – ☏ 020 7908 9696 – www.electriccinema.co.uk. Why not enjoy an evening in London by catching a film at one of the city's oldest (opened 1910) and most beautiful cinemas? Relax with a drink in hand or, even better, lie down on a sofa bed. Book ahead.

Camden Town

Map p. 91

⑩ Jazz Café – Off the detachable map – 5 Parkway – NW1 7PG – ⊖

An Evening at the Theater

Enjoy your stay in London by spending an evening at the theater, a concert, or a music hall. **Musical theater** is showcased in the **West End theaters**, around Leicester Square, particularly on the Strand (Savoy, Adelphi); on Shaftesbury Avenue (Sondheim, Palace, Lyric, Gielgud); Charing Cross Road (Phoenix, Garrick, Wyndham's); Haymarket (His Majesty's, Haymarket); Catherine Street (Drury Lane); Wellington Street (Lyceum).
☺ For listings, check the websites www.timeout.com/london or officiallondontheatre.co.uk. Half-price tickets for same-day shows are on sale at the TKTS booth (www.tkts.co.uk) at Leicester Square.

Soho by night.

Camden Town – 📞 020 7485 6834 – www.thejazzcafelondon.com. One of the best jazz clubs in the capital. Also features a variety of soul, RnB, funk, electro, and hip-hop concerts every evening starting at 7PM. On Fri. and Sat., the venue transforms into a dance floor starting at 10:30PM. Restaurant on the 1st floor.

22 **Electric Ballroom** – **Off the detachable map** *– 184 Camden High St. – NW1 8QP – ⊖ Camden Town – 📞 020 7485 9007 – www. electricballroom.co.uk. Since 1938, this legendary venue has hosted the likes of Sid Vicious, Madness, The Clash... and continues to welcome artists from all genres. Club nights on weekends.*

King's Cross-St Pancras

Map p. 91

24 **Spiritland** – **E1** *– 9–10 Stable St. – N1C 4AB – ⊖ King's Cross – St Pancras – 📞 020 3319 0050 – www.spiritland. com – 9AM–11PM, Fri. 9AM–1AM, Sat. 10AM–1AM, Sun. 10AM–7PM. This concept bar for audiophiles prides itself on having a cutting-edge sound system. High-quality programming (jazz, dub, etc.), DJ sets every night, album launches, recording studio... Perfect for enjoying good music while sipping a cocktail with friends.*

The Old Queen's Head – **Off the detachable map** *– 44 Essex Rd – N1 8LN – ⊖ Angel – 📞 020 7354 9993 – www.theoldqueenshead.com –*

12PM–12AM, Thu. 12PM–1AM, Fri. 12PM–2AM, Sat. 12PM–3AM, Sun. 12PM–12AM. This multi-floor pub in the Islington area, north of St Pancras, hosts concerts, DJ sets, and other music nights. On the top floor, a karaoke room can be booked.

East End

Map p. 98

11 **The Book Club** – **H2** – *100–106 Leonard St. – EC2A 4RH – Old Street or Shoreditch High Street (Overground) – 020 7684 8618 – www.wearetbc.com – Wed. 5PM–12AM, Thu. 5PM–2AM, Fri. 4PM–3AM, Sat. 12PM–3AM.* Talks, exhibitions, parties, music sessions: this popular bar-club in the East End is multi-functional. You can even play ping-pong! The clientele is often young and highly fashionable.

❤ **18** **Queen of Hoxton** – **H2** – *1–5 Curtain Road – EC2A 3JX – Shoreditch High Street (Overground) – 020 7422 0958 – www.queenofhoxton.com – Thu.–Sat. 5PM–2AM; rooftop: Thu.–Fri. 5PM–9:30PM, Sat. 2PM–9:30PM.* A bar, a club, and an art gallery in one, this venue has a relaxed, underground vibe, with graffiti on the walls and occasional raves in the basement. When the weather is nice, the rooftop is covered with grass, flowers, and multicolored tables; in the fall, a giant heated tipi welcomes guests.

19 **Xoyo** – **G2** – *32–37 Cowper St. – EC2A 4AP – Old Street – 020 7608 2878 – www.xoyo.co.uk – from 10PM, varying hours.* A highly regarded club combining concerts on weekdays and clubbing nights with renowned DJs on weekends. Music programming is varied but always high quality. Come in pairs or more: guests are not permitted to enter alone.

The Southern Neighborhoods

Dogstar – **Off the map** – *389 Coldharbour Lane – SW9 8LQ – Brixton – 020 7733 7515 – www.dogstarbrixton.com – Wed.–Thu. 4PM–11PM, Fri. 4PM–3AM, Sat. 12PM–3AM, Sun. 12PM–10PM.* A three-floor grand pub and the first DJ bar in the capital, this is the perfect spot to party late into the night. Early birds can also enjoy concerts, stand-up comedy shows, and sports broadcasts. There's something for everyone at all hours!

Accommodation

Accommodation in London is very expensive. To get better rates, book your stays well in advance, ideally during the week or on Sunday, and watch out for promotions on hotel booking sites.

The most central upscale neighborhoods (Mayfair, St James's, The Strand) are home to luxury hotels. Very residential, Kensington and Notting Hill boast a series of charming hotels set in 19th-century homes. Bayswater, their neighbor, is filled with more budget-friendly hotels. Those traveling by train can settle near King's Cross and St Pancras stations, toward Bloomsbury. This pleasant and central neighborhood offers numerous accommodations across all price ranges, often housed in former Georgian residences. Earl's Court and Victoria have simple hotels and relatively affordable B&Bs. *The price ranges mentioned correspond to a double room. Please note: rates can vary greatly depending on the day and the hotel's occupancy rate.*

 Find addresses on the detachable map using the numbered tabs (e.g. ❶). The coordinates in red (e.g. D2) refer to the same map.

Covent Garden

Map p. 34

From £150 to £250

❽ **Hub by Premier Inn Covent Garden** – **E4** – *110 St Martin's Ln – WC2N 4BA –* ⊖ *Leicester Square or Charing Cross –* ☎ *020 3728 8373 – www.premierinn.com –* ✕ ♿ *– 163 rooms £187/£242 –* ☕ *£5.* "Compact and connected": this is the formula for Hub Hotels, offering small but ultra-functional rooms. About fifteen other addresses in London: Westminster, Tower Bridge, King's Cross, Spitalfields, City, and more.

Bloomsbury

From £50 to £100

❸ **Generator London** – **E2** – *37 Tavistock Pl. – WC1H 9SE –* ⊖ *King's Cross-St Pancras or Russel Square –* ☎ *020 7388 7666 – www. staygenerator.com – starting from £38, in dorm style –* ☕ *£9.50.* A bit of an industrial atmosphere for this large youth hostel but perfectly located between the British Museum and King's Cross and St Pancras stations.

Over £400

❻ **Bloomsbury Hotel** – **E3** – *16–22 Great Russell St. – WC1B 3NN –* ⊖ *Tottenham Court Road –* ☎ *020 7347 1000 – www.doylecollection. com –* ✕ ♿ *–* 🅿 *charges apply – 153 rooms £475/£665 –* ☕ *£29.* Close to Covent Garden, a chic hotel with a typically English atmosphere. Relaxing setting and contemporary rooms. Friendly and highly professional service.

South Bank

Map pp. 66–67

From £200 to £300

12 The Mad Hatter – F5 – *3–7 Stamford St. – SE1 9NY – Southwark – ☏ 020 7401 9222 – www.madhatterhotel.co.uk – ✗ ♿ – 🅿 charges apply – 30 rooms £224/£249 – ☕.* On the south bank of the Thames, close to the Tate Modern, this establishment is located in a beautiful Victorian pub and offers cozy and well-soundproofed rooms.

Belgravia

From £150 to £250

2 The Z Hotel Victoria – C6 – *5 Lower Belgrave St. – SW1W 0NR – Victoria – ☏ 020 3589 3990 – www.thezhotels.com – ♿ – 106 rooms £160/£240 – ☕ £11.95.* Clean and functional, a stone's throw from Victoria Station. Be aware, rooms are tiny (107 to 150 sq. ft.) and not all have windows. Friendly service.

South Kensington

Map pp. 72–73

From £200 to £300

4 The Resident Kensington – A6 – *25 Courtfield Gardens – SW5 0PG – Earls Court or Gloucester Road – ☏ 020 7244 2255 – www.residenthotels.com – 🅿 charges apply – 65 rooms £182/£258.* In a quiet neighborhood, warm rooms with small kitchens (fridge, microwave, kettle). Some rooms overlook greenery.

148

North Kensington

From £50 to £100

Safestay – Off the map – *Holland Park – W8 7QU – Holland Park – ☏ 020 7870 9629 – www.safestay.com/venue/safestay-london-kensington-holland-park/ – 11 rooms and 26 dorms 4–12 beds each – from £25, in dorm style – ☕ £8.* A very popular hostel for its setting: a listed Jacobean building in a large wooded park.

Notting Hill

From £200 to £250

Vancouver Studios – Off the map – *30 Prince's Square – W2 4NJ – Bayswater – ☏ 077 5428 6145 – www.vancouverstudios.co.uk – 47 studios and apartments £200/£250 – ☕ £8.50.* This charming spot offers pleasant studios with kitchenettes. You can even order a few groceries for your arrival.

Garden Court Hotel – Off the map – *30–31 Kensington Gardens Square – W2 4BG – Bayswater – ☏ 020 7229 2553 – www.gardencourthotel.co.uk – 40 rooms £239/£285 ☕.* This hotel with a bright facade has been family-run since 1954. Simply furnished rooms, good value for money.

Marylebone – Regent's Park

Map p. 87

From £200 to £300

1 Gunmakers – C3 – *33 Aybrook St. – W1U 4AP – Baker Street – ☏ 020 7935 5291 – www.gunmakershouse.co.uk – ✗ – 5 rooms £220 – ☕.* This pub with traditional decor doubles as a charming small hotel with new and comfortable rooms. Well-located, between Regent's Park and the Wallace Collection, it makes a good base for exploring the city. Be sure to dine here too: the atmosphere is welcoming and the food delicious!

King's Cross-St Pancras

Map p. 91

From £150 to £250

16 **The Angus Hotel** – **E2** – *31–32 Argyle Square – WC1H8AP – King's Cross-St Pancras – 020 7837 3388 – www.angushotel kingscross.com – 35 rooms £149/£168.* In a beautiful Georgian-style building, this small hotel has been run by the same family for over 40 years. It's well-located, very clean, and quiet. The rooms are on the small side — but that's typical in the city! Great value for the price.

18 **The Crestfield Hotel** – **E1** – *2–4 Crestfield St. – WC1H 8AT – King's Cross-St Pancras – 020 7837 0500 – www.crestfieldhotel.co.uk – 52 rooms £139/£172.* A clean and functional establishment, situated on a quiet street just steps away from the major train stations. The rooms aren't very spacious, but the well-maintained setting makes it a great option.

17 **Studios2Let** – **E2** – *36–37 Cartwright Gardens – WC1H 9EH – King's Cross-St Pancras – 020 7380 8450 – www.studios2let. com – studios £149/£180.* Compact, clean, and well-equipped studios (107–204 sq. ft.) for an independent stay, just a 5-minute walk from St Pancras Station.

East End

Map p. 98

From £200 to £300

5 **Point A Hotel Liverpool Street** – **H3** – *13–15 Folgate St. – E1 6BX – Liverpool Street or Shoreditch (DLR) – 020 7456 0400 – www. pointahotels.com – 212 rooms £214/£274 – .* A compact hotel offering minimal facilities (bed, shower, TV, and that's all!) to guarantee the lowest rates. Great location. Ask for a room with a window.

From £400 to £500

15 **The Hoxton Shoreditch** – **H2** – *81 Great Eastern St. – EC2A 3HU – Old Street – 020 7550 1000 – www.thehoxton.com – 210 rooms £389/£449 – £20.* In a rapidly developing neighborhood, this beautiful hotel has an industrial design, comfortable furnishings and offers room service. Bike rentals are available.

Docklands

Map pp. 106–107

From £100 to £300

20 **Novotel Canary Wharf** – **Off the detachable map** – *40 Marsh Wall, Isle of Dogs – E14 9TP – Canary Wharf (DLR) – 020 3530 0500 – www. all.accor.com – 313 rooms £326/£353 – £25.* This 39-floor building, with its functional and appealing modern interior design, offers fully equipped rooms with breathtaking views of the city. The breakfast served at Bokan bar (*p. 135*) is very successful.

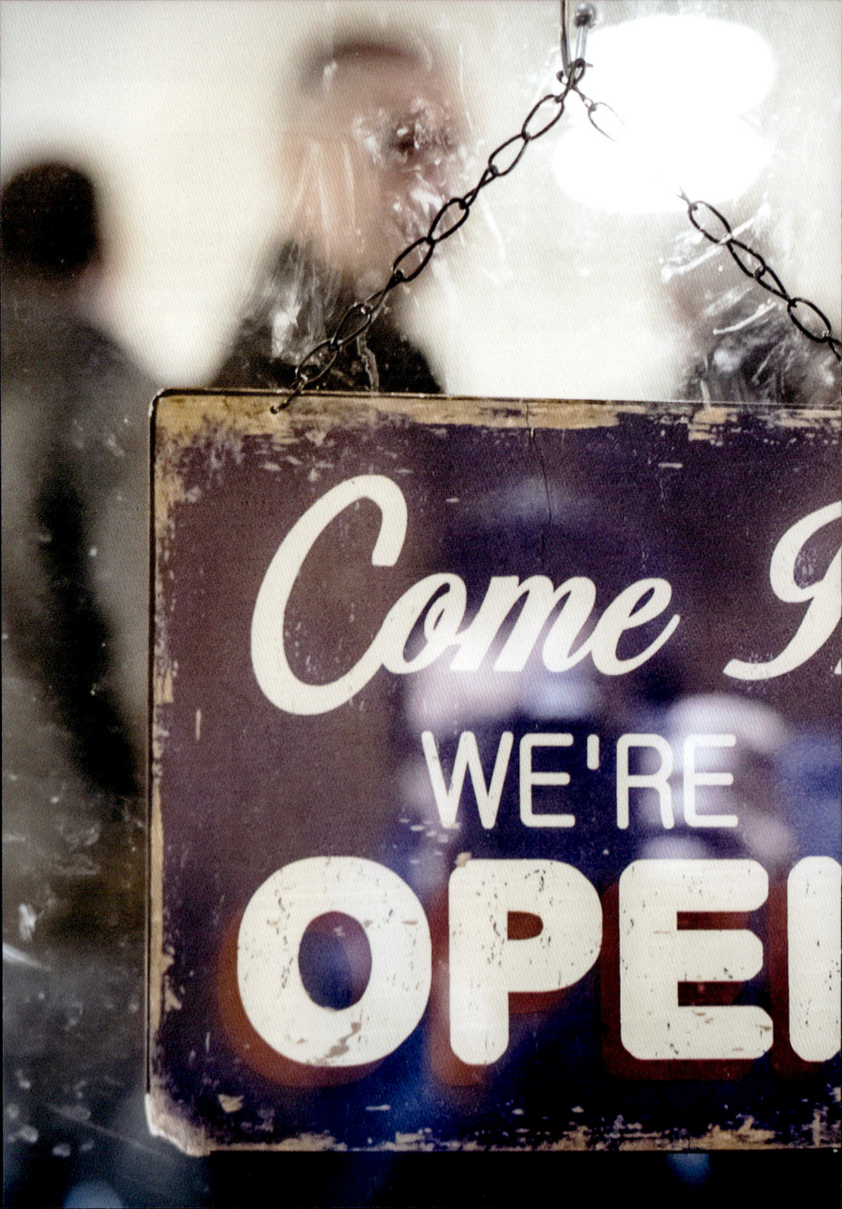
Come
WE'RE

PRACTICAL GUIDE

"Come in, we're open."
mauro_grigollo/Getty Images Plus

Plan your trip

Entry requirements

On January 1st, 2021, the UK left the European Union, which has changed certain travel requirements.

Identification documents

A **valid passport** is required to travel to the UK. Each child must have their own passport, regardless of age. If your **child** has a different last name than you, as well as for minors traveling alone, there are extra documentation requirements. For the latest information, see www.gov.uk/standard-visitor/if-youre-under-18.

Visa

Visa exemption remains valid for tourist stays of less than 6 months, simple business visits, training, conferences, seminars, etc.
For any type of extended stay (work, studies longer than 6 months, etc.), a visa is required.
☞ **www.gov.uk/check-uk-visa**

ETA (Electronic Travel Authorization)

An **Electronic Travel Authorization (ETA)** is now required for all travelers: check www.gov.uk/guidance/apply-for-an-electronic-travel-authorisation-eta to apply online (cost: £16, valid for 2 years).

Climate and seasons

London experiences a **temperate maritime climate**: moderate temperatures and high humidity all year round.
Though showers are frequent, **spring** is enjoyable for its mild temperatures (averaging 52–59°F from late March to late May).
In **summer**, the climate is generally pleasant (64–68°F from June to August), with peaks at 86°F, though cool and foggy days can occur.
Fall is relatively mild and sunny (52–59°F in September to October).
Winter is never too severe (39–43°F from November to March) and snowfall is quite rare, but wind and humidity can make it feel much colder. The weeks leading up to **Christmas** see a high influx of tourists, as does the **sale** season (from late December onward).

For more information

www.visitbritain.com – The Great Britain Tourist Board.
www.visitlondon.com – The London Tourist Board.
www.timeout.com/london – For planning your cultural outings. There are lots of blogs on the city, like the popular **www.londonist.com**.
Also download the Visit London – Official Guide app.

SHansche/Getty Images Plus

Christmas decorations in the streets of London.

153

Your stay

Embassies

United States – 33 Nine Elms Lane – London SW11 7US – ⊖ Vauxhall – ✆ 44 20 7499 9000 – www. uk.usembassy.gov.

Canada – Canada House, Trafalgar Square – London SW1Y 5BJ – ⊖ Charing Cross – ✆ 44 20 7004 6000 – www.international.gc.ca.

Money

Currency

The official currency is the **British pound** (£), divided into 100 pence (p). In early 2025, $1 = £0.81 (£1 = $1.24). There are notes of £50, £20, £10, and £5, and coins of £2, £1, 50p, 20p, 10p, 5p, 2p, and 1p.

Banks

Banks are generally open from Mon. to Sat. 9:30AM to 4:30PM.

Credit cards

An international credit card remains the most flexible means of payment. **In most places, it is even the only accepted method**: more and more stores, restaurants, cafés, bakeries, and museums no longer accept cash, and contactless payment (up to £100) is offered almost everywhere. Even street performers often have a payment terminal! So there's no need to withdraw too much cash from the ATM.

Check with your bank about the fees applied on payments and withdrawals (subject to a limit). If applicable, a one-time international option might be the most economical solution.

Currency exchange

You won't need it. Besides ATMs being omnipresent, both in the airport and around the city, most everything can be paid for by contactless credit card (*see above*).

Time difference

All year round, London is five hours ahead of New York.

Electricity

The standard voltage is 230 volts AC (50 Hz), so you may need a converter for devices running on 220 V. Some places still have three-pin sockets, in which case you will need an **adapter** for your electrical devices. Check with your hotel (most lend adapters).

Don't panic!
Emergencies – ✆ 112 or ✆ 999 (free call)
Police – ✆ 101 (free call)
Lost Bank Cards – Amex: ✆ 1 (801) 849 2124
Visa: ✆ 1 (800) 847-2911
Mastercard: ✆ 1 (800) 627-8372
Lost Property in Transport (Transport for London) – ✆ 0343 222 1234

Opening hours

Stores

Mon.–Sat. from 9:30/10AM to 6/7PM, sometimes later (8/9PM) on major shopping streets (Oxford Street, Kensington High Street, etc.). Open on Sun. (from 10/11AM to 4/5PM) in tourist areas.

ℭ *"Where to Go/Shopping" p. 136.*

Museums and monuments

Many open every day of the week (10AM–6PM), sometimes with reduced hours on Sun. and public holidays (bank holidays). Most close on Jan. 1st, Dec. 25th and 26th, and the first Monday in May.

☺ *Take advantage of night openings to explore the major museums: National Gallery (Fri. until 9PM), National Portrait Gallery (Fri.–Sat. 9PM), Victoria and Albert Museum (Fri. 10PM), British Museum (Fri. 8:30PM), etc.*

Thematic evenings are also regularly organized at Tate Britain and Tate Modern, the Science Museum, and the Natural History Museum, as well as candlelit tours at Sir John Soane's Museum and Dennis Severs' House.

Pharmacies

Most open from 9AM to 6PM.
Boots Piccadilly – 44–46 Regent St. – ⊖ Piccadilly Circus – ℘ 020 7734 6126 – Mon.–Sat. 8AM–11PM.

Zafash – 233–235 Old Brompton Rd – ⊖ West Brompton – ℘ 020 7373 2798 – daily 8AM–midnight.

Public holidays

- January 1st (New Year's Day)
- Good Friday
- Easter Monday
- Early May Bank Holiday (First Monday in May)
- Spring Bank Holiday (Last Monday in May)
- Summer Bank Holiday (Last Monday in August)
- Christmas Day (December 25th*)
- Boxing Day (December 26th*)

If these dates fall on a weekend, the following Monday or Tuesday are public holidays.

London Pass

Available in tourism information centers (ℭ *see next page*) or online (www.londonpass.com), this pass offers access to over 80 sites, museums, and attractions, a Hop-On Hop-Off bus ride, and a mini-cruise on the Thames.

Prices – 1 day £85, 2 days £115, 3 days £128, up to 10 days. Online discounts available.

It is up to you to calculate whether this card is advantageous, noting that several major museums are already free.

Museums and attractions

Most major museums in the city are free and encourage visitors to make a donation. For those that charge an entrance fee, a reduced rate is always offered to children. The last admission is generally between 30 and 60 minutes before closing time.

London museums are well-equipped: quality restaurants and cafés, unique stores, themed tours of the permanent collections, late openings (☾ *"Hours," opposite),* audioguides and multi-language materials are all typical features.

☺ *The free **Bloomberg Connects** app serves as an audioguide with quality audio and/or video content for more than thirty museums and galleries in London.*

Tourism offices

London Tourist Office – www.visitlondon.com. It gathers several **Information & Visitor Centres**, in Victoria and King's Cross-St Pancras stations and at Piccadilly Circus.
City of London Information Centre – St Paul's Churchyard – ⊖ St Paul's – ✆ 020 7332 3456 – www.cityoflondon.gov.uk.
Greenwich Tourist Information Centre – Pepys House – 2 Cutty Sark Gardens – ⊖ Cutty Sark (DLR) – ✆ 020 8305 5235 – www.visitgreenwich.org.uk.

Post

Stamps are available in post offices and from newsagents. A stamp for an international postcard costs £1.90.
☾ www.royalmail.com

Tipping

The service charge is most often included in the bill at **restaurants** and bars, where it is added to the price of dishes and drinks on the menu (approx. 12.5%). If not, it is customary to tip 10–15% of the bill.

Service is also included in your **hotel** bill.
For **taxis,** plan on tipping 10–15% of the fare.

Press

National daily press

This includes serious newspapers such as *The Telegraph*, *The Financial Times*, *The Guardian*, *The i Paper*, and *The Times*, as opposed to more sensational tabloids like *The Daily Mail*, *The Daily Express*, *The Daily Star*, *The Daily Mirror*, and *The Sun*. All are available online.

Local daily press

London Standard is the main free London daily. In addition to national news, it focuses on life in London. You can find it at the entrance of certain subway stations.

Dining

The traditional **English breakfast** is mostly reserved for weekends but is often served in hotels and Bed & Breakfasts (B&Bs).
At noon, Londoners opt for a light lunch: a sandwich, salad, or soup. When the weather's nice, a **picnic** is a must! Consider the food sections in department stores selling sandwiches and salads, or take advantage of **food trucks** and **global cuisine stalls** that set up in London's markets, plazas, and festivals. Some restaurants offer a **lunch menu** with two or three courses that are good value for money, providing an opportunity to enjoy fine dining on a budget! Most serve from 12PM to around 2/2:30PM.

Some Typical "British" Dishes

The traditional breakfast consists of eggs, bacon, and toast, with orange juice and tea or coffee. A full English breakfast should also include sausages, tomatoes, and **beans** (white beans cooked in a sweet tomato sauce).

Among other main dishes, a classic is beef in sauce, topped with puff pastry and baked with kidneys (**steak and kidney pie**) or with mushrooms (**steak and mushroom pie**). The **Cornish pasty**, a pastry filled with meat and potatoes, is ideal for eating on the go, just like **fish and chips**: battered fish fillet served with fries. Another specialty is **fish pie**: haddock pie with peas. As for seafood, the English enjoy **shrimp** and **oysters**, often cooked hot. Cheese, like cheddar or stilton, is traditionally enjoyed after dessert, with a glass of port. It is also a staple of the **Ploughman's lunch**, served in pubs.

On the dessert side, you won't be disappointed by classics like **apple pie**, **crumble**, **lemon tart** or **trifle** (sponge cake, custard, whipped cream and fruit). As for **pudding**, there are more than a hundred recipes.

At 4PM, Britain switches to **tea time**. Pastries and mini sandwiches accompany the cup of tea (*☾ pp. 130 and 185*).

It's customary to grab a beer at a **pub** after work at 5 or 6PM, before heading out to dinner around 7:30 to 9PM. Dinner is the most substantial meal of the day. Most restaurants don't serve beyond 10 or 10:30PM, and it's advisable to book a table before the weekend.

☾ "Where to Go/Dining" p. 116 and "London Dining" p. 185.

Etiquette

Queuing Up – Londoners stand in line in an orderly and calm manner.

At the Pub – Aside from in some that serve food, you must order and pay at the counter.

Evening Attire – If dining at a nice restaurant and going to the theater, a concert, or the opera, dress smartly. You won't, however, need to dress very formally to go dancing, except at exclusive venues. When in doubt, go for smart casual. And never forget that some rock clubs won't let those dressed too formally in...

Taxi

Though quite pricey, the London cab is an attraction in itself.

Black cabs

The traditional black London taxis now sport vibrant colors. You can hail them when the orange "For hire" sign on the roof is lit. All are equipped with meters (*starting fare £3.90, additional charges after 8PM, and on weekends and holidays).* The fleet, which is reportedly responsible for 20% of London's pollution, is being gradually replaced by low-emissions vehicles.

Minicabs

For long distances, it's better to book a minicab. Negotiate the fare in advance as they don't have meters.

Beware, some private taxis are unlicensed: those that are licensed display a yellow disc from the Public Carriage Office on the front and rear of the vehicle.

Reservations – Dial-A-Cab – ✆ 020 7253 5000; **London Radio Cars** – ✆ 020 8204 4444.

Phone

From abroad

✆ 00 + 44 (UK country code) + recipient's number without the initial 0 (10 digits total).

From London to abroad

✆ 00 + country code (United States 1, Canada 1) + recipient's number (without the 0).

Internal calls

All calls, local or long-distance, are composed of 11 digits.

Phone booths

Though you can still make calls from some traditional red booths (with a bank card, coins, or phone card), many have been dismantled or converted to other uses: mini-libraries, art installations, coffee shops, defibrillator stations, smart device repair kiosks... or selfie spots!

Smartphone apps

The most useful ones: **Visit London** (city guide, offline maps, great spots, and plenty of info to help organize your stay), **Citymapper** or **Tfl Go** (route planners for public transport, biking, scooting), **Tube Map** (subway map).

Public restrooms

There are plenty in London, and most are wheelchair accessible.

Public transport

Transport for London – ✆ 0343 222 1234 (24/7 – charges apply) – www.tfl.gov.uk.

Bus

The iconic red double-decker buses add to London's charm and offer a great way to see the city. The network is dense and convenient (with frequent service), featuring nearly 130 lines covering just the city center. Get the *Key Bus Routes in Central London* map, free at subway stations or downloadable at www.tfl.gov.uk/maps/bus, or use the TfL Go or Citymapper apps to plan your routes.

Fare: The Hopper fare £1.75 includes any transfers within an hour.
About sixty night buses, identified by the letter N (night) before their number, take over from the subway and day buses between midnight and 7AM. However, their schedules remain somewhat irregular, and you need to signal the driver to stop.

Subway (Tube, Underground)

☞ *Subway map on the back of the detachable map.*

The **Tube** is the fastest way to get around the capital, with a network of 11 underground lines identified by name and color. Directions *Northbound*, *Southbound*, *Eastbound* or *Westbound* indicate the line's direction. The final destination is displayed at the front of the train and on the platform's display board.

☺ *Many Tube lines have multiple routes that end at different stations. Make sure to check the destination of your train before you get on.*

Keep your ticket: you need to validate it to exit the subway.

Hours: Mon.–Sat. from 5/5:30AM to 12:30/1AM, Sun. from 7AM to 12/12:30AM.

The Victoria, Central, Jubilee, Northern, and Piccadilly lines operate 24 hours on Fri. and Sat.

Dockland Light Railway (DLR)

An independent driverless subway line serving East London from the City. DLR stations are accessible to people with reduced mobility.

Overground

This above-ground rail network serves the London area, with several stations in the city, particularly in the east (Liverpool Street, Shoreditch, etc.); some are connected to the subway. Night service (24 hours on Fri. and Sat.: Night Overground) between Highbury & Islington and New Cross Gate.

Fares

Public transport is very expensive. A single ticket for the subway/DLR costs £6.70! The goal of this prohibitive price? To avoid paper tickets. So choose contactless payment, a Travelcard, or an Oyster Card *(see opposite)*.

Prices vary depending on the **zones**, as well as the **time** you travel: during **peak hours** (Mon.–Thu. 6:30AM–9:30AM and 4PM–7PM), or outside of those times. The full fare ticket *(£3.40 zones 1–2)* allows travel at any time; the off-peak ticket *(£2.80 zones 1–2)* can be used without restrictions outside of peak times.

☺ *Children under 11 travel free on buses, the subway, DLR, and Overground.*

Tickets can be purchased at subway stations. If you are caught without a ticket, you are liable for an £80 fine.

😊 *Warning: Regardless of the payment method chosen, make sure you validate your ticket or bank card at the start AND at the end of your journey (except on buses), to ensure the correct fare is charged; otherwise, you may be charged for a journey across the entire line.*

Contactless Payment – Contactless payment with a bank card is the most convenient option for visitors. It is programmed to charge the most advantageous rates, with caps not exceeding £8.10/day or £40.70/week for travel in zones 1 and 2, for example.

😊 *However, beware of potential banking fees. Note also that contactless payment can only be used for one person at a time.*

Travelcard – This provides unlimited access to subway, buses (day and night), DLR, and Overground. One Day Travelcard: £15.20 in zones 1 to 4.

Oyster Card – A prepaid magnetic card that can be used across the entire London transport network (including on some suburban trains). You load the amount of money you want and top it up as needed, using cash or credit card, at subway station counters, online (www.tfl.gov.uk/oyster), via the TfL Oyster app, or at many retailers. You can even store a Travelcard on it.

The Oyster Card is available at subway stations for £7 (non-refundable); any credit below £10 left on the card at the end of your stay can be refunded: inquire at the station. Plan for a credit of £10 for 1 day, £15 for 2 days, and £20 for 3 days. Whatever the number of trips made during the day, the card is programmed to charge the most advantageous rates (capped at £8.10/day for journeys in zones 1 and 2). You can also purchase a weekly card for £40.70 (zones 1 and 2).

Visitor Oyster Card – Sold exclusively online (www.visitorshop.tfl.gov.uk – £5 non-refundable), this allows you to get prepared before departure and works in a similar way to the Oyster Card except you cannot load a Travelcard onto it. Any credit below £10 remaining on the card is refundable. The card is sent to your address by mail: make sure to buy it well ahead of your departure.
☞ *"London pass" p. 155.*

Boat

Why not take the boat to get around London? Enjoy the regular service of **river buses** operated by **Uber Boat by Thames Clippers**. Several lines serve 24 stops along the Thames, allowing you to travel from Tate Britain to Tate Modern, for example, or from Westminster to Greenwich. Discounts with the Oyster Card, payment possible with the Uber app or with a contactless card.

🧭 *www.thamesclippers.com. For a guided cruise, see "Guided Tours" below.*

Bike

The network of bike lanes is well-developed in certain areas of the capital, and it's very pleasant to ride a bike along the Thames or in some parks. Stay alert in the city center as traffic can be particularly busy. Many resources for cyclists, including route suggestions with detailed maps, are available at **www.tfl.gov.uk/modes/cycling/**. You'll also find information on how to travel with your bike on public transport.

Santander Cycles – www.tfl.gov.uk/modes/cycling/santander-cycles. Self-service bike stations are scattered throughout the downtown area (credit card payment – £1.65/30min). Several private companies, including **Lime** (www.li.me), offer self-service electric bikes and scooters, which can be geolocated and unlocked with your smartphone.

Guided tours

On foot

London Walks – www.walks.com. Casual or themed walks around a neighborhood or even museum.

Bowl of Chalk – www.bowlofchalk.net. A guide with a *very* British sense of humor offering several tours during the weekend in central and East London. Price at the visitor's discretion.

Alternative London Tours – www.alternativeldn.co.uk. Themed walks in the East End focusing on gastronomy, pubs, or street art.

Shoreditch Street Art Tour – www.shoreditchstreetarttours.co.uk, **Street Art London Tour** – www.streetartlondon.co.uk, **Strawberry Tours** – www.strawberrytours.com. Guided tours dedicated to street art.

By boat

In addition to the Thames Clippers river shuttles (🧭 *mentioned above*), several companies offer guided cruises of the Thames.

City Cruises – www.cityexperiences.com/london/city-cruises. Numerous options; for example, from Westminster to Greenwich (1h20, £15.95 one way).

Jason's Trip – www.jasons.co.uk. From late March to October, barge cruises on the Grand Union Canal between Camden Lock and Little Venice (45min, £18 one way, £23 round trip).

By bus

Some agencies organize guided tours, while others offer the flexibility to hop on and hop off at will with the same ticket, so you can plan your own visits.

Big Bus Tours – www.bigbustours.com. Three "hop-on, hop-off" routes. Tickets start at £45 for 24 hours, including walking tours and a Thames cruise.

LeoPatrizi/Getty Images Plus

Pedestrians in London.

By cab

London Cab Tours – www.londoncabtours.co.uk. Tours of 3 hours (£200 per car) or a full day (starting from £400); many themed options.

By bike

BrakeAway Bike Tours – www.biketouroflondon.com. Meeting point at platforms 1 and 2 of Waterloo Station. Two tours available (3h30): "Grand London" and "Secret London" (£32).

Cultural agenda

To follow London's vibrant cultural life, check **www.timeout.com/london** or the Culture section of **The Guardian** (www.theguardian.com) and the **London Standard** (www.standard.co.uk).

Annual events

January
▶**New Year's Day Parade** – Starts at noon from Parliament Square (Westminster) to Piccadilly – www.lnydp.com.
▶**London International Mime Festival** – Visual theater: mime, circus, etc. – www.mimelondon.com.
▶**Burns Night** – Tribute on Jan. 25 to Scottish poet Robert Burns (1759–1796), with a traditional meal and various city events, especially aboard the *Golden Hinde* (ⓒ p. 62).
▶**Charles I Commemoration** – Costume procession starting at 11:30AM from St James's Palace to Banqueting House (last Sun.).
▶**London Art Fair** – London Art Fair at the Business Design Centre in Islington – www.londonartfair.co.uk.

January–February
▶**Chinese New Year** – In Chinatown, in the Soho area (date varies).

March
▶**St Patrick's Day** – Irish parade on March 17 at South Bank.

Easter
▶**Hot Cross Buns Service** – Church service and distribution of Easter buns at St Bartholomew-the-Great (Good Friday).
▶**Easter Parade** – Carnival parade on Easter Monday at Battersea Park.
▶**London Harness Horse Parade** – Horse parade on Easter Monday at Battersea Park – www.lhhp.co.uk.

Late March–Early April
▶**Oxford-Cambridge Boat Race** – Since 1829, Oxford and Cambridge universities have competed in a rowing race on the Thames – www.theboatrace.org.

April
▶**London Marathon – The Course** – Between the Docklands and Westminster – www.tcslondonmarathon.com.
▶**Vaisakhi (Baisakhi)** – Punjabi dances and songs celebrating the Sikh New Year in Trafalgar Square.
▶**Boishakhi Mela** – Bengali New Year is celebrated in the East End – www.towerhamlets.gov.uk/mela.

May
▶**Open Air Theatre** – Start of the open-air theatre season at Regent's Park – www.openairtheatre.com.
▶**RHS Chelsea Flower Show** – Flower show at the Royal Hospital in Chelsea – www.rhs.org.uk.

June
▶**Trooping the Colour** – Parade celebrating the sovereign's birthday – kbp.army.mod.uk.

163

▶**Horse Guards Parade** – Whitehall (2nd Sat.).

▶**Hampton Court Festival** – Various concerts at Hampton Court Palace – www.hamptoncourtpalacefestival.com.

▶**London Open Gardens** – Celebrations in public and private gardens – www.londongardenstrust.org.

▶**Wimbledon Tennis Championships** (2 weeks)– www.wimbledon.org.

▶**Taste of London** – Food festival at Regent's Park - www.london.tastefestivals.com.

▶**Royal Ascot** – Popular horse races – www.ascot.com.

▶**London Festival of Architecture** – Open houses, guided tours throughout the city – www.londonfestivalofarchitecture.org.

June–July

▶**Pride in London** – London LGBTQ+ pride march – www.prideinlondon.org.

▶**Hampstead Summer Festival** – Concerts, food, graphic arts, etc. – www.hampsteadsummerfestival.com.

▶**Spitalfields Festival** – Late June to early July. Classical, contemporary, world music concerts, etc. – www.spitalfieldsmusic.org.uk

June–August

▶**Royal Academy Summer Exhibition** – Summer exhibition at the Royal Academy of Arts, Burlington House – www.royalacademy.org.uk.

July

▶**Wireless Festival** – Major festival of music and dance at Crystal Palace Park and Finsbury Park – www.wirelessfestival.co.uk.

▶**RHS Hampton Court Garden Festival** – Flower show at Hampton Court Palace – www.rhs.org.uk.

▶**The BBC Proms** – Classical music at the Royal Albert Hall (until September) – www.bbc.co.uk/proms.

August

▶**Notting Hill Carnival** – Major Caribbean carnival, starts at Portobello Road (last weekend of the month).

▶**Greenwich + Docklands International Festival** – Concerts, performances, outdoor theater – www.festival.org/gdif.

September

▶**Totally Thames** – A festival celebrating the Thames, with artistic and cultural events along the riverbank, including the famous Doggett Coat and Badge Race between London Bridge and Chelsea Bridge – www.thamesfestivaltrust.org.

▶**Open House Festival** – Heritage Open Days – www.open-city.org.uk.

▶**The London Design Festival** – Over a hundred events throughout the city – www.londondesignfestival.com.

▶**Goldsmiths' Fair** – Exhibition and sale of jewelry at Goldsmiths' Hall (St Paul's) – www.goldsmithsfair.co.uk.

▶**Pearly Kings and Queens Harvest Festival** – On harvest festival day, the Pearly Kings and Queens parade from Guildhall to St Mary-le-Bow Church in handmade costumes embroidered with thousands of pearl buttons, each weighing up to 66 lb – www.pearlysociety.co.uk.

October

▶**Michaelmas Law Term** – Opening of the legal session, with judges in robes laying flowers at Westminster Abbey.

▶**Trafalgar Day Parade** – Parade commemorating the Battle of Trafalgar (on the 21st).

▶**London Film Festival** – At the National Film Theatre – www.bfi.org.uk/lff.

November

▶**Bonfire Night** – Fireworks in major city parks (on the 5th), commemorating the Gunpowder Plot (1605) – www.bonfirenight.net.

▶**London Jazz Festival** – Throughout the city – www.efglondonjazzfestival. org.uk.

Flora Luna/Getty Images Plus

Pride in London.

▶**London to Brighton Veteran Car Run** – Vintage car race starting at Hyde Park (1st Sunday) – www.vccofgb. co.uk/lontobri.

▶**Lord Mayor's Show** – Lord Mayor's parade in the City (2nd Saturday) – www.lordmayorsshow.london.

▶**Remembrance Day Service and Parade** – Remembrance Sunday (Sunday near 11th Nov.), ceremonies at the Cenotaph in Whitehall and most churches in the city.

▶**Start of Christmas Lights** – Regent Street in mid-November.

December

▶**Street lights and Christmas caroling in churches.**

▶**Trafalgar Square Christmas Tree** – Installation of the Christmas tree donated by Norway.

▶**Winter Wonderland** – Grand Christmas-themed fair in Hyde Park – www.hydeparkwinterwonderland .com.

Art galleries

Some galleries play a prominent role in London's artistic life:

St James's

▶**White Cube** – 25–26 Mason's Yard – ⊖ Piccadilly Circus – www.whitecube. com. Also at: 144–152 Bermondsey St. – ⊖ Bermondsey.

Soho

▶**The Photographer's Gallery** – 16–18 Ramillies St. – ⊖ Oxford Circus – www.thephotographersgallery .org.uk.

The City
▶ Barbican Art Gallery – *☾ p. 52.*

Chelsea
▶ Saatchi Gallery – *☾ p. 74.*

Kensington
▶ Serpentine Gallery – *☾ p. 80.*

East London
▶ Whitechapel Gallery – *☾ p. 99.*

Hoxton
▶ Victoria Miro Gallery – *☾ p. 99.*

DISCOVER MORE

When music rules.
Jon Arnold Images/hemis.fr

London in a few dates

43 – Foundation of Roman *Londinium*.
2nd c. – Construction of the Roman wall.
5th c. – Romans evacuate the city.
8th–10th c. – Viking raids and invasions.
1065 – Foundation of **Westminster Abbey**.
1066 – Norman invasion: defeat of Harold II's troops at Hastings and coronation of William I.
1067–1097 – Construction of the **Tower of London**.
1157 – Arrival of Hanseatic merchants in the **City** of London.
1192 – Election of the first mayor of the City, Henry FitzAilwin.
1209 – **London Bridge**, the first stone bridge, replaces the Roman bridge.
1216 – Barons force King John Lackland to ratify the **Great Charter** (Magna Carta), the foundation of English institutions.
1349 – The **Black Death** devastates London.
1530–1532 – Construction of **St James's Palace**.
1536–1539 – **Reformation**: the English Church breaks from the Papacy.
1555 – Brief restoration of Catholicism: 300 Protestants perish at the stake in Smithfield.
1558 – Restoration of the English Protestant Church with the ascension of Elizabeth I.
1567 – Creation of the 1st **Stock Exchange**.
1599 – Opening of the **Globe Theatre** in Southwark.
1600 – Establishment of the English East India Company.

1642 – Start of the civil war. Cavaliers (royalists) and Roundheads (parliamentarians) clash.
1649 – Execution of **Charles I** in front of Whitehall Palace.
1649–1660 – Republic, known as the "Commonwealth of England."
1653 – **Cromwell** becomes Lord Protector of the Republic.
1655 – Return of the Jewish people, banned from the city since the 13th c.
1660 – Restoration; the king allows theatrical performances in **Covent Garden**.
1665 – **Great Plague**: 75,000 victims out of 460,000 inhabitants.
1666 – **Great Fire** and birth of the first London newspaper.
1666–1723 – Rebuilding of **St Paul's Cathedral** and city churches by Christopher Wren.
1685 – Arrival of French Huguenots (revocation of the Edict of Nantes).
1688 – Civil war: exile of James II; the throne is offered to **William of Orange**.
1750 – Construction of **Westminster Bridge**.
1753 – Foundation of the **British Museum**.
1756–1763 – Seven Years' War pits Britain and Prussia against France and Austria.
1812 – John Nash designs and builds **Regent Street**.
1824 – Opening of the **National Gallery**.
1835–1860 – Reconstruction of the **Houses of Parliament**.

1836 – Foundation of the University of London.

1851 – First World's Fair in Hyde Park.

1852–1909 – Construction of the **South Kensington** museums, including the Victoria and Albert Museum.

1863 – Opening of the first **subway line**.

1894 – Inauguration of **Tower Bridge**.

1938 – Creation of the **Green Belt**.

1940–1941 – **Blitz**: the bombing of London by the Germans marks the beginning of the Battle of Britain.

1958 – The first women enter the House of Lords.

1979 – **Margaret Thatcher** becomes the country's first female Prime Minister.

1981 – Establishment of the **London Docklands Development Corporation** to revitalize the docks; marriage of Prince Charles and Diana Spencer.

1982 – Opening of the **Barbican Centre**. Construction of the Thames Barrier.

1990 – **John Major** becomes Prime Minister.

1994 – Inauguration of the Channel Tunnel.

1997 – Return of the Labour Party to power with **Tony Blair**. Death of Princess Diana in Paris.

1998 – Reopening of the **Globe Theatre**; inauguration of the **British Library**. Referendum: Londoners now elect their mayor.

1999 – Millennium projects: Dome (Greenwich), extension of the Jubilee line, **Millennium Bridge** and **Tate Modern**, London Eye, Great Court of the **British Museum**.

2003 – London becomes the first city in Europe to introduce urban congestion charges.

2005 – Terrorist attacks.

2008 – **Financial crisis**.

2010 – **David Cameron** becomes Prime Minister.

2011 – Marriage of Prince William and Kate Middleton.

2012 – London hosts the **Olympic Games**. Diamond Jubilee of Elizabeth II.

2013 – Opening of **The Shard** to the public.

2015 – Elizabeth II becomes the longest-reigning monarch: 63 years, 7 months, and 2 days.

2016 – Labour's **Sadiq Khan** becomes Mayor of London. Victory of **Brexit** by referendum; **Theresa May** becomes Prime Minister.

2017 – Wave of terrorist attacks in central London; Grenfell Tower fire.

2018 – Marriage of Prince Harry and Meghan Markle.

2019 – Brexit Party's victory in European elections; resignation of Theresa May, replaced by **Boris Johnson**.

2020 – January 31st: the UK officially leaves the European Union; **Covid-19 pandemic**.

2021 – January 1st: the UK leaves the European Customs Union and single market.

2022 – Queen's Platinum Jubilee (70 years on the throne). Boris Johnson resigns, succeeded by Liz Truss, then **Rishi Sunak. Death of Queen Elizabeth II**.

2023 – Coronation of King Charles III.

2024 – Sadiq Khan re-elected as Mayor of London for a third term. After early general elections, Labour returns to power with **Keir Starmer** as head of the government.

London, the center of the world?

On January 1st, 2021, the United Kingdom exited the European Customs Union and the single market. This marked the end of the Brexit process initiated after the 2016 vote, and also the end of the free movement of goods and people to and from the country. Despite the resulting difficulties and uncertainties, London remains an extraordinary cultural melting pot.

Goodbye EU, hello world!

"Goodbye Europe, hello world!" is the slogan under which **Boris Johnson** and the supporters of **Brexit** approach this new era. They plan to reposition themselves economically and geopolitically at the heart of the world, strengthening ties with the Commonwealth member states, with India, Canada, and Australia leading the charge. They also aim to find their place between two economic giants: China and the United States.

To solidify this "**Global Britain**" strategy, London has embarked on a vast market search, signing trade partnerships with over 60 countries.

Obstacle course

For now, social, economic, and political difficulties are continuing. The combined effects of Brexit and the **Covid-19 pandemic** led to the departure of some residents from Central and Eastern Europe, causing a **labor shortage** in road transport, healthcare, hospitality, and agriculture. Repeated **scandals** ultimately led to Boris Johnson's resignation as head of the Conservative Party (July 2022). His successor as Prime Minister, Conservative **Rishi Sunak**, was met with a massive and unprecedented **wave of strikes** that began in summer 2022. Railroad workers, dockers, garbage collectors, postal workers, lawyers, teachers, and others demanded wage increases to cope with **record inflation** exceeding 10% and unprecedented increases in energy and food prices, exacerbated since the war in Ukraine began. **Keir Starmer**, the leader of the Labour Party, became Prime Minister in July 2024.

Neighborhood troubles

The return of customs checks at borders and new trade agreements imposed by Brexit have heightened tensions within the United Kingdom. Having voted predominantly against Brexit, the **Scots** and **Northern Irish** are even more dissatisfied with the current economic challenges, reviving independence desires for the former and reunification desires for the latter with the Republic of Ireland.

The City, a leading financial center

Even alone and weakened, the United Kingdom remains the **6th-largest economy in the world**. Although the current difficulties and the projections of the Bank of England do not bode well for the coming years, London can still rely on its banks, insurance companies, and investment firms, which make the **City** the second-largest financial center in the world after New York. In London, other leading sectors include **tourism**, **media**, and **advertising**.

A city open to all

Great Britain has always promoted freedom of expression and political tolerance toward minorities, enabling peaceful coexistence between communities. In London, the very presence of Mayor **Sadiq Khan**, the son of Pakistani immigrants, who has served as the head of the municipality since 2016, testifies to the city's extraordinary **multiculturalism**. More than a third of the population was born outside the United Kingdom, with nearly 270 nationalities represented in the capital and over 300 languages spoken. Indians, Pakistanis, Bangladeshis, Sub-Saharan Africans, and Jamaicans form the largest communities.

Neighborhoods and communities

London is home to a number of thriving cultural communities, many of whom have left an indelible mark on the city's culture. Some prominent ethnic enclaves in London include the sizable Bangladeshi population in the East End, a prominent Caribbean community in central London and Brixton, Lithuanians in Beckton, Sub-Saharan Africans in the north and also downtown, Chinese in Soho, and Polish in Ealing. Throughout the year, celebrations of heritage abound: Notting Hill's Caribbean Carnival is a can't-miss event, and Chinese New Year parties bring the streets to life. In Greater London, near Wembley, visitors can also see the largest Hindu temple outside India, the **Neasden Temple** (BAPS Shri Swaminarayan Mandir).

Passport, please!

A work or study permit is now necessary for long-term settlement in London. While the majority of Europeans previously established on British soil have applied for resident status or dual nationality, others have decided to leave the country. However, the feared "Brexodus" has failed to meaningfully materialize, and London has not lost its status as a global city, nor its captivating power.

Architecture and urbanism

London's diversity of architectural styles and influences is one of its most striking attributes. The city's turbulent history, its near-total destruction during the Great Fire of 1666, the monstrous damage from German bombings during World War II, and the unique nature of its urban geography have all contributed to this. As a result, truly long-standing relics of the city's architectural past are rare. From the **Norman period**, the Tower of London remains. The palace and Westminster Abbey bear witness to the **Gothic period**.

A confounded urbanism

London is not a city, but a patchwork of villages, each growing until it meets its neighbor – without concerted plans seeming to guide development. The irrigation system, a network of streams draining the villages and carrying waste, long defied urban planners and was not systematically coordinated until the end of the 19th century. Administratively, the capital has two seats of power, torn between Westminster and the City. Today, it's hard to find a district that doesn't feature architectural ruptures, which results in surprising juxtapositions.

Palladian renaissance

In England, the Gothic style came late, and the Renaissance first made its mark in the late 16th century, thanks to the work of **Inigo Jones** (1573–1652). This urban planner, considered the founder of English architecture, admired the classical Renaissance style initiated by **Andrea Palladio** (1508–1580). Jones is credited with Covent Garden and the Banqueting House in Whitehall. The Palladian style is inspired by antiquity, with simple, symmetrical facades rhythmically adorned with tall windows, columns, and arcades, and topped with balustrades, cornices, or pediments and domes.

English Baroque

In the early 17th century, with the Counter-Reformation in continental Europe, the Renaissance gradually evolved toward the Baroque. The intention was to soften the austerity of architecture by making it less symmetrical and more ornate. After the Great Fire of 1666, the reconstruction of London provided an opportunity to apply this new style under the guidance of a major architect, **Christopher Wren** (1632-1723). A commission set the street widths, building heights, and materials to be used. Wren notably built St Paul's Cathedral.

TonyBaggett/Getty Images plus

Georgian-style architecture.

His inspiration was a balanced blend of Italian Baroque and Palladian. His style features grand colonnades, domes, and pediments.

Neoclassicism

Eighteenth–century architects bridged the gap between Wren's version of Baroque and the Palladian legacy, resulting in the neoclassical style, which harks back to ancient temples with discreet additions. Among them were Colen Campbell (1676–1729), William Kent (1685–1748), and **James Gibbs** (1682–1754), who created St Martin-in-the-Fields.

Georgian style

Part of the broader neoclassical movement, Georgian style is typical of England and spans the reigns of the Hanoverian Kings George during the 18th century. Its most famous representatives are **William Chambers** (1723–1796) and **Robert Adam** (1728–1792). It is a reinterpretation of ancient styles gradually infused with whimsies, small follies, and fake ruins that embellish parks. The British Museum dates back to this era. Moreover, London is experiencing a demographic explosion and there's a need to house families: the **terraced houses**, those rows of adjoining and similar houses that give unity to

English streets and mark the Georgian character, are multiplying.

Regency style

Starting in 1811, the Prince Regent, the future George IV, was in power. It was an era of grand developments. Among the architects of the Regency style: **Henry Holland** (1745–1806), **John Soane** (1753–1837), and Thomas Cubitt (1788–1855). But the most important is undoubtedly **John Nash** (1752–1835), who is credited with Regent Street, the terraces along Regent's Park, Carlton House Terrace, and the west wing of Buckingham Palace. Nash distinguished himself by presenting a comprehensive vision for the development of an entire area of London, extending from Regent's Park to Regent Street, Trafalgar Square, and St James's Park.

Victorian eclecticism

Architects seek inspiration from national heritage. They reinvent references and mix them in often outrageous ways. After the advent of Gothic architecture, there followed an interest in Romanesque and English Norman styles. The most imposing example of **neo-Gothic** architecture in London can be seen in the Houses of Parliament. Other style combinations are on show at the Natural History Museum and Tower Bridge.

The 19th century also saw the construction of **residential neighborhoods**: simple adjoining red brick houses in modest areas, or more elaborate styles for wealthier locales. Cadogan Square, near Knightsbridge, is among the most remarkable ensembles.

Until the 1870s, buildings teemed with details and ornaments; then there was a shift toward greater simplicity. The **Arts & Crafts** movement spearheaded by **William Morris** (1834–1896) emphasized the value of craftsmanship over industry.

The 20th century

This century marked the gradual abandonment of eclectic heaviness in favor of forms evoking nature. In Europe, this was known as Art Nouveau; in England, it is referred to as **Modern Style**.

Starting in the 1920s, the **International Style** broke with the excesses of the 19th century. The aim became the functionality of buildings. The favored materials were concrete, glass, and steel; the geometric forms were meant to be efficient, with space and light optimized.

However, England struggled to let go of its nostalgic styles, especially neo-Gothic for official buildings. Modernism was slow to assert itself in residential developments as well.

The massive destruction of the Blitz did not seem to make room for creativity either. The heavy mass of the **Barbican Arts Centre** is enough to prove this, or, more interesting but equally contested, the **Lloyd's building** by Richard Rogers.

Among urban developments, one must mention the area of **Canary Wharf**, elegant and futuristic with its glass and steel towers. But it's the redevelopments that are the most striking: those of **St Katharine's Docks**, **Butler's Wharf**, and the buildings along **South Bank**.

The 21st century

The proliferation of towers

The first decade of the 21st century saw the number of **skyscrapers** multiply in London. Since the early 2000s, more than a hundred towers exceeding 328 feet in height have sprung up. Some are still under construction, and several dozen projects of equal scale are in the pipeline. The skyline has been transformed to the extent that in 2007, the city had to legislate to protect certain "**viewing corridors**." St Paul's Cathedral, Parliament, the Tower of London, and Buckingham Palace are among the monuments whose silhouettes must remain clearly visible. The boundary remains delicate. For instance, the sleek form of Richard Rogers' **Cheesegrater** doesn't obstruct the view of St Paul's Cathedral from Fleet Street. However, Renzo Piano's **The Shard** (2012) sparked controversy. As the tallest tower in Europe (1,017 feet), it is said to "dwarf" the cathedral according to English Heritage authorities.

Green style

Sometimes, the choice of curves, shapes, and dimensions is driven by ecological considerations. Take 30 St Mary Axe, a landmark of the City, which has been nicknamed **The Gherkin**. Its aerodynamic lines actually serve to channel the wind, enabling natural ventilation for the offices inside. Similarly, while the oval structure of **City Hall**, built on the banks of the Thames, may seem unusual, it is explained by highly technical systems for wind and sun exposure

and material conservation. Another example: it is thanks to its 486-feet height that the **Strata Tower** (2010) in south London accommodates wind turbines capable of generating 8% of its electricity needs. Solar panels, rainwater harvesting systems, and the use of sustainable materials (recycled concrete, UV-filtering glass) are becoming widespread in the latest constructions.

Stratford, an Olympic form !

The skyline five miles east of the City also underwent significant changes following the **XXX Olympics** (2012). The derelict industrial area that was chosen to host the games, which at 543 acres exceeded the size of Hyde Park, presented a major challenge. To make this new Stratford hub more attractive, **Westfield Stratford City**, the largest shopping center in Europe, opened in 2011. Most of the park's infrastructures are being repurposed or are under redevelopment (some have also been dismantled) in service of a venue now known as **Queen Elizabeth Olympic Park**. The emblem of the Olympics, **The ArcelorMittal Orbit**, a 377-foot sculpture designed by Anish Kapoor, has housed the world's longest steel slide since 2016 and offers an impressive view from its observation deck. The **Aquatics Centre**, built by Zaha Hadid, continues to host competitions and training sessions. The works are expected to be completed by 2025, notably with the opening of a new wing of the Victoria and Albert Museum, the **V&A East Storehouse**. While residential projects multiply around it, the former

Rapid Gentrification

In the 1960s, the poor and working-class neighborhoods of North London, such as **Islington**, began to attract a new population of the middle classes, artists, and intellectuals. By moving in and renovating homes, stores, and public spaces, this middle class gradually drove up real estate prices, forcing the original working-class residents to leave and thereby completely changing the socio-economic profile of the area. This trend of urban turnover was dubbed "gentrification" in 1964 – from the English word "gentry" (which refers to the class of people just beneath the nobility) – by Ruth Glass, an American sociologist then residing in Islington. Since then, London's gentrification has spread to the East End and is now advancing rapidly toward the popular neighborhoods south of the Thames, like Brixton and Peckham.

Olympic Park is set to become a new district, **Stratford Riverfront – East Bank**, centered on culture, creativity, and education. The University College London (UCL East) campus opened its first buildings at the end of 2022; Sadler's Wells theater inaugurates a hip-hop academy in 2024; and the BBC Symphony Orchestra is expected to move there in 2025.

And always more projects...

The second-largest urban renewal project in Europe is currently taking place on the south bank of the Thames, opposite Chelsea. It is the **Nine Elms** (*www.nineelmslondon.com*) district, a massive project centered around the former **Battersea** power station. Over forty projects are underway or planned: construction of new skyscrapers, including several towers between 525 and 656 feet already built in Vauxhall; complete renovation of the vast New Covent Garden Market; development of green spaces; the new U.S. Embassy (2018); and more. In short, a new city within the city, connected by the Northern Line subway with its two new stations (2021), Battersea Power Station and Nine Elms.

Over in **Canary Wharf**, architects continue to outdo each other, launching their constructions into the clouds, like the **Landmark Pinnacle**, which became one of Europe's tallest residential towers in 2020 with its height of 764.5 feet.

The same goes for the **City**, where the skyline will be further transformed by 2026, with the addition of a dozen new skyscrapers. The tallest one, **1 Undershaft**, is expected to have 73 floors and reach a total height of 951.5 feet.

The Gherkin, designed by the architects Foster + Partners. xavierarnau/Getty Images Plus

Rock, pop, and more

What if we had to sum up the love story between London and music? In no particular order, it could be the photo of the punk band the **Sex Pistols** signing a contract with the A&M label in front of Buckingham Palace, or the concert scene of the **Yardbirds** in *Blow Up*, Michelangelo Antonioni's film, which won the Palme d'Or at Cannes in 1967. And of course, all those record covers tied to the English capital: the jokers of **Madness**, laughing in front of Chalk Farm station in the heart of Camden; Battersea Power Station – the former power station now rehabilitated – proudly illustrating *Animals* by **Pink Floyd**; **David Bowie** posing on tiny Heddon Street for the cover of one of his great albums, *The Rise & Fall Of Ziggy Stardust*; the Beatles crossing Abbey Road to reach the legendary recording studios of the same name; or even Paul McCartney's **Wings**, hair blowing in the wind with Tower Bridge in the background. So yes, we could do it this way. But that wouldn't tell the whole story.

The rock epicenter

While other British cities may have vividly marked the imagination of music lovers – starting with the two northern rivals, Liverpool and Manchester – the British capital remains the epicenter of national and international movements, as well as the birthplace of labels, stores, studios, and concert halls, without which the history of rock would not have been written in quite the same way.

If the **Beatles** remain the epitome of the 1960s music scene and those who greatly contributed to the invention of the concept of **"pop music"** – "pop" being short for "popular" – London will be the first to claim their evil twin, five bad boys who take their name from a Muddy Waters song. This quintet draws from American blues to shape a rebellious new voice in rock music, led by **Mick Jagger**. Mick's pouty lips and suggestive hip movements stir the public to the point where the music weekly *Melody Maker* asks this crucial question: "Would you let your sister go out with a **Rolling Stone**?"

Swinging London

Between 1962 and 1967, London is also the privileged zone of the Mod movement, dominated by young people from working or middle-class backgrounds who work during the week to better enjoy the weekend: they wear the suits of New Wave actors, ride Italian scooters, and stay at the forefront of musical novelties. **The Who** is their go-to band, with the electric anthem *My Generation*. **The Kinks** are also part of the scene, and the Davies brothers' band takes the opportunity to write one of history's most beautiful songs about the English capital, *Waterloo Sunset*. It's the era of Swinging London, with models like Twiggy and Penelope Tree donning Mary Quant skirts, and photographer David Bailey capturing the pop stars of the time…

The punk generation and its children

Then, we have to wait a decade, marked by the multiple identities of Bowie and the emergence of glam rock, followed by hard rock – from the ashes of the Yardbirds, **Led Zeppelin**, godfather of the genre, is born – before London reconnects with a youthful exuberance.

As early as 1976, punks become known for their disdain of the system, their leftist leanings, their embrace of the "Do It Yourself" ethic, and their righteous belief that ideas trump technique. Following the Sex Pistols, a slew of bands like **The Clash**, **The Jam**, **Subway Sect**, and **Generation X** arrive to shake up an industry that had become complacent. Fanzines and independent structures, such as the essential Rough Trade, support this musical excitement that seems like it will never die down, giving rise to sub-movements like New Romanticism – with the band **Visage** as an ambassador – or new-wave and Goth scenes, with **Siouxsie** as the high priestess and Robert Smith of **The Cure** as the prince.

An inherited influence

London, a hub of musical media that set trends throughout the early 2000s, is now home to indie labels that rival powerful mainstream labels and venues that have made history – the Marquee Club in the 1960s, a Britpop hotspot in Camden called The Good Mixer (**Blur**, among others), and St Martin's School of Art. London has often achieved the improbable feat of blending avant-garde scenes (such as industrial music) with XXL commercial successes like the vibrant **Spice Girls** and the unmissable **Robbie Williams**. Because it's a city where the past blends effortlessly with the present, artists have skillfully taken this legacy to transcendent heights, such as **Adele**, seen as the rightful heir to the legendary Dusty Springfield; the late **Amy Winehouse**, keeper of an ageless soul; or the band **The Libertines**, champions of an imagined England.

In the 21st century, London is also the birthplace of a thriving underground electronic scene: **grime**, a style drawing from dancehall music and drum and bass, perfectly illustrates the cultural blend that has long been a creative force of the British capital, as the Notting Hill Carnival reminds us every year at the end of August. A sprawling city with distinct neighborhoods, London may not be the birthplace of rock and its various offshoots, but for 60 years it has been one of its most active hearts.

London on screen

From the 19th-century city shrouded in fog and poverty, to the royal city dotted with castles and mysteries, to the vibrant cosmopolitan metropolis of the 21st century, countless films and series have used London as their backdrop. Here's our selection.

10 films to watch before leaving

David Lean: **Oliver Twist** (1948). This adaptation of Dickens's novel features settings inspired by Gustave Doré's Illustrations of London (1870).
George Cukor: **My Fair Lady** (1964). An innocent and sentimental depiction of class differences in London at the start of the 20th century.
Michelangelo Antonioni: **Blow Up** (1967). A cult film capturing the essence of 1960s London. Palme d'Or 1967.
Stephen Frears: **My Beautiful Laundrette** (1986). This film set in South London explores racial tensions and a romance between two young men.
Roger Michell: **Notting Hill** (1999). The quintessential romantic comedy that introduced the world to London's Notting Hill neighborhood.
Woody Allen: **Match Point** (2005). A delicious thriller where passion and social climbing compete within London's high society.
Christopher Nolan: **Batman Begins** (2005). University College of London transformed into Gotham City.

Ron Howard: **Da Vinci Code** (2006). The search for an incredible secret takes us through historic sites in London.
Tom Hooper: **The King's Speech** (2010). The true story of the future George VI, father of Elizabeth II.
Sam Mendes: **Skyfall** (2013). The 23rd James Bond film, set against the backdrop of the London Underground and the National Gallery.

5 series to watch on returning

The Crown (2016–2024). This biographical saga dedicated to the reign of Elizabeth II helped popularize her image. 6 seasons.
Bridgerton (2020–2024) offers a modernized portrait of London's high society during the Regency era.
Fleabag (2016), a mini-series of 12 episodes that became an instant cult classic. Captures the daily life of a confused yet endearing London thirty-something.
It's a Sin (6 episodes, 2021) follows young gay men in 1980s London, battling the AIDS epidemic.
EastEnders started in 1985 and is still going strong. For 39 seasons and almost 7,000 episodes, it has followed the lives of several fictional working-class families in East London.

Fashion

London is one of the world's undisputed fashion capitals, alongside New York, Milan, and Paris. It offers a diverse style palette, from the most classic – dare we say old-school – to innovative designer creations, street style, and vintage. London boldly and inventively embraces fashion, unafraid of eccentricity. Every day, both young and older folks don outfits that range from posh to unique to rebellious, the result of a blend of cultures and countercultures.

British chic

Two streets are legendary for typical British masculine elegance: **Jermyn Street** (St James's), famous for shirts, hatmakers, and shoemakers, and **Savile Row** (Mayfair), where princes, statesmen, and international stars frequent houses like Henry Poole & Co, Gieves & Hawkes, Dege & Skinner, and Richard James. They have bespoke suits made there, unique pieces crafted from fabrics that are showcased like jewels, be it the famed English tweeds or other marvels from elsewhere.

From swinging London to the punk era

Some extraordinary figures have marked the fashion scene: avant-garde **Mary Quant** (1930–2023) introduced the miniskirt and colorful tights in 1955. By 1975, the punk movement was championed by designer **Vivienne Westwood** (1941–2022), long established in major fashion shows, always with a touch of irreverence. Another renowned designer, **Sir Paul Smith** (born in 1946), cultivates a classic style with a twist: a colorful detail, a floral pattern, and those iconic colorful stripes.

Fashion chic, green, or "chav"

The unconventional collections of **Alexander McQueen** (1969–2010) and **John Galliano** (born in 1960) long dominated runways. **Stella McCartney**, a committed environmentalist, established her ethical brand eschewing leather and fur. In the 2000s, the former Spice Girl **Victoria Beckham** made her entry into the English fashion scene. Her classy and understated brand dresses stars like Beyoncé and Kate Winslet.

On the streets, the vogue for big brands indirectly gave rise to the **chav**. The term refers to young people of modest backgrounds aiming to display their social savvy with high-end sportswear and flashy jewelry. Conversely, since the 1990s, vintage has enjoyed increasing popularity among a section of the population more concerned with recycling and sustainability than brands. In the East End, around Brick Lane, numerous stores highlight clothing and accessories from the 1920s to the 1980s.

The royal family

How can one talk about London without mentioning the monarchy? Among the major tourist attractions of the capital are the parades of unflappable guards under their bearskin hats and the kitschy souvenir stores bearing images of the royal family. Royalty means Buckingham Palace, the Tower of London, and the Crown Jewels, as well as celebrations like **Trooping the Colour**, the celebration of the monarch's birthday.

God save the king!

On September 8, 2022, after 70 years of reign, Queen **Elizabeth II** passed away at the age of 96 at her Scottish residence in Balmoral. Ascending the throne in 1952, she was the "senior" of British monarchs – she had broken the record of her ancestor Victoria (63 years, 7 months, and 2 days on the throne) on September 9, 2015, and celebrated her Platinum Jubilee in June 2022. Her eldest son, **Charles III**, succeeded her at the age of 73, amidst a particularly tense economic and geopolitical context. A great many Britons flocked to his coronation, showing their attachment to the royal family.

Division of roles

In practice, the **British monarchy** is **constitutional** and real power belongs to the **Prime Minister**, but the sovereign still plays an important role. He is the head of state, the Commonwealth, and the Church of England. He presides over the opening of the parliamentary session and meets weekly with the Prime Minister. He retains the constitutional right to dismiss the Prime Minister and dissolve Parliament.

Always in the headlines

Public opinion toward the royal family has always been ambivalent, ranging from slightly voyeuristic fascination to unconditional support, to exasperation at the frivolity or legal problems of some of its members.

The royal couple, Charles III and queen consort Camilla, enjoys the sympathy of a large part of the population. The same goes for **Prince William**, the first heir to the throne, who embodies the face of a more modern monarchy. His marriage to **Kate Middleton** in 2011, and then his brother **Harry**'s marriage to American actress **Meghan Markle** in 2018, as well as the birth of their children, have captured the country's enthusiasm. On the downside, the young family recently decided to relocate across the Atlantic.

The royal family has been going through difficult times since 2024, when several of its members announced they were fighting against illness, starting with Kate Middleton and King Charles himself.

London dining

"Modern British"

For a long time, good food and Great Britain didn't mix well... But then came the 1990s and a new British cuisine, which revived traditional dishes by lightening them up and taking inspiration from abroad. To be fair, the old British Empire, given its many bouts of colonization and waves of migration, had already adopted a great many recipes from such territories as South Asia, Africa, the Caribbean, the Middle East, and the Far East. "Modern British" is a label for a cuisine freely inspired by global flavors, showcasing fresh organic products and refined presentation. It's innovative, championed by chefs like Gordon Ramsay, Marcus Wareing, Bruce Poole, and the very popular **Jamie Oliver**. Not to mention Anglo-Israeli chef **Yotam Ottolenghi**, who heads six restaurants in London (**☉** Dine pp. 122 and 124), and whose cookbooks are bestsellers worldwide. Since the 2000s, chefs have increasingly embraced the trend of street food and **pop-up restaurants**, temporary establishments that open for a season or even just an evening. To keep up, you have to check social media! There is no shortage of websites listing the latest in the capital, such as London Eater (www.london.eater.com).

Culinary enthusiasm is also popularized through numerous **gastronomic festivals**, like Taste of London (www.london.tastefestivals.com), the Foodies (www.foodiesfestival.com), and the Street Feast night markets (www.streetfeast.com).

The ritual of afternoon tea

In grand hotels and renowned tea rooms, tea time is observed in the afternoon (**☉** Grab a Drink p. 130), this moment of sociability dating back to the early 19th century. Your drink – preferably a black tea, but you can order coffee or a glass of champagne instead! – generally comes with a delicious snack: soft scones served with strawberry jam and lightly whipped cream (clotted cream), an assortment of biscuits, pastries, and finger (or tea) sandwiches, or thin slices of white bread with fillings like cucumber, eggs, or salmon. After that, you should be satisfied until supper!

Paradise for veggies

Vegetarians or vegans, London caters to all. All diets are easily accommodated all over the capital, which has more than 500 "green" restaurants! Even junk food is getting in on the action, with vegan fried chicken and vegan kebabs.

INDEX

Collection under the direction of Philippe Orain

Publication Manager and Editor-in-Chief of the guide: Lucie Fontaine

Editorial Secretary	Élisabeth Cautru
Editorial Team	Christine Barrely, Christophe Basterra, Jonathan Burteaux, Séverine Cachat, Élisabeth Cautru, Mélanie Cornière, Sandrine Favre, Laurent Gontier, Anath Klipper, Hélène Le Tac, Laura Pertuy, Jérôme Saglio, Julie Subtil, Ronald Wood, Catherine Zerdoun
Contributors to this guide	Costina-Ionela Lungu, Theodor Cepraga, Leonard Pandrea (Cartography), Véronique Aissani, Carole Diascorn (Cover), Marie Simonet, Marion Capéra (Iconography), Bogdan Gheorghiu, Cristian Catona, Gabriel Dragu, Hervé Dubois, Pascal Grougon (Pre-press), Dominique Auclair (Guide)
	Maps: © MICHELIN 2024 and Contains Ordnance Survey data © Crown copyright and database right 2018. Code-Point® Open data: Contains Royal Mail data © Royal Mail copyright and database right 2018
Graphic Design	Laurent Muller (interior layout), Véronique Aissani (cover)
Advertising Management and partnerships	contact.clients@editions.michelin.com
	The content of advertisement pages inserted in this guide is solely the responsibility of the advertisers.
Contacts	Want to reach us? Visit the contact section of our website: editions. michelin.com
	Publication 2025

MICHELIN Editions

57 rue Gaston Tessier – 75019 Paris (France)
R.C.S. Paris 882 639 354

Copyright © 2025 MICHELIN Editions

Published in 2025 by Abrams Books, an imprint of ABRAMS. All rights reserved. No portion of this book may be reproduced, stored in a retrieval system, or transmitted in any form or by any means, mechanical, electronic, photocopying, recording, or otherwise, without written permission from the publisher.

Library of Congress Control Number: 2025932362

ISBN: 978-1-4197-8426-2
eISBN: 979-8-88707-862-5

Printed and bound in China
10 9 8 7 6 5 4 3 2 1

Abrams books are available at special discounts when purchased in quantity for premiums and promotions as well as fundraising or educational use. Special editions can also be created to specification. For details, contact specialsales@abramsbooks.com or the address below.

Abrams Books® is a registered trademark of Harry N. Abrams, Inc.

ABRAMS is represented in the UK and Europe by Abrams & Chronicle Books, 1 West Smithfield, London EC1A 9JU and Media Participations, 57 rue Gaston Tessier, 75166 Paris, France. abramsandchronicle.co.uk and media-participations.com info@abramsandchronicle.co.uk

Photographic Credits pp. 4-5
(from left to right and top to bottom)
Mauro_Repossini/Getty Images Plus
Jon Arnold Images/hemis.fr
majaiva/Getty Images Plus
Jon Arnold Images/hemis.fr
Vito_Elefante/Getty Images Plus
asmithers/Getty Images Plus
W. Bibikow/hemis.fr
Jon Arnold Images/hemis.fr
Cultura/hemis.fr (architects Herzog & de Meuron)
scottyh/Getty Images Plus

195 Broadway
New York, NY 10007
abramsbooks.com